THE FILMS OF STEPHEN KING

The Films of Stephen King

From *Carrie* to *The Mist*

Edited by
Tony Magistrale

First published in hardcover in 2008 by
PALGRAVE MACMILLAN®
in the United States—a division of St. Martin's Press LLC,
175 Fifth Avenue, New York, NY 10010.

Where this book is distributed in the UK, Europe and the rest of the world,
this is by Palgrave Macmillan, a division of Macmillan Publishers Limited,
registered in England, company number 785998, of Houndmills,
Basingstoke, Hampshire RG21 6XS.

Palgrave Macmillan is the global academic imprint of the above
companies and has companies and representatives throughout the world.

Palgrave® and Macmillan® are registered trademarks in the United States,
the United Kingdom, Europe and other countries.

ISBN: 978–0–230–33830–2

The Library of Congress Cataloging-in-Publication Data is available from
the Library of Congress.

A catalogue record of the book is available from the British Library.

Design by Newgen Imaging Systems

First PALGRAVE MACMILLAN paperback edition: January 2012

10 9 8 7 6 5 4 3 2 1

Printed in the United States of America.

Once again, for Katherine and Norman Tederous, the aunt and uncle who introduced me to drive-in horror movies at the earliest possible age

Contents

Notes on Contributors   ix

Introduction   1

1 The Queen Bee, the Prom Queen, and the Girl
   Next Door: Teen Hierarchical Structures in *Carrie*   13
   Alison M. Kelly

2 *Apt Pupil*: The Making of a "Bogeyboy"   27
   Dennis F. Mahoney

3 Maybe It Shouldn't Be a Party: Kids, Keds, and Death
   in Stephen King's *Stand By Me* and *Pet Sematary*   41
   Jeffrey A. Weinstock

4 The Lonesome Autoerotic Death of Arnie
   Cunningham in John Carpenter's *Christine*   53
   Philip Simpson

5 Tonka Terrors: The Humor and Horror of "Trucks"
   and *Maximum Overdrive*   67
   Michael A. Arnzen

6 The Long Dream of Hopeless Sorrow: The Failure
   of the Communist Myth in Kubrick's *The Shining*   83
   Michael J. Blouin

7 The Prisoner, the Pen, and the Number One Fan:
   Misery as a Prison Film   93
   Mary Findley

8 Redemption through the Feminine in *The Shawshank
   Redemption*; Or, Why Rita Hayworth's Name
   Belongs in the Title   103
   Tony Magistrale

9   Christian Martyr or Grateful Slave?
    The Magical Negro as Uncle Tom in
    Frank Darabont's *The Green Mile*   117
    Brian Kent

10 White Soul: The "Magical Negro" in the Films
    of Stephen King   131
    Sarah Nilsen

11 Reaganomics, Cocaine, and Race: David Cronenberg's
    Off-Kilter America and *The Dead Zone*   143
    Sarah E. Turner

12 The Feminist King: *Dolores Claiborne*   155
    Colleen Dolan

13 Only Theoretical: Postmodern Ambiguity
    in *Needful Things* and *Storm of the Century*   167
    Mary Pharr

14 *Rose Red* and Stephen King's Hybrid House
    of Horrors   179
    Dennis R. Perry and Carl H. Sederholm

15 Gardening for a New Generation of
    Horror in *Secret Window*   191
    Benjamin Szumskyj

16 Plucking Stems, Pulling Strings, and Pushing Agendas:
    The Consistency of Personal Failure and Mental Frailty
    in *The Mist*   201
    Patrick McAleer

Bibliography   221

Index   233

Notes on Contributors

Michael A. Arnzen is associate professor of English at Seton Hill University, near Pittsburgh. He has published work on King and the horror film in such venues as *Paradoxa, The Journal of Popular Film and Television, New York Review of Science Fiction, Narrative,* and the recent book *Horror Film: Creating and Marketing Fear.* Arnzen is also a three-time winner of the Bram Stoker Award.

Michael J. Blouin is a PhD candidate at Michigan State University writing a dissertation comparing horror images in Japan and America. This is his first publication.

Colleen Dolan is a feminist writer and educational therapist living in St. Thomas, Virgin Islands. She is currently researching the influence of gender bias in the diagnosis of learning disabilities.

Mary Findley teaches in the Humanities and Social Science Department at Vermont Technical College. Her background is in Gothic literature and her research focuses on Stephen King, the prevalence of the vampire in literature, culture, and film, and what horror's manifestation in popular culture reveals about the American psyche. She chairs the Stephen King Area of the Popular Culture Association and is published in *Spectral America: Phantoms and the National Imagination* (2004).

Alison M. Kelly teaches American and British literature at Deerfield Academy, where she frequently presents Brian De Palma's *Carrie* to adolescent boys and girls quite capable of identifying with characters in the film. She has published articles on *American Psycho, The Exorcist,* and teaching Poe in the high school curriculum.

Brian Kent is senior lecturer in the English Department at the University of Vermont. He has published essays on Stephen King's novels, *The Stand* and *The Shining.* He is currently writing a book on Gore Vidal.

Patrick McAleer is ABD at Indiana University of Pennsylvania. He currently teaches Composition and Literature at Inver Hills Community College in Minnesota. He is the author of *Inside the Dark Tower Series: Art, Evil and Intertextuality in the Stephen King Novels* (2009) and *The Writing Family of Stephen King: A Critical Study of the Fiction of Tabitha King, Joe Hill and Owen King* (2011). He is also co-chair of the Stephen King Area at the Popular Culture Association's annual national conference (with volume contributor Philip L. Simpson).

Tony Magistrale is professor of English and chair of the English department at the University of Vermont. He is the author of 20 books on horror films, Edgar Allan Poe, the history of the Gothic, and the work of Stephen King, including *Hollywood's Stephen King*, published by Palgrave in 2003.

Dennis F. Mahoney is professor of German and director of the "Global Village" Residential Learning Community at the University of Vermont. In addition to his books, articles, and book chapters on German literature from the Enlightenment through Romanticism, he has also published on German film and has been guest editor of the journal *Historical Reflections* (Fall 2000).

Sarah Nilsen is associate professor of English at the University of Vermont. Her areas of research include Walt Disney, cultural diplomacy, race and popular culture, and cultural studies.

Dennis R. Perry is associate professor of English who teaches American Literature and Literature and Film at Brigham Young University. His publications include articles on Melville, Whitman, Poe, and others, and the book *Hitchcock and Poe: The Legacy of Delight and Fear*.

Mary Pharr is professor of English at Florida Southern College. Coeditor of *The Blood Is the Life: Vampires in Literature* (1999), she has also edited the anthology *Fantastic Odysseys* (2003). She has presented and published extensively on the novels and films of Stephen King, speculative cinema, and fiction.

Carl H. Sederholm is assistant professor of Humanities at Brigham Young University. His publications include articles on Hawthorne, Irving, and H. P. Lovecraft. He is currently working with Dennis Perry on a book concerning Poe's influence on the modern Gothic tale.

Philip Simpson is academic dean of Humanities, Fine Arts, and Social/Behavioral Sciences at the Melbourne campus of Brevard Community College in Florida. He is currently the vice president, as well as Area Chair in Horror, for the Popular Culture Association. He is the author of *Psycho Paths: Tracking the Serial Killer through Contemporary American Fiction and Film* (2000) and numerous published essays on horror and popular culture.

Benjamin Szumskyj currently teaches at a private Christian high school in Australia. He has written dozens of essays and articles on literary criticism as well as editing and coediting books on critical studies, including *Fritz Leiber & H.P. Lovecraft: Writers of the Dark* (with S. T. Joshi); *Robert E. Howard: Power of the Writing Mind* (with Leo Grin); and *Fantasy Commentator # 57/58: Fritz Leiber Theme Issue* (with A. Langley Searles). He is the general editor of the MLA Indexed journal *Studies in Fantasy Literature*.

Sarah E. Turner is a senior lecturer in English at the University of Vermont. Her areas of research and teaching include popular culture, constructions of race, hip-hop literature, and book clubs.

Jeffrey A. Weinstock associate professor at Central Michigan University, is the editor of four published collections: *Spectral America: Phantoms and the National Imagination; The Nothing That Is: Millennial Cinema and the* Blair Witch *Controversies; Approaches to Teaching the Prose and Poetry of Edgar Allan Poe;* and *The Pedagogical Wallpaper: Teaching Charlotte Perkins Gilman's "The Yellow Wall-Paper."*

Introduction

Since the release of Brian De Palma's film *Carrie* in 1976, Hollywood's involvement with adapting Stephen King's fictional universe into film for both theatrical release and made-for-television miniseries has been nothing less than obsessive. At this writing, over seventy films have been made either based on Stephen King narratives or screen/teleplay scripts that King himself authored. The artistic quality of this collective work is remarkably mixed, ranging from the simply insulting (*Children of the Corn* and *Dreamcatcher*) to the brilliantly nuanced (*The Shawshank Redemption* and *Stand By Me*). Many of the world's major directors have produced movies based on King stories, and their films have also attracted a range of the most accomplished actors and actresses in Hollywood today. Since the "King film industry" has involved some of the most influential and talented names in Hollywood, it seems high time that more critical attention should be directed specifically at the films themselves, especially in light of the fact that King's writing is so cinematic—that is, plot driven, visually oriented, and character centered.

Given King's generous propensity to make his literary properties available to potential filmmakers at a reasonable cost (he regularly sells his work for a dollar and then takes five percent of the box office receipts [Magistrale, *Hollywood's Stephen King*, 7]), young, neophyte directors have also been drawn to King adaptations. Thus, Mary Lambert found her feature film directorial debut in *Pet Sematary*, while in 2001 Jay Holben produced a fine, eight-minute version of *Paranoid*, an adaptation of a rare King poem, as an independent film project that never attained theatrical release. Just as King's literature has now inspired a generation of young writers around the world, it is no exaggeration to suggest that his prose has also birthed a phenomenon unique in the long history of Hollywood's efforts at adapting literature into film.

Perhaps because of his best-seller popularity, his strong, plot-dominated narratives, his deftly drawn characters, or a combination of these elements, by the 1980s Hollywood discovered that any Stephen King work is a bankable project. Few of the 80-plus films from his literary canon theatrically released or televised in a miniseries format have failed to make money. Even short stories such as "Sometimes They Come Back," "The Mangler," and "Children of the Corn" have joined King's often behemoth-sized novels in attracting Hollywood's cinematic interest. Hollywood's attention to Stephen King helps to make us realize that this writer is more than just a remarkably popular and a readily recognizable cultural icon; it confirms his status as one of America's greatest storytellers, a versatile artist capable of producing narratives so compelling that they translate well into a variety of visual mediums. Moreover, very few novelists, even best-selling writers, manage to attain King's degree of success when their work is adapted to the big screen. King's narratives-into-films stand in sharp contrast to other, equally talented authors working in the same genres as King, such as Dean Koontz, Joyce Carol Oates, Peter Straub, and Anne Rice, among others, who simply have had precious little of even their best fiction translated into important films. To find adequate comparisons to the success King has attained on screen, we must look to writers working in genres other than horror. Ian Fleming's James Bond spy novels and the action thrillers of Michael Crichton and Robert Ludlum are his only real rivals.

One hundred years from now, several of King's novels will likely endure—*The Shining, The Stand, The Dark Tower* series, the magnificent novellas in *Different Seasons*, perhaps even his testament to domestic abuse and resiliency, *Dolores Claiborne*—as evidence of America's late twentieth-century struggle with its own internal monsters. I also believe, however, it will be the Stephen King films, even more than the novels that have inspired them, that will eventually crystallize into King's greatest artistic legacy. Perhaps the only occasion in which I have found myself in agreement with an assessment made by critic Harold Bloom is when he writes that King's books "are visually oriented scenarios, and they tend to improve when filmed" ("Afterthought" 208). Without entering the debate about the merits of comparing novels to films, the movie versions of *The Shining, Carrie, The Shawshank Redemption, Stand By Me,* and a handful of other titles have now, for various reasons unique to the films themselves, entered into the cinematic pantheon; according to the Internet Movie Database and Allmovie.com, for example, *The Shawshank Redemption* is eclipsed only by *The Godfather* as the most popular movie of all time. As good a novella as *Rita Hayworth and the Shawshank Redemption* is, the book never attained the same cultural resonance as the film. In fact, I am always impressed by the number of people who still do not recognize that the film version of *Shawshank* is adapted from a King narrative. Similarly, Stanley Kubrick's *The Shining* continues to be the subject of active scholarly discourse, amassing a critical bibliography that is larger than the combined attention of all the other films based on King's oeuvre. It is, however, Kubrick's *film* that has maintained this level of scholarly appreciation; the gothic *novel* on which it was based still awaits a comparable level of critical attention.

Although the stories of Stephen King have piqued Hollywood's interest for the past four decades, it is notable that the most impressive (i.e., popular, financially successful, critically engaged) adaptations made from his work have not come from King-authored screenplays. In fact, the best King films are born from the art of other writers (and directors) interpreting King for the screen. King supplies effective plot lines that are, in turn, often condensed and reconfigured by others. When King authors the screenplays for his own work, generally speaking, there are problems with pacing and focus. The lackluster televised miniseries of *The Shining, Rose Red*, and *Desperation* are cases in point. All three filmic texts feature teleplays written by King, and each is sluggish in its plot development, lingering too excessively over issues perhaps better suited to novels rather than motion pictures. This is not to say that screenplays of King's work authored by other writers are always successful—*Dreamcatcher* is a case in point—but Hollywood seems to sense that King's tendency toward loquacious prose requires severe editing, particularly by way of condensing, if his narratives are to have a chance at becoming successful cinematic adaptations. Despite the amount of money lavished on a production, what works on paper as a novel does not always translate well into visual cinema, as *The Da Vinci Code* aptly illustrated.

There are several examples that might be summoned to illustrate these points. In 1979, King published *The Dead Zone*, a long, loosely plotted, interwoven pastiche that brought together a psychic, a serial killer, and a zealous political demagogue. The book is still a powerful read, but director David Cronenberg and screenwriter Jeffrey Boam essentially reduced the scope of the novel by a third, and, while still retaining its episodic nature, they rendered the story into a tighter and more fast-paced narrative. I think something similar happens as well in Brandon Boyce's screenplay and Bryan Singer's cinematic direction of the novella *Apt Pupil*. King's story is probably a third too long and its ending—the random killing spree of Todd Bowden, all-American boy turned Nazi—is, in the movie, rendered far more chilling, as Todd uses the manipulative skills he has gained from steady contact with an ex-Nazi commandant to intimidate, rather than to execute, his high school guidance counselor, Mr. French. Additionally, the visceral killing of the homeless man in the film represents another very successful condensation of action that transpires over several years in King's novella, wherein Todd and Dussander learn to hone their murderous impulses.

Thus, the deft hand of a director or screenwriter better acquainted with the pacing required in the art of filmmaking often appears to enrich Stephen King's work; there are numerous instances where the collaboration between a creative screenwriter and a director has actually embellished the original King best seller. In *The Shawshank Redemption*, for example, King's text is enhanced by Frank Darabont's decisions to include the scene texturing the soprano duet from *The Marriage of Figaro* and the concluding scene on the Mexican beach where Andy and Red are reunited, neither of which is present in the King text. The film's inclusion of these shots turns out to be two of the most frequently cited by critics and general film audiences alike. Moreover, both scenes are integral to the film's meaning, highlighting, respectively, Andy's deepening affiliation with unruly women and a denouement that presents a visually satisfying moment of open sand, sea, and sky in contrast with the severely claustrophobic atmosphere of the rest of the film.

Given the immense worldwide popularity of the Stephen King film corpus and its relevance to the field of American cultural studies, it is truly remarkable that neither an academic journal nor, for that matter, any publication specializing in film studies, has yet to devote an entire issue to these cinematic adaptations. Though many of the King films have been examined in isolation (e.g., Frank Kermode's BFI edition on *The Shawshank Redemption*), as individual essays appearing in academic journals, or as chapters within edited volumes on topics treating general subjects such as the horror film or feminism (e.g., the Lant and Thompson edited collection *Imagining the Worst: Stephen King and the Representations of Women*), this book is the first collection of critical essays devoted exclusively to films adapted from the narratives of Stephen King.

Since the publication of the hardcover edition of this book in 2008, Mark Browning has addressed the King film corpus in *Stephen King on the Big Screen* (2009), and he has certainly made a contribution to the existing body of critical work in this field. Browning's book "attempts to look at King's adaptations on their own terms and see how they succeed or fail in generic terms" (26). By "generic terms" he means to interpret King's films in the context of the larger horror genre.

The book's problems are twofold, and both are related to Browning's claim for a generic approach to these movies. As the author himself admits, "Of all the films in this book, less than half have an entity that might be deemed a monster at all . . . [and] at least nine films here are explicitly not horror" (15). Because so many of King's films bend genres, Browning is left without a unifying approach—or a viable thesis—to map the work he interprets. Consequently, films bear no relationship to one another, and, just as egregious, his interpretations are usually devoid of a context—even a generic one. While Browning claims, for example, to have read psychoanalytic criticism of horror (e.g., Robin Wood) and Carol Clover's feminist analysis, their insights into the genre never find their way into *Stephen King on the Big Screen*. Unfortunately, neither do any of the other possible theoretical formulations available for interpreting the horror genre.

Which brings us to the second liability in Browning's book. Without a sustained commitment—generic, theoretical, and the intertextuality of the King film canon itself—informing this book, the author is left with a collection of unconnected ruminations, and he often resorts to expansive plot summaries. Moreover, Browning's insights are often suspect, as when he posits absurdly that "matters of gender are almost irrelevant" in *The Shawshank Redemption* (153), or when he ignores completely the crux of what the film *1408* is really about: a father confronting his repression over the death of his daughter (218–222).

While Browning's book joins this present collection in expanding a critical awareness of King's cinematic adaptations, it is clear that the scholarship in this area of film/cultural studies is still woefully underdeveloped.

I remain at a loss to explain this, especially in light of the fact that over the past twenty years horror film in general has received more than its fair share of critical explication. Given that, why have only *The Shining* and *Carrie*, directed by well-known and heavily analyzed auteurs, received an adequate level of scholarly attention? Perhaps King's extraordinary popular reputation has spilled over to defray efforts to treat these films as serious works of cinematic art. Perhaps the lack of critical attention to these films reflects the uneven quality of the King movie canon itself, as I have mentioned already. Perhaps the King films are on the whole still too young to have amassed a critical dialogue. Or, perhaps the sheer size of this film bibliography, replete with its inclusion of multiple screenwriters, directors, and production staffs and companies, makes the task of discussing these movies as a coherent body of work with a cohesive vision more difficult, if not impossible.

All these arguments notwithstanding, it is my conviction that film scholarship has been both prejudicial and deliberately exclusionary when dealing with filmic art associated with Stephen King. Film critics have rightly been unable to ignore *any* film directed by Stanley Kubrick, but how else to explain the general lack of interest in cinema as significant as *Dolores Claiborne, The Dead Zone, Stand By Me, The Green Mile*, and *The Shawshank Redemption*? These films, like King's literary canon, do not fit neatly into a singular film genre, and this is why so many of them have not found inclusion in recent film scholarship on the horror film. Ironically, this omission underscores the larger academic prejudice to dismiss King's writing—and the films made from it—as merely the work of a "hack horror writer."

The present collection, containing original essays that are published here for the first time, seeks not only to redress the lack of serious interpretative analysis most of the films under discussion have yet to receive, but also to encourage others to join in a critical dialogue that is long overdue. In the age of cultural and popular studies, this book is a reminder that the Stephen King movie industry, now worth well over a billion dollars in generated revenue and possessing a huge worldwide fan base, is a valuable focus of study and critical explication. Moreover, the majority of films under discussion in this volume are worthy of critical exegesis, reflecting as they do issues of immediate relevance in a profoundly anxious world. One important reason for King's enormous success is his attention to societal problems—our overreliance on technology and drugs, and the moral erosion of social institutions through racism, gender inequality, and the excesses of capitalism. Vampires and demons may be the great popular attractions of King films, but at the heart of his universe is a deep-seated awareness of American anxieties about how we live and where we are going, as a nation and as individuals. As many of the authors in this book point out, these are cautionary narratives about the dangers inherent in living selfish and irresponsible lives, whether as parents and spouses or as global citizens.

This collection begins with several essays examining the important role of adolescents in Stephen King's cinematic microcosm. King's children embody the full spectrum of human experience; many are at the centers of the films that feature them, and from them all other actions seem to radiate. Some of these young people are the nucleus for familial love as they are portrayed in the first halves of *Firestarter, Pet Sematary, The Shining*, and *Cujo*. But just as often, King's adolescents are troubled and troubling.

Alison M. Kelly's chapter on *Carrie* provides a useful set of sociological categories for the various characters in the film, defining their place in the American high school social hierarchy. Since these categories are rigidly demarcated, interaction among members of different groups is either tumultuous or impossible. Dennis Mahoney's treatment of the high school student in *Apt Pupil* follows in a similar vein, as he compares the apt pupil's fascination with Nazism and descent into evil to King's own ruminations on the Columbine killings and the sobering emergence of what King himself has called America's "Bogey Boys."

Commencing with the reminder that a child's bloody sneaker connects *Stand By Me* and *Pet Sematary*, Jeffrey A. Weinstock develops this grisly symbol in his chapter as a means for discussing the loss of childhood, innocence, and life that are common to both films. From this point of comparison, however, Weinstock then surmises that the more mainstream *Stand By Me* is actually more terrifying than the supernaturally animated horror in *Pet Sematary* because the former—unlike the latter—poses a nihilistic rejection of the afterlife in the finality of a dead child and the sobering acceptance that neither God nor fate governs the course of human existence.

When most people think of Stephen King's fiction or the films based on his canon, they typically think of the evil affiliations forged between supernatural agencies and the humans manipulated by them, or the unsavory bonds formed between two humans, often between a younger male and an older one, such as those found in *Apt Pupil* or *Pet Sematary*, that result in mutual corruption based on a shared secret. However, there are also extremely positive unions formed between individuals in many of the films made from King's works. Although they appear initially as unlikely candidates for friendship, the interpersonal connections established between Gordie Lachance and Chris Chambers (*Stand By Me*), Dolores Claiborne and Vera Donovan (*Dolores Claiborne*), Andy Dufresne and Red Redding (*The Shawshank Redemption*), and even Paul Edgecomb and John Coffey (*The Green Mile*) suggest that shared secrets in King's universe are not always doomed to disastrous consequences. In the films cited above, the secret knowledge of criminality—two murders in *Dolores Claiborne*, the location of an escaped felon in *Shawshank*—is maintained because the respective crimes are viewed as morally, if not legally, condoned.

In her treatment of Taylor Hackford's film adaptation of *Dolores Claiborne*, Colleen Dolan explores the connections between novel and cinematic adaptation and finds that the latter, as represented by Selena, Dolores, and Vera, offers an exploration of the archetypal life cycle of woman as daughter, mother, and, finally, crone. Also considering the major symbols in the film—the solar eclipse and the abandoned well—Dolan employs these montages as a means for explicating the tragic salvation that Dolores manages to carve out for herself and her daughter. She reads the film as a vehicle for illustrating the incomplete evolution of American feminism.

Friendships in King's fiction transcend age, class, gender, and racial barriers as often as they cross legal and ethical lines of conduct. Like the feminist bond Dolores establishes with Selena and Vera, Tony Magistrale's essay on *The Shawshank Redemption* discusses another subversive friendship in King's movies—this one crossing racial and class lines—that is equally as instrumental in the survival of the film's respective characters. His chapter posits that Andy and Red gain strength from subverting traditional gender affiliations and aligning themselves with various constructions of femininity—cinematic, musical, and marital—that exist at the margins of the film's central action and stand in opposition to the masculine oppression that dominates life in Shawshank prison. One need not be incarcerated inside an actual prison, however, to experience life as a prisoner. So argues Mary Findley in her chapter that interprets *Misery* as a prison film. Positing that *Misery* is best understood as the first part of a prison trilogy that includes *Shawshank* and *The Green Mile*, Findley establishes points of comparison that illuminate the interrelationships among these three movies.

The King film corpus raises interesting issues about the political ideology underlining many of these films: are they subversive texts, challenging traditional constructions of gender and race, or are these explorations restricted by the limits of a liberal sentimentalism? Unlike *Shawshank*, where the bond of friendship transcends racial and class differences, Brian Kent's reading of *The Green Mile* challenges the film's premise that Coffey receives his just Christian reward in passively accepting his role as suffering agent bearing the sins of others. Viewing Coffey in light of a literary tradition that includes Stowe's Uncle Tom and Twain's Jim, Kent links Coffey to these earlier racial stereotypes of the selfless, spiritually minded Afro-American who appears to exist in order to help white people work out their self-esteem issues and other assorted guilts. The racial dynamics and excessive self-sacrifice associated with Coffey complicate our response to both whites and blacks in this film; indeed, the film, despite its strong liberal overtures against corporeal punishment and racist profiling, ultimately fails to engage the attendant racism inherent in Coffey being black.

The racial tension that undermines the complacent ending of *The Green Mile* is revisited in the chapters written by Sarah Nilson and Sarah Turner. Nilson undertakes a discussion of race in her analysis of various Afro-American characters in the King film oeuvre. Like Kent's chapter, Nilson's concern is in tracing the concept of the "magical negro"—typically a black male character who aids whites in their physical and moral struggles to survive in seminal films such as *The Green Mile* and *The Shining*. In addition to these films, however, Nilson addresses the racial implications in an obscure production called *Ghosts*, a short film written by Stephen King starring Michael Jackson. Turner's essay on *The Dead Zone* reads its main character, John Smith, in racial terms, as the monstrous "other" typically found in classic horror cinema. While his character is located at the center of this film, she argues that Smith is simultaneously pushed to its periphery because of his supernatural estrangement—which parallels racial otherness—from the white mainstream.

Critic James Egan has asserted that "from the beginning of his career, King has concerned himself with the complex implications of science and technology, so much so that the horror he evokes often seems inseparable from the dangers of imperious science and runaway machinery of many sorts" (140). Two chapters in this volume examine the unholy nexus between horror and technology. Philip Simpson reads *Christine* as a vampiric machine that merges voracious capitalism with lethal femininity. Applying a psychoanalytic paradigm to Carpenter's film, Simpson views the car as a metallic rendition of the *vagina dentata*; the machine forces to the surface of the narrative the feminized Arnie Cunningham's misgivings toward sexuality and his doomed effort to remedy them through identification with Christine's siren song. In his reading of the King-directed film *Maximum Overdrive*, Michael A. Arnzen likewise discusses King's perspective on mechanical technology. In his treatment of both the film and "Trucks," the short story (and made-for-television movie) that is the basis for *Maximum Overdrive*, Arnzen argues for a reconsideration of King's cult-status film as a techno-horror-humor hybrid that mocks the gods of technology worshipped by America and most of the rest of the world. Especially intriguing is Arnzen's effort to compare *Maximum Overdrive* with the carnivalesque ritual of the automobile demolition derby, wherein extreme levels of mechanized violence displace rules of social behavior.

Of all the films treated in this collection, Stanley Kubrick's version of *The Shining* is in the popular imagination arguably the best-known King adaptation as well as the title to have received the most attention from film and cultural scholars. Michael J. Blouin's essay runs counter to the often-argued position first put forth by Fredric Jameson that the Overlook Hotel embodies the spirit of American capitalism run amok and that Jack Torrance, through the process of his identification with the hotel, aligns himself with a similar ideological ethos. Instead, Blouin proposes that the ghosts at the Overlook are less capitalist incarnations and representations and more appropriately aligned with a communist politburo; Torrance's fatal misreading of the social mobility actually available to him at the Overlook as well as his desire to be part of the hotel's "collective" reflect his urge to dissolve the rigid class hierarchy in place among the ghosts and in larger American society.

Many of Stephen King's celluloid adaptations first appeared in televised miniseries (primarily on the ABC Network). Two of the chapters in this collection deal specifically with a couple of these King miniseries: Pharr on *Storm of the Century* and Perry and Sederholm on *Rose Red*. Pharr writes about *Storm of the Century*, arguably the best of the King miniseries, and *Needful Things*, a film that might have fared better in a miniseries format instead of via theatrical release. *Storm* and *Needful Things*, like *'Salem's Lot*, continue King's fascination with detailing the deconstruction of ethics in contemporary America, and all three of these films are commentaries on corrupt small-town communities and communal values. Perry and Sederholm view *Rose Red* as a work best understood as a "hybrid"—that is, viewing the miniseries as a merging of genres (comedy and horror), interwoven literary and filmic allusions (*Midsummer Night's Dream, Moby-Dick, The Haunting of Hill House*, and "The Fall of the House of Usher"), and through a constant self-referential awareness of the movie's place in the haunted house tradition.

In the penultimate chapter of this collection, Benjamin Szumskyj addresses one of the more recent King film adaptations, *Secret Window*. His analysis begins with a comparison between the film and the novella upon which it is based. He concludes with a Bakhtinian reading of the multiple personality disorder that afflicts the film's central protagonist.

In the final chapter of this collection, Patrick McAleer addresses the most recent of King's filmic adaptations, *The Mist*. His reading posits a sociopolitical analysis of "failure" as it operates in many King novels and films, including *The Mist*. He reads Darabont's film as a highly pessimistic adaptation of King's novella, perhaps underscoring the general erosion of American confidence since King authored the original text.

For over three decades, Stephen King has worked hard to capture in prose some of the most essential facets of what it means to be American—the good, the bad, and the ugly. The best cinematic adaptations of this prose have likewise captured the *Americanness* of King's art: from the personal tragedies associated with divorce and alcoholism to the violence of the supernatural and paranormal, to the bonds of unlikely friendships that transcend race, class, and age. His horror aesthetic, with its inordinate attention to car crashes, drug dependency, and dysfunctional behavior, provides an oddly eccentric yet somehow appropriate lens for viewing postmodern American culture. There also remains, on the other hand, a particular resiliency to the heroes and heroines featured in the films discussed in this book. King maintains a nearly sentimental faith that the individual can and will survive, even as the social institutions that individuals assemble may prove wholly untenable. American audiences come to these films for the same reason the rest of the world does: to see ourselves portrayed honestly, the foibles and scars as well as those moments of unselfish love. In an era where politicians deathlessly trumpet superficial American virtues at the expense of reality, the films of Stephen King, as many of the chapters in this book argue, provide a more accurate—albeit sobering—national portrait.

Chapter 1

The Queen Bee, the Prom Queen, and the Girl Next Door

Teen Hierarchical Structures in *Carrie*

Alison M. Kelly

High school is your adolescent world.

Brian De Palma

I was frightened . . . both of the world of girls I would have to inhabit . . . . and of the level of cruelty I would have to describe.

Stephen King, on writing *Carrie*

In her best-selling book *Odd Girl Out: The Hidden Culture of Aggression in Girls*, Rachel Simmons examines the seething female anger and frustration that writhes just beneath the façade of "sugar and spice and all things nice" (101). In response to the various cinematic manifestations of this theme, she claims, "*Heathers* was the first in a string of movies depicting the clandestine politics of popular girl cliques" (75). However, this theme was first addressed more than a decade prior to the release of *Heathers. Carrie* has passed its thirtieth anniversary as a novel and a film, and in both texts, Stephen King and Brian De Palma predicted with frightening accuracy what our girls would become in subsequent decades. The horror of *Carrie* is that her world is now the norm. If her telekinesis is downplayed, a new kind of horror emerges: the metamorphosis of our daughters from kind and loving little girls into cruel, calculating destroyers of self-esteem and identity. This then spawns a pecking order that is near impossible to challenge or change. Chris Hargensen, as Bates High's "Queen Bee," is our real horror. Though Carrie physically destroys the school, she is merely completing a destruction that Chris began years before and has honed to perfection through puberty and privilege.

Table 1.1 has defined the six major teen characters in *Carrie* according to Rosalind Wiseman's criteria in her 2002 groundbreaking study of teens and power, entitled *Queen Bees and Wannabees*. Each represents a different rung on the ladder of teen hierarchy, from the very bottom—"Target"—to the most coveted position: "Queen Bee." Although Tommy Ross and Billy Nolan do not naturally fall within the boundaries of the female hierarchy, they meet the male criteria Wiseman has laid out and actively contribute to the downfalls of Bates High and Carrie White. However, this tragedy is clearly meant to be seen as girl-motivated, girl-activated, and the product of Girl-World.

Table 1.1 Carrie's cast of characters as defined by *Queen Bees and Wannabees*

Name	Title	Characteristics	Description
Chris	Queen Bee	"Through a combination of charisma, force, money, looks, will, and manipulation, this girl reigns supreme. . . . Never underestimate her power." (Wiseman 25)	"Seventy-four assigned detentions. She skipped out on fifty-one of [them]." (King 72) "Everything was for Chris . . . [Billy] would have done murder for her, and more." (King 117)
Norma	Sidekick	"The girl who's closest to the Queen Bee and will back her no matter what because her power depends on the confidence she gets from the Queen Bee." (Wiseman 28)	"Chris had been doing a little quiet promoting among her friends." (King 148) "That was when they all started laughing. I did too." (King 174)
Sue	Torn Bystander	"Constantly conflicted between doing the right thing and her allegiance to the clique . . . . she's the one most likely to be caught in the middle of a conflict between two girls." (Wiseman 31)	"The upset inside her was very great, too great yet for either tears or anger. She was a get- along girl, and it was the first fight she had been in." (King 78)
Carrie	Target	"She's the victim, set up by the other girls to be	"Her hair stuck to her cheeks in a curving helmet

Continued

Table 1.1 Continued

Name	Title	Characteristics	Description
		humiliated, made fun of, excluded . . . . [her] style of dress, behavior, and such are outside the norms acceptable to the clique." (Wiseman 35)	shape. There was a cluster of acne on one shoulder. At sixteen, the elusive stamp of hurt was already marked clearly in her eyes." (King 7)
Tommy	Leader	"This is usually the one everybody wants to be. . . . He's well-respected among boys. He doesn't always have to obviously display his power." (Wiseman 183)	"He apparently had a high enough tolerance to verbal abuse and enough independence from his peer group to ask Carrie in the first place . . . [He] appears to have been something of a rarity: a socially conscious young man." (King 93)
Billy	Bad Boy/ Thug	"A really dangerous guy who often says disrespectful things to and about girls. [A girl] dates [him] *because* she knows he's bad. She gets to tick off her parents, flirt with danger." (Wiseman 180; emphasis in the original)	"Something about him excited [Chris] . . . she thought it might have been his car—at least at the start. Billy's car was old, dark, somehow sinister." (King 134)

The female hierarchy in *Carrie* is immediately established in the opening scene: the P.E. volleyball game. In the DVD documentary, "Visualizing *Carrie*," screenwriter Lawrence D. Cohen explains, "You understand immediately that this is a character who's a loner, who's picked on and feels terrible about it." As the camera slowly hovers over the court and then moves in to focus on Carrie White, two things are obvious to the viewer. First, Carrie is, at best, a peripheral member of the team. She is positioned in the lower right-hand corner of the court, and as the girls play, Norma backs up into Carrie's space, forcing her to retreat further into the corner. Second, most of the girls on the court consciously attempt to make this as miserable an experience as possible for Carrie. As they bat the ball around during the game point, various cries are heard: "Hit it to Carrie—she'll blow it!" After Carrie ineffectively swats at the ball and misses for the final point in the game (which is exactly what both teams *expected* her to do), there is a chorus of disappointed voices: "You can't win a game with *her* on the team," "*Look* at her!" and "Moron!" Norma even hits Carrie on the head with her red baseball cap. Finally, Chris Hargensen makes a parting shot to her on the way to the locker room: "*You eat shit.*"

This film still demonstrates a great deal about the female power dynamics at Bates High School.

1. Chris is larger than Carrie; she leans down and forward to insult her, which increases the level of intimidation.
2. Carrie also looks down. She cannot meet Chris's eye.
3. Chris is clearly furious with Carrie. Carrie, on the other hand, looks like she is about to burst into tears. P.E. class and one volleyball point have become something far more significant.
4. Carrie's hands hover near her ears. Is she literally trying to block out Chris's insults?
5. Chris's shirt is tucked in to show off her figure. She is proud of her female assets.
6. Carrie's shirt is oversized, with another layer underneath. Is this to hide the fact that she is well along into puberty, or is it a kind of armor to help protect her from Chris's wrath? Is she trying to mask her femininity in as obvious a way as Chris flaunts hers?

7. The girls in the background do not pay any attention to the confrontation because "anyone can torment Carrie because no one could possibly be less popular" (Holland-Toll 77).

8. Bates High School's colors are yellow and black and their mascot is the Stinger. According to art director Jack Fisk, "We didn't want anything cuddly or too friendly." This further emphasizes that Chris, as the Queen Bee, rules the school, just as a Queen Bee has complete control over her hive. This description perfectly suits Chris's temperament and control issues.

Carrie's role as Target is then immediately reinforced in the infamous locker room scene. When Carrie finds blood on her hand and is unable to connect the sight of it to the knowledge that she has gotten her first period, she emerges from the shower stall panicked and in search of help. Her first response is to go to Sue Snell, who has already established herself as a "kinder" peer to Carrie, since she did not openly participate in Carrie's harassment on the volleyball court.

True to her form, Chris sets things in motion. Dangling a tampon from her fingers, she taunts Carrie: "Have a Tampax, Carrie . . . hey, Norma, Carrie's got her period!" An examination of the screenplay provides insight into this scene. When Chris begins to chant "Period," the screenplay has spelled it "PEERiod," a direct reference to Carrie finally behaving within the norms of Girl-World. Her first menstrual period *should* make her "one of the girls." Instead, because of Carrie's terrified reaction and Chris's preexisting frustration over the outcome of the volleyball game, Carrie's initiation into womanhood becomes one more reason to torment her. In the DVD documentary, "Acting *Carrie*," Nancy Allen (Chris) describes her experience filming the locker room scene: "To shoot it, I have to say, was maybe the most disturbing thing I've ever shot because it's like a gang, it's like a tribe and a ritual or some kind of horrible thing, and we did work ourselves into this sort of frenzied state, and I did start to feel like I hated [Carrie]."

Given Chris's authority over the other girls, it is natural for the rest of the members of the P.E. class to join in. Chris throws the first sanitary pad, quickly followed by Norma who, as the Sidekick, will do anything her Queen Bee does, providing that Chris does it first. Sue pulls the cover off of the sanitary pad dispenser, indicating that even a responsible girl can get sucked into the group mentality. Then the other girls join in, quickly turning a female prank into something far darker and more psychologically damaging to Carrie. She entered the locker room as the Target, and now she is literally a target as the girls bombard her with tampons and sanitary pads while she cowers in the corner of her shower stall.

Sue, Chris, Norma, and Carrie's roles in the hierarchy further develop when Miss Collins discovers what is going on. Just as Carrie initially went to Sue for help, Miss Collins grabs Sue and asks, "Sue, what are you doing?" before she addresses any of the other girls involved. Sue is a girl who has earned the trust of adults as well as her peers. She is the one expected to help Carrie, and she is the one Miss Collins looks to for insight into this locker room hazing. Meanwhile, Chris and Norma have not yet realized that they have gone too far. Their cries of "Plug it up! Plug it up!" echo through the locker room long after Miss Collins arrives. The girls only cease their chanting and throwing when Miss Collins slaps Carrie, and the camera immediately cuts to close-ups of Chris and Norma, who are grinning, and Sue, who looks shocked by what has just happened and her contribution to it.

This pivotal scene sets the stage for the film's most crucial theme in both Lawrence D. Cohen's screenplay and in Girl-World: betrayal. Carrie White's body has committed a physical betrayal of sorts, with the advent of her period at the wrong time, in the wrong place, and under the wrong circumstances. Furthermore, her mother views her first menstrual period as a direct physical betrayal of her soul. She tells Carrie, "if [you] had remained sinless, the curse of blood would never have come on [you]."

The girls are also betrayed when Miss Collins refuses to view their behavior as a joke. According to Amy Irving (Sue), when Miss Collins views her line-up of teen offenders, "Brian [De Palma] really wanted me to be the most guilty of all." This is visible in the expression on Sue's face; she does not like having to hear what Miss Collins is saying—"Now I want you all to know that you did a really shitty thing yesterday, a really shitty thing. Did any of you stop to think that Carrie White has feelings?"—because it's exactly what she has been saying to herself when she mentally assesses her role in tormenting Carrie over the years. As the group's "good girl," Sue is the one least likely to get in trouble; thus, her betrayal of Carrie's trust hurts the most.

Meanwhile, Chris and Norma can barely keep straight faces throughout Miss Collins's angry response. But during an afternoon of jumping jacks, sit-ups, and push-ups, when Chris blurts out, "Stick it up your a . . ." to Miss Collins, she is finally put in her place with a well-placed slap to the face. Chris's offensive and influential mouth is now temporarily silenced. However, while this could have easily become an "Us (The Girls) vs. Them (The Adults)" scenario, Chris is suddenly forced to come to terms with the unreliable conformity of her peers. Physically located at a midpoint between the girls and Miss Collins, Chris turns to them and pleads, "She can't get away with this if we all stick together. Norma? Helen? Sue?" While Norma cannot meet Chris's eyes and Helen shakes her head like a wounded puppy, Sue hits *her* breaking point and responds, "Shut up, Chris . . . just shut up."

This is devastating to Chris. The Girl-World she has reigned over has been upended, and she must now question her place in it, since "[W]omen have long relied upon their affiliations with others to enhance social status, and at its core, popularity is a mean and merciless competition for relationships" (Simmons 157). Chris's loyal Sidekick, Norma, has refused to stand by her, her drone bees will not acknowledge their Queen's presence, and Sue, who was the Torn Bystander up until this point, begins to align herself with what she knows is right. Her verbal response to Chris seals the deal: Chris is out of the Prom, Sue and the other girls are in, they've chosen the Establishment over a friend in need, it's all Carrie's fault, and as Chris promises, "This isn't over. This isn't over by a long shot!"

What has upset Chris the most is not Miss Collins's slap, or her friends' fear of standing up for her; rather, Chris finally comes to the unpleasant realization that "someone from Carrie's social caste can have an influence on her life" (Newhouse 52). Meek, unassuming Carrie White has deprived Chris of the thing she wants the most: to have her Queen Bee status affirmed in the most social and significant way possible. Chris wants to be Prom Queen. Thus, Chris will be looking for some kind of retribution; as Wiseman warns parents, "If your daughter is in a position of power, she'll likely have an eye-for-an-eye outlook on life" (Wiseman 47).

Chris's response to this experience is a result of her inability to "just shut up." As Tony Magistrale asserts in *Hollywood's Stephen King*, "Chris' obsessive attention to her mouth—compulsively darkening it with lipstick, employing it as a manipulative aid for persuading Billy Nolan to help her further humiliate Carrie, licking her lips wantonly before pulling the cord that releases the bucket of blood" (29)—connects specifically to Chris's role as a female bully who is accustomed to getting what she wants. Although boys are more likely to respond to adverse situations with physical violence, which is then soon forgotten, girls are more likely to carry a grudge and "use back-biting, exclusion, rumors, name-calling, and manipulation to inflict psychological pain on targeted victims" (Simmons 3). Hence, it is natural for Chris to use her mouth to inflict further harm, just as Sue uses hers to make amends. Standing up to Chris is not enough to assuage Sue's guilty conscience; she "understands that a small and meaningless act of atonement will not do . . . this gesture must hurt [her] as much as she has hurt Carrie" (Holland-Toll 79). Thus, Sue feels compelled to offer Carrie the one thing she would never have otherwise: a date to the Prom. At the core of Sue's decision to deprive herself of the Prom so that Carrie might attend lies yet another personal agenda: "her kindness to Carrie is really an act of social rebellion; by treating Carrie humanely, she hopes to save herself from a future of unconscionable conformity" (Magistrale, *Landscape of Fear*, 97). Sue believes having Carrie attend the Prom will help both of them to determine what kind of women they want to be, in comparison to the girls they currently are.

Despite their differences, Sue's steady boyfriend, Tommy Ross ("Leader"), and Chris's current beau, Billy Nolan ("Bad Boy/ Thug"), are little more than a means to an end that their girlfriends have already decided upon; they exist so that the girls can manipulate them into assisting them with their respective Prom schemes. As the scenes following Chris's outburst in detention bounce back and forth between the two couples, we see how similar Sue and Chris actually are, despite their oppositional motivations; both young ladies use oral methods of persuasion on their boyfriends in order to assure their complicity in their respective schemes.

Convincing Tommy Ross is no easy task for Sue. However, our initial impressions of Tommy are favorable in terms of his role as Leader at Bates High School. He is the athlete who writes poetry, is above his peers' immature behavior, and challenges his English teacher's goading of Carrie in class when she musters up the nerve to comment that his poem is "beautiful." When Sue approaches Tommy at track practice, he stands out from his peers; in contrast to their yellow-and-black uniforms, he wears solid black, with his blond hair in a halo around his head. As "the only truly stable and reliable character" (Kakmi 1) in the film, Tommy is a man among boys, and the only one who does not have any sort of ulterior motive regarding Carrie. When Sue meets with him behind the bleachers, she asks, "Tommy, if I asked you to do something very special for me, would you do it?" Without hesitation, Tommy responds, "Yeah." Sue continues, "I want you to take Carrie White to the Prom." It is interesting to note that Sue does not *ask* Tommy to do this for her; rather, she phrases her question in terms of what she *wants* from him.

While we do not witness Tommy's immediate reaction to Sue's request, we are meant to understand that Sue "convinces" him in a later scene by using the silent treatment while she dutifully does her homework, leaving him to watch television. It isn't until he says, "Okay, I'll do it," that she rewards him with a smile. Given Tommy's status as Leader, he is the only male in school who can successfully orchestrate Carrie's initiation into acceptable teen society. This scene also ends Sue's role as Torn Bystander; once she has made the decision to introduce Carrie to high school society on what is arguably the biggest night of the year, she has sided with the Target and rejected the Queen Bee.

Chris, on the other hand, decides on an equally effective approach which clearly defines her as the "bad girl." Sue's depriving Tommy of *anything* oral is in direct contradiction to Chris's overuse of *all things* oral: she is a masterful combination of mixed messages, which only serve to confuse and frustrate Billy. For example, she sucks on his finger, kisses him, and then shoves him away, calling him a "dumb shit." However, she makes her meaning apparent when she kisses him yet again, and breathily tells him, "I want you to do something . . . something important . . . [*her head descends into his lap*] oh Billy . . . I hate Carrie White."

This scene reinforces Leonard Sax's analysis of female bullies in his best-selling work, *Why Gender Matters*. He has analyzed bullying according to the following gender roles and criteria:

GIRLS who bully typically	BOYS who bully typically
have many friends	have few friends
are socially skilled	are socially inept
act in groups to isolate a single girl	act alone
are doing well in school	are doing poorly in school
know the girls they are bullying	do not know the boys (or girls) they bully

Through her behavior toward Carrie, her sexual manipulation of Billy and his acquiescence in her plot to ruin Carrie, Chris Hargensen demonstrates almost every criteria Sax sets out (75). Billy also meets the criteria laid out for him, most notably the final one; when Chris begins to fellate him, his response to her hating Carrie is a dumb-founded "Who?" Billy has no clue who Carrie is, and even says, "That Carrie White, she sure is cute," when he sees her at the Prom, yet he agrees to whatever Chris asks of him. Of significance is that Chris phrases her request to Billy in almost the same wording as Sue uses on Tommy: "I want you to . . ." Given the forcible quality of Sue's and

Chris's requests, and the resulting oral consequences, the boys are putty in their hands. Considering Tommy's status as Leader and Billy's as Bad Boy/Thug, their girlfriends have chosen their specific methods of persuasion well.

While Sue and Chris are busy with their boys, Carrie is undergoing a metamorphosis. An examination of Carrie's bedroom demonstrates the shift from the girl Carrie was obligated to be under her mother's abusive tutelage to the woman she is becoming under Sue's and Miss Collins's guidance. Although Miss Collins's efforts will result in her death at the Prom, her motivations behind encouraging Carrie are indicative of a woman who has correctly read the group dynamics in her P.E. class and is making an honest attempt to break a mold that she views as damaging and hurtful. In Miss Collins's eyes, the Prom is the perfect chance to begin social integration for Carrie, as well as an opportunity for her to provide some adult guidance in breaking down Chris's infrastructure of abuse and intolerance. Miss Collins understands that Chris will not change . . . but perhaps Carrie can.

In the beginning of the film, Carrie is a teenager who gives no indication that she has an identity outside of the one her mother has forced upon her. For example, when Carrie first examines herself in her bedroom mirror, Jesus is reflected in the upper left-hand corner of the mirror, watching over her. In this scene, "Carietta White is concerned with finding anything beyond the utter emptiness that is her soul. She looks at herself in the mirror and sees only ugliness and then a void" (Weller 13). This "void" is emphasized by the overwhelming blackness reflected in the mirror, with Carrie at the center of nothingness. When she shatters her own reflection out of frustration and angst, the mirror's pieces fall onto her dresser. The only discernible items on it are a cross, a Bible, and a Jesus and Mary nightlight. There is nothing in the room to indicate that a teenaged girl inhabits it. Several scenes later, when Carrie is again looking into the mirror, this time while getting ready for the Prom, the picture of Jesus is no longer visible, the room is aglow and a rose and a newspaper clipping of Tommy Ross are taped next to the mirror. Carrie is coming into the light and evolving . . . which is what Sue and Miss Collins are hoping for, what Chris resents, and what Margaret White fears.

However, in *Danse Macabre*, Stephen King states, "[H]igh school is a place of almost bottomless conservatism and bigotry, a place where the adolescents who attend are no more allowed to rise 'above their station' than a Hindu would be allowed to rise above his or her caste" (169). Carrie's station in life seems to be inherently ingrained in her society. Margaret White is horrified by her daughter's newfound independence and subsequent defiance, the student body is bound to be confused by Carrie's appearance at the Prom, and with Sue's determination to "make things right" and Chris's vow that things "aren't over," both girls engage in a power struggle over the fate of Carrie White and her status in their world. Because of these conflicting forces, it is obvious that Carrie's attempts to conform are the beginning of the end.

Yet, when Carrie arrives at the Prom, she and Tommy contradict King's statement about the caste system in high schools, because "when she brings her behavior and appearance into accord with [her peers], the other girls are ready to welcome Carrie into their group" (Strengell 166). However, this is because of Chris's noticeable absence at the Prom. She was Carrie's greatest tormenter, and now that Carrie is at the Prom and Chris is not, her followers are beginning to connect with the new and improved Carrie . . . a Carrie they can approve of and relate to, since she now looks like and is behaving like them.

Unfortunately, "the Carrie who became sociable suffer[s] as a result . . ." (Bliss 64). Norma, the ever-faithful Sidekick and Chris's self-proclaimed "best friend," is the true catalyst for Carrie's downfall. While Billy and Chris have obtained the desired bucket of blood, Norma is the only one who can ensure that Carrie is crowned Queen. As we follow Norma through the gymnasium, she bustles from table to table, filled with self-importance as she proves her complete allegiance to her Queen by substituting the actual ballots with "Carrie" ballots. Interestingly, in this scene, Chris is virtually powerless, since she has been banned from the Prom and can only huddle under the stage while she waits to pull the rope that will release the bucket of blood.

When Tommy and Carrie are conveniently named King and Queen, we are shown what the world can be like without Chris. With the literal and figurative removal of the Queen Bee, the entire hierarchy begins to collapse. Carrie receives legitimate praise and applause, and instead of the mocking and jeering she has grown up with and has come to expect from her peers, she sees only smiling faces as she makes her way to the stage. As she and Tommy are officially crowned, her face radiates beauty and hope. For a brief moment, Carrie White becomes the high school success story. She has overcome the humiliation of the locker room and has finally assimilated herself with her peers, who indicate that they are more than willing to accept her on these terms. For a brief moment, the Target has usurped the role of the Queen.

Obviously, this cannot last because even though the school might be willing to accept Carrie for the night, Chris Hargensen cannot. When Chris releases the bucket of blood on Carrie and Tommy, ending Tommy's life and Bates High School as she knows it, this "prank" is enough to confirm the following: "Our fundamental social institutions—school, marriage, the workplace, and the church—have, beneath their veneers of respectability, evolved into perverse manifestations of narcissism, greed and violence" (Magistrale, *Landscape of Fear*, 75). Hope for a better, more accepting future is short-lived, and a return to the corrupt norm is guaranteed. As the pig blood covers Carrie from head to toe, she is once again a target and *the* Target.

So Carrie wreaks havoc on her world. While this includes the entire town of Chamberlain in King's novel, De Palma limits Carrie's destruction to those who represent *her* world: her peers and her mother. Most of her senior class perishes as a result of fire and water in biblical proportions, and Carrie saves "special" punishments for those who have affected her the most: Chris, Billy, her mother, and Sue.

Once again, Chris is punished through betrayal. Unlike King's novel, which has Billy behind the wheel, *Chris* is the one driving as she and Billy speed away from the high school in Billy's car. While Billy sits in the passenger seat, drunk and drooling, Chris spots Carrie in the road up ahead and speeds up in an attempt to run Carrie down. Although Billy has rightfully earned the title of Bad Boy/Thug, he looks horrified at what Chris intends to do. Chris, on the other hand, is full of anticipation as she excitedly chews on her gum. In this scene, it is clear that Chris is the true "monster" of Chamberlain. *She* is the reason why most of her peers are dead. The years of abuse she has inflicted upon Carrie, her total disregard for humanity and authority, her ability to convince Norma to fix the Prom election, combined with the fact that *she pulled the rope*, all prove that spoiled Chris Hargensen has brought this upon herself. And so Chris is betrayed by Billy's car. She cannot manipulate an inhuman object in the same way she manipulates people; the car must respond to natural (and supernatural) physical forces, unlike the emotional forces Chris is able to dictate at will through her status.

After destroying Chris and Billy, "Carrie returns home, rejected by the outside world, only to be rejected by her inner world as well; her mother, the one person who should protect and understand her, stabs her" (Collings 38). Although this needs no reinforcement, Carrie again proves that she is the Target. As Margaret attempts to end Carrie's life through a physical form of betrayal (backstabbing), Carrie hits her breaking point and kills Margaret with a variety of kitchen implements. At this point, she finally gives up and gives in: "Carrie has pushed her isolation as far as possible. She has killed everyone who has touched her life, dissolving all social bonds until there are literally no groups left" (Collings 38–39). Just as the ladder of teen hierarchy had collapsed in on itself at Bates High School before Chris's prank, and is now destroyed through the massive death toll, Carrie brings her house down on herself and her mother. As her home folds itself into the ground, sociological destruction is complete . . . at least temporarily.

In perhaps the film's greatest departure from the novel, Sue Snell has a special torment reserved for her. Unlike most of her peers, Sue has been spared Carrie's telekinetic wrath. Perhaps this is because of her kind nature and well-meaning gestures toward helping Carrie to achieve some measure of happiness, or her attempt to expose Chris at the Prom before Miss Collins misinterprets her actions and throws her out of the gym. Regardless, Sue is left to experience the aftermath of Chamberlain's destruction. As she goes to place flowers on Carrie's former home, we are able to read, "Carrie White burns in Hell" scrawled on a white "FOR SALE" cross on the lawn. Chamberlain clearly has not learned any lessons about *why* Carrie White had finally had enough at the Prom.

In "Acting Carrie," actress P. J. Soles (Norma) explains, "*Carrie* is more than just a teenage horror film; it is about young kids trying to find themselves as adults in the world. They're making that transition . . . wanting to be respected by your peers, and not knowing quite where you fit in society, wanting to make a name for yourself." By deviating from the standard horror genre to include some very real statements and portrayals about the unforgiving nature of the teen experience, De Palma's *Carrie* is a film that not only stands the test of time, but it has also predicted a future that is all too grim. According to Jürgen Müller, "real reports of rampant violence repeatedly hit the headlines, a testament to the fact that the social microcosms within schools are no place for kids who journey the path less traveled" (386). Chris Hargensen is alive, well, and thriving in various cinematic reincarnations of her original form; there have been at least 14 high school massacres in the past 5 years, and the term "Intermittent Explosive Disorder" (http://www.mayhem.net/Crime/intermittent. html) has been added to our vocabularies. Yet, we are still wondering *why* our high schools have become the way they are. King's novel and De Palma's film have answered that question; now, in the role of Sue Snell, it is up to *us* to decide how to respond to our girls.

Chapter 2

Apt Pupil

The Making of a "Bogeyboy"

Dennis F. Mahoney

On May 26, 1999, in his keynote address at the annual meeting of the Vermont Library Conference, Stephen King reflected on the spate of adolescent violence in American schools that had culminated the previous month in the massacre of 12 students and a teacher at Columbine High School in Littleton, Colorado. Without condoning the acts of individuals like Eric Harris and Dylan Klebold, he saw them as part of a pattern rooted in American history and embedded in contemporary society's easy access to guns and the culture of violence in America's entertainment industry—from which latter point he did not exempt his own work. With teenage killers well on their way to becoming the new "bogeyboys" of American culture, objects of fear whom we claim not to understand, King argued that "perhaps the real first step in making them go away is to decide what it is about them that frightens us so much."[1]

A seemingly unlikely candidate for becoming such a bogeyboy is Todd Bowden, the suburban, solidly bourgeois, high-achieving, and athletic protagonist in the novella *Apt Pupil* (1982), who discovers a Nazi war criminal in his neighborhood and becomes increasingly corrupted by the stories of mass murder he hears in exchange for not revealing his discovery to the authorities: "On the surface, Todd is the perfect California high school kid. Beneath, he's fascinated by the Holocaust and the power wielded by the Nazis; a member of the Trenchcoat Mafia, in fact, without the trenchcoat." Although King did not develop the point in his speech, other parallels exist between the fictional character Todd Bowden and the actual perpetrators of the Columbine Massacre. The recently released diaries and school essays of Eric Harris, the older and more dominating figure, reveal a self-destructive fascination with Nazism that helps explain why Harris and Klebold chose April 20, the birthday of Adolf Hitler, as the time to launch their assault on Columbine High School, even though Klebold himself was of Jewish descent; indeed, Harris's nickname for Klebold was "V" (as in *Vergeltung*, German for vengeance), Hitler's designation for the unmanned planes and missiles launched against England in 1944 after the Allied invasion of Normandy. As in *Apt Pupil*, two individuals melded their identities into a lethal composite at Columbine High School, with one half serving more as the planner and the other as the implementer of violent fantasies that otherwise might have remained dormant. In this regard, both fiction and life share a pattern that Tony Magistrale has observed throughout Stephen King's work: "King's portrayal of evil most often appears to require an active, illicit bond between a male (often in the role of a father or father surrogate) and a younger, formerly innocent individual (often in the role of biological or surrogate progeny) who is initiated into sin" (*Hollywood's Stephen King*, 85).

As King observed in his speech, the conclusion to his novella, where Todd Bowden takes a high-powered rifle to a nearby freeway and shoots at anything that moves until he is killed by police, differs substantially from that of the 1998 film adaptation by Bryan Singer. Perhaps Singer and his crew were fearful of providing unwitting stimuli to troubled youths—the reason why Stephen King withdrew his "Richard Bachmann"—novel *Rage* (1977) from circulation after learning it had been in the locker of Michael Carneal, who murdered three of his classmates as they prayed before school in Paducah, Kentucky. Likewise, Singer's film is scrupulous in refraining from the cinematic depiction of the atrocities that Kurt Dussander (Ian McKellan) recounts to Todd (Brad Renfro), concentrating instead on their nefarious effect on Todd's psyche and behavior. At the end of Singer's film, we do not know what will become of Todd now that he has graduated from high school as class valedictorian—but the concluding scene encourages us to assume the worst. In this regard, I argue, the film *Apt Pupil* gives better expression to fears King conjures up at the end of his keynote address than if it had followed the script of the novella:

> [T]he unstated idea is that we have lived well while most of the world lives badly, eaten well while too much of the world goes hungry or actually starves, dressed our children in the best, much of it made by children in other countries who have little but their dreams, many of which are the violent American dreams that they see on TV. We have

had all this, some of us—maybe a lot of us—seem to think, and there must be a price. There must be a payment. Perhaps there must even be a judgment. Then into our uneasy minds come the images of the bogeyboys, who shot so well because they had trained on their home computers, and on the video games down at the mall.

In King's tale, which starts in 1974 with Todd Bowden as a student in Santo Donato Junior High and concludes after his graduation from high school, the initial sources of Todd's information on and fascination with concentration camp atrocities are the war magazines in his friend's garage that presumably also provide the address for the mail-order SS uniform that he later will compel Dussander to wear. Without being able to come up with a concept for what he calls "the gooshy stuff,"[2] Todd senses the commercialization and fetishicization of the Holocaust displayed in actual films of the mid-1970s such as Liliana Cavani's *The Night Porter* (1974) and in a whole genre of pornography featuring Nazi trappings for sado-masochistic "games." Dussander, meanwhile, decries the hypocrisy of Vietnam-era American politicians who "speak of morality while they douse screaming children and old women in burning napalm" (130). At the start of the film *Apt Pupil*, Todd is already a senior in high school, and the year is 1984. This date is significant for at least three reasons. It situates the story at the height of the Reagan era, when Bruce Springsteen's "Born in the USA" could be used inappropriately as a feel-good campaign song. Its Orwellian overtones accord well with Todd's mastery of surveillance tactics and inquisitorial skills in his blackmailing of Dussander. Finally, it indicates that by this point in American history the Holocaust was beginning to be regarded as subject matter fit for instruction in schools like Santo Donato High, if only for a week, with no further time to address the questions as to whether it was caused by economics, society, culture, or simply human nature, much less why our fascination with the Holocaust needs to be tempered with self-questioning as to the motivations behind it.[3] As Todd's social studies teacher returns his A-level paper, he wipes away the blackboard's pie-chart listing of types of victims and recommends to the class the Santo Donato library as an excellent source of further information.

Be it the war magazines in the novella or the piles of books on topics such as "Hitler's Henchmen" that we see Todd avidly reading while the opening credits flash by, they serve as the equivalents of the secret history of the Overlook Hotel in King's *The Shining*, recorded in the infamous scrapbook that Jack Torrance uncovers in chapter 17. All these "(un)holy gifts" entrap people who think they are on the verge of a sensational disclosure about something that does not involve them. Stephen King situates such a plot device within the tradition of gothic literature, including his own, "wherein the past has this unbreakable hold on the present" (Magistrale, *Stephen King: The Second Decade*, 10). The opening sequence to the film *Apt Pupil* also makes quite clear that for Todd, "history" is a simulacrum that will soon become "his story" as well. As Tony Magistrale observes, "At one point, the camera superimposes Todd's face alongside black-and-white headshots of several Nazi officers [one of them proves to be a youthful portrait of Kurt Dussander] . . . The effect, albeit momentary, creates for the audience a merging between Todd's head and those of the men he is studying" (*Hollywood's Stephen King*, 110–111). Claudia Eppert similarly points out that history comes alive for Todd "through the encounter not with eyewitness survivor testimony but rather, more disturbingly and unconventionally, with perpetrator testimony" (72). By increasingly coming to identify himself not with the victims of the Holocaust, but rather with perpetrators like Dussander, Todd proves himself to be "apt" in more than one sense of the word—not only "quick to learn or understand," but also possessing "a natural tendency to error or undesirable behavior" (*Webster's II New Riverside Dictionary*, 120).

When Todd Bowden first crosses the threshold into Kurt Dussander's bungalow, the bright yellow California sunlight of *Apt Pupil* is replaced by a nicotine-brown and green patina that feels dirty without actually being so; it is as if Jonathan Harker had entered Dracula's castle. Dussander, as played by Ian McKellan, is no repulsive silent-screen Nosferatu, however, not even the "cross between Albert Einstein and Boris Karloff" (112) described by King. Initially, he appears as a pathetic old man who assures Todd that he votes, as if that were sufficient proof of his Americanized identity, and who appears genuinely shocked when he learns that the only way to prevent Todd from turning him in is to tell the tales of wartime atrocities that Todd's teachers were afraid to reveal at school. But just as Todd has to talk his way into Dussander's house, language also serves as the vehicle for his corruption, as he increasingly becomes a vampiric extension of the evil that Dussander implants within him and that will become "undead" through him. During the night after Dussander describes the time there was a leak in the hose leading into the gas chamber and he had to send five of his men with rifles to finish off the twitching victims after two hours of listening to their moans and high-pitched giggles, alternating shots of Dussander and Todd at home in their beds show that both of them are haunted by this tale; Todd even dreams of looking inside a gas-chamber portal and seeing shorn victims staring back at him. As in the opening sequence of the film, Todd has entered a past that is becoming ever more present. On the other hand, Todd also learns from Dussander, in his public persona as "Arthur Denker" ("thinker," in German), how language can be used to create the very useful fictions that have served him well for four decades. When invited to dinner by Todd's mother, who clearly wants to meet the old man with whom Todd now spends most of his waking hours after school, he displays an old-world charm that enchants parents and grandparents alike, making use of his extreme near-sightedness in a way that suggests he has learned a lesson or two from the "Mister Magoo" Saturday morning cartoons that Todd finds running when he comes to deliver his "Christmas present." Also, he has no trouble responding to a question by Todd's grandfather, on a Thanksgiving visit from North Carolina, as to what he did during the war by claiming to have worked in a military hospital cleaning bed linens and nurses' uniforms—a truly sanitized version of war stories fit for normal American consumption in a household where only the mounted deer-head on the wall serves as a reminder that Todd comes from a family of hunters.

Todd knows better, of course. As his mother unwittingly says about her son at this point in the dinner party, "He's good at other things." He continues to hunt for more titillating disclosures, wanting to know "How did it feel?" to have been a participant of massacres such as Baby Yar outside of Kiev. In contrast to King's novella, within the film *Apt Pupil* neither Dussander nor Todd display any animosity toward Jews. Dussander shrugs off his murder of 90,000 individuals during his tenure as camp commandant at the Death Camp of Patin as being simply a matter of carrying out orders, although he does confess that thereby "a door was opened that could not be shut"—one of the key motifs within the film. Shortly thereafter, while showering after a basketball game at school where a bigger and taller player has knocked him off the court, Todd imagines himself surrounded by naked older men, transposing himself into the tales he has solicited from Dussander. At this point in the film, Todd still seems to have the capacity to picture himself as a Holocaust victim; or do the stares he receives from the inmates suggest that he is one of the soldiers that Dussander has sent into the showers? Given the choice, would he rather be "victim" or "perpetrator"? This is a question that is answered later in the film, when Todd to his horror finds himself trapped in the basement of Dussander's house with a "dead victim" who refuses to die and who wants to get out of this room as desperately as Todd.

That Todd is developing a pleasure for ordering about his prisoner becomes clear in the very next scene when he forces Dussander to put on the SS uniform that he has bought for him and to march to his commands. In the figurative and literal turning point in the film, Dussander automatically gives a Nazi salute and continues marching even after Todd tells him to stop. King's narrative expresses Todd's mounting dismay with the help of the following comparison: "He felt like the sorcerer's apprentice, who had brought the brooms to life but who had not possessed enough wit to stop them once they got started. The old man living in genteel poverty was gone. Dussander was here" (143). For Todd, whose first name in German is one letter away from "Tod" (death),[4] the point of reference is probably the "Mickey Mouse" sequence in the Walt Disney film *Fantasia*, but the literary source of the tone poem by Dukas is Goethe's ballad "Der Zauberlehrling," written in June of 1797, immediately before he resumed his work on *Faust*, the man who thought he could control the devil and who ultimately finds himself to be the agent of Mephisto's diabolical machinations. Bryan Singer's film omits such literary references, although the DVD subtitle for this scene is the proverb "Clothes Make the Man"—an apt reflection of King's penchant for using such proverbial remarks to characterize the psychic disposition of his characters.[5] Within the movie screenplay (by Brandon Boyce), Dussander warns the horrified Todd, "Be careful boy, you play with fire," but the fire Todd has ignited is already out of his control. Later that evening, Dussander lights up his gas oven and makes an unsuccessful attempt to place within it a live cat which in the novella he attracts by a bowl of milk—the same type of ruse he had perfected in his interrogations as commandant in the Death Camp of Patin.[6] By the end of the film, he will have succeeded in luring a more compliant human victim into his kitchen.

That same evening Todd attends a party with Becky Trask (Heather McComb), the girl who has wanted to go out with him since the beginning of the film. The cross-cutting between this scene and Dussander's tryst with "Timmy" brings to the fore questions of identity—which in the case of a teenager and star baseball pitcher like Todd involves his sexual identity—and the highlighting of sado-masochism, homoeroticism, and homophobia in Singer's retelling of King's tale. Becky has driven Todd to the party, and she is also "in the driver's seat" in terms of initiating sexual advances that the distracted boy, fresh from his encounter with Dussander, barely reciprocates. As they take a break from kissing, Todd takes a risk and asks a question that she clearly is not expecting: whether she ever wonders why people do the things they do. Depending on her answer, this might have given Todd an opportunity to reveal his experiences with Dussander before the two of them became bound inextricably to one another. But in this sexually charged setting, she answers that she prefers not to think and just do, lowering her head into his lap for what clearly is intended to be an act of fellatio. At this point, the scene cuts to Dussander slumped half-drunk on his back porch, whispering terms of endearment to the "kitty" he picks up and brings into his house, licking his lips as he does. The camera returns to the young couple in the car, both discomfited after Becky's unsuccessful attempt to arouse Todd: it is all too evident that the grisly tales he has been hearing in recent months are affecting not only his sleep and his grades. With an embarrassed smirk followed by a howl of laughter, Becky remarks that maybe he does not like her; maybe he does not like girls. Immediately after Todd's humiliation when he fails to perform sexually, the scene returns to Dussander seeking his thrills by thrusting the struggling cat in the oven and turning on the flames. Given Dussander's evident knowledge of German culture—a favorite piece of music that he plays at critical moments in the movie is the "Liebestod" (Love-Death) music from Wagner's *Tristan und Isolde*—he might well know, and most certainly would appreciate the following apercu by the Romantic writer Novalis: "Sonderbar, daß der eigentliche Grund der Grausamkeit Wollust ist" ([It is] Strange that the actual basis for cruelty is pleasure).[7] This pleasure in cruelty takes on active physical expression when Todd—frantic that his parents will learn about his bad grades this quarter and even more upset when his friend Joey (Joshua Jackson) asks him how things are going with him and Becky Trask—kills a pigeon with an injured wing, using the basketball he had been struggling in vain to shoot into the basket. Singer employs both the word and the image of "balls" throughout the film as a metaphor for virility, nerve, and skill. Todd's lack of "touch" with the basketball early on evolves into smooth shooting at the end of the film. That Todd succeeds in killing his animal victim before Dussander does is already an indication that this "apt pupil" one day may rival or even surpass his master in monstrosity.

First, though, he needs to develop his "shooting touch" in deception, blackmail, and murderous resolve. This is where Dussander still has lessons to teach, as when he impersonates Todd's grandfather and visits his high school guidance counselor Edward French (David Schwimmer), who has sent out a warning letter about Todd's grades and requested a parental conference. Inventing a story of work and drinking problems involving Todd's parents, grandfather "Victor" promises to supervise Todd's study habits and persuades French to let Todd's grades rest with his final exams if he can bring these up to straight As. When Todd later protests that he cannot turn around a half year of bad grades in 3 weeks, Dussander tells him that he can and he will, canceling any more "stories" and ordering Todd to study during vacation as well. The former camp commandant now has a new inmate to control. "Arbeit macht frei!"—the grimly ironic slogan hanging over the entrance of Dachau—here takes on a revivified meaning.

This concern for Todd's grades, of course, is anything but grandfatherly benevolence; Todd has threatened to reveal his knowledge of Dussander's identity if the news about his bad grades reaches his parents, who are expecting their son to graduate first in his class. Dussander, in turn, makes amply clear that blackmail works both ways by announcing that he has placed in a safe-deposit box at a bank—to be opened on the occasion of his death—a full account of Todd's dealings with him, including the visit to the guidance counselor, designed to ruin Todd's reputation for life if it ever sees the light of day. Dussander reveals this news at a point in the novella and film when Todd, after the enforced study sessions have succeeded in raising his grades, crosses the kitchen with the intent of pushing his tormentor down the cellar stairs as Dussander strains to reach for a fresh bottle of bourbon (191–197). In the film, Todd stops dead in his tracks as Dussander turns around with the bottle in one hand and a long knife in the other; perhaps the "old man," as Dussander calls himself in this final tale for Todd, is not as weak as "the boy" imagines. Offering a drink to celebrate the beginning and end of their life together, Dussander moves his arm around Todd's head as if he were about to embrace him, but instead reaches for the glass into which he pours Todd—who hitherto has consumed only milk or coke in this kitchen—a swig of bourbon. When Todd, instead of a toast, tells him he should fuck himself, Dussander responds in the film, as he does in the novella, with the rejoinder "we are fucking each other—didn't you know that" (197), but here prefaces it with "My dear boy"—a form of address indicating possession as well as endearment. Todd is making the transition from boyhood to adulthood, with all the negative ramifications this carries in Stephen King's canon—the next time he comes to Dussander's home he will be driving a car, not riding a bike—but he has one more crucial test to pass before his Nazi apprenticeship is completed.

Whereas at the beginning of both the novella and film Todd carried out more than he was capable of controlling—the "Sorcerer's

Apprentice" syndrome, so to speak—"Denker/Dussander" had grown so cautious that he remained trapped in his house, "thinking" but no longer "doing." Like the combination of Harris and Klebold at Columbine High School or of Victor Frankenstein and his creation, the symbiotic union of Todd and Dussander enables them to combine "thinking" and "doing," but in a very malevolent way. In the following 3 years of King's novella, they independently murder a sizeable number of hobos and transients on the edges of Santo Donato society. The film condenses these killings into one horrific incident involving "Archie" (Elias Koteas), a homeless person living in a ravine a short distance from Dussander's house who offers him sexual favors in exchange for money and a shower; it is significant that "homosexuals" were listed among the Nazi victims on that pie chart that Todd was studying so intently at the beginning of the film. Dussander fears Archie (who receives a name only in the film credits) because the latter, in the process of rooting through his trash can, had caught a glimpse of him in his bedroom dressed in his Nazi uniform, which he has taken to wearing even when Todd is not in the house. Archie, though, also has seen Dussander with his young boy "friend," and it is this that he "knows" about him, as he tells him after the two of them get off the bus they are riding. This suggests not only Dussander's paranoia, but also the (homoerotic) attraction that at least subliminally connects Todd and the old man. Earlier in the film, it was on a similar bus ride that Todd, fresh from a study session at the Santo Donato library, had first encountered Dussander. While the incriminating news that Todd bore to the door was far more dangerous to Dussander, at that point he was still a frightened old man with shaking hands and a tremulous voice; by this point in the film, his murderous impulses are fully reactivated. After plying the hobo with liquor, he stabs him in the back and pushes him down the cellar stairs—carrying out what Todd had intended to do to Dussander before their drink together. In the process, Dussander suffers a heart attack that not only sets in motion the final stages of his life but also leads to Todd carrying out the same sort of killing duty that Dussander once had been unable to complete in Patin.

Summoned to Dussander's house on the pretense that he needs to read him an important letter, Todd is instead ordered to call an ambulance—but only after cleaning up the bloody mess in the kitchen and the body down below. After Dussander locks him in a cellar with what appears to be a glowing red furnace in the background—a composite of hellfire and the death camp crematoria—Todd receives a further shock when what he thought was a corpse stands up and stumbles toward him with the same gaunt features and shaven head of the shower inmates from his earlier dream visions. Todd's response is to swing a shovel repeatedly until his struggling opponent—whose only words to him are "Why are you doing this?"—lies in a pool of blood.[8] Dussander, listening on the other side of the basement door, opens it and sees Todd standing below with his face blood-spattered. "How did it feel?" is the question that he will ask Todd later at the hospital following his successful heart surgery. By this point in the film, he and Todd have switched places, with Todd being the perpetrator and Dussander the interrogator. Here we have Todd's truest initiation into the club of "Hitler's Henchmen." Dussander's repetition of Todd's earlier question to him forges a blood bond between two murderers and imparts the confidence in his abilities that Todd will soon display when he tells his former guidance counselor Edward French: "You have no idea of what I am capable of doing." This scene is the analogue to the dream sequence in the novella where Dussander records Todd's levels of sexual excitement as the latter penetrates a young Jewish girl strapped to a table (189–190). But King and Singer take care to remind us that such infernal "experiments" had a basis in fact. In the neighboring hospital bed lies Benjamin Kramer—in the film an elderly gentleman who praises Todd for being such a good friend to someone he first thinks is his grandfather. Kramer, we later learn, was an inmate at Patin for 10 months whose wife and two daughters died there. The look of horror on his face as he recognizes the identity of his roommate provides mute testimony to what he has witnessed in Patin. Would that fictional characters like Todd Bowden or actual individuals like Eric Harris had been given the opportunity to have their fantasies of death and destruction confronted with the effects of their implementation, either through survivor testimony or else the critical, not exploitive examination of Holocaust perpetrators as undertaken by King and Singer. As Eppert observes, "Had his school implemented such a curriculum, Todd might have acquired the agency to arrest himself and exercise vigilance with regard to his pedagogical encounters with Dussander" (101).

Shortly before the novella's lethal conclusion, Dr Isaac Weiskopf, the Israeli special operative who arrives at the hospital to arrange for the transport of Dussander for his war crimes trial in Jerusalem, speculates that perhaps "the very atrocities in which Dussander took part formed the basis of some attraction" between him and Todd Bowden:

> But maybe there is something about what the Germans did that exercises a deadly fascination over us—something that opens the

catacombs of the imagination. Maybe part of our dread and horror comes from a secret knowledge that under the right—or wrong—set of circumstances, we ourselves would be willing to build such places and staff them. Maybe we know that under the right set of circumstances the things that live in the catacombs would be glad to crawl out. (282–283)

Weiskopf—who in the film teaches at the Judaic Institute in Munich—is "wise" in including himself in these reflections, indicating that all human beings have a fascination with and a capacity to commit what we prefer to call "inhuman" acts.[9] As with the Columbine killers or with the hierarchy of male ghosts in *The Shining*, the fact that Todd and Dussander share and maintain a secret knowledge helps to fuel its enticement and enactment. The illicit nature of their behavior acts like a drug—demanding more details, greater levels of barbarism, until narrative crosses into action, past merges with present, and history becomes "their story." Seen in this context, King's "Summer of Corruption" is not only a key component of the overall concept of the collection *Different Seasons*, but also a worthy successor to such tales as Poe's "The Fall of the House of Usher" and Melville's "Benito Cereno," which likewise make it clear that "American innocence" cannot gaze upon "old world" horror and remain unaffected.

Although Weiskopf's role in the film is not quite so prominent as in the book, Singer provides other suggestions that Southern California and the Holocaust are linked by more than the presence of perpetrators like Dussander and survivors like Kramer. Todd's school setting and home environment, it becomes clear, are breeding grounds for the infectious disease that Dussander has brought with him from the death camps, although not quite in the way that Claudia Eppert indicates when trying to explain Todd's fascination with Nazism: "Part of his motivation comes from an attempt to understand what is behind the fascist symbols and Germanic slogans he sees spray-painted onto school walls" (71). Although Todd does discern a swastika sprayed on the culvert through which he bicycles on his way to and from Dussander's home, the only Nazi symbols we see in Santo Donato High are the ones that Todd scribbles on the top of one of his papers, rather than taking notes on the meaning of "sociology." The "Germanic slogan" we see in his school at the beginning of the film is "Dare to be a leader," but with iconic images of the presidential figures on Mt Rushmore, not Adolf Hitler, as the models to be imitated. Most intriguingly, the team icon of the Santo Donato High School "Pirates," for which Todd is the star pitcher, is a skull-and-crossbones figure eerily similar to the Death's Head emblem on the SS officer's uniform that Todd makes Dussander wear. "Clothes Make the Man," after all.

By the end of the film, Todd Bowden has learned well his lessons in piracy. He quotes verbatim phrases that Dussander once had used against him when he blackmails Edward French into not revealing that Dussander came to a meeting in the guise of Todd's grandfather. After Dussander's suicide in order to evade deportation and then prosecution in Israel for his crimes, his former high school guidance counselor is the only individual with conclusive proof of Todd's complicity in keeping Dussander's location unknown to the world. In the novella, Todd "solves" the problem by murdering French in cold blood and then embarking on the shooting spree alongside the freeway that will end only with his own death 5 hours later. In the film, Todd Bowden has much better nerves and a far more chilling ability to seize upon and exploit any suggestion of human weakness. After the meeting with Todd and his "grandfather," French displayed a willingness to help even beyond the matter of grades when he offered Todd the chance to talk about problems he might be having with his parents or with girls, confiding that he has just gone through a nasty divorce with his wife and hence has an appreciation for the trials people undergo. Under other circumstances, his guidance counselor could have become the type of confidant that Todd sought in vain from his girlfriend. But by this point in his development, Todd develops this information and French's offer of his home telephone number into an accusation that French was attempting to start up a homosexual relation with a student, threatening that he will drag "Ed" down with him if the latter reveals what he knows about Todd's interactions with Dussander. As Dussander is expiring in his hospital bed at this very moment, the suggestion of the crosscutting is that his spirit has taken new refuge in a young boy whose blond hair and Aryan features would qualify him for the Hitler Youth, but who preaches his gospel of hate and homophobia with an American flag flying in the background of the Bowden family driveway.

The "Icarus speech" that Todd delivers at his high school graduation ceremony likewise contains a hidden message. In his "Bogeyboys" talk, King expressed sympathy for young people whose high school experiences of isolation and torment lead them to do horrible things: "In Iroquois trials of manhood, naked warriors were sent running down a gauntlet of braves swinging clubs and jabbing with the butt end of spears. In high school the goal is Graduation Day instead of a manhood feather, and the weapons are replaced by insults, slights, and epithets, many of them racial, but I imagine the feelings are about the same." Film viewers either familiar with King's novella or seeing *Apt Pupil* in a post-Columbine world probably are bracing themselves for a cataclysmic conclusion to the film: Todd self-destructing at his high school graduation ceremony, for example, and taking down as many people as possible with him. Instead, he gives his "Icarus speech," showing off his classical erudition. Within the context of the myth, Daedalus—the inventor of the labyrinth in which the King of Crete keeps the Minotaur—escapes the island by making wings for himself and his son Icarus. The latter, however, flies too close to the Sun, which melts the wax holding the feathers together, and plunges to his death into the sea. In Singer's film, interestingly enough, it is "Icarus" who survives his surrogate father's death. Rather than using the talents he has been given for a "joyride" (like the earlier self who blackmails Dussander in exchange for titillating tales), he instead flies away to freedom with the help of his newly acquired skills. This is anything but a happy ending. As Kim Newman observes, the film's finale poses "the truly terrifying question of what the kid is up to these days" (35).[10] Singer invites the viewer to imagine the path in American society that Todd Bowden could take should his dreams of becoming a "leader" ever come to fruition. What might he be doing some 20 years after graduation from high school, about the age that the real-life Kurt Dussanders of the Nazi era were playing key roles in the implementation of the Holocaust? Judging from recent newspaper headlines, there must be many American "Apt Pupils" in the world nowadays—those experiencing their own "joyride" moments in places like Guantanamo and Abu Ghurib, and those who prefer the more refined pleasure of developing policies that facilitate torture, rape, and murder in the guise of defending "freedom."[11]

Notes

1. "The Bogeyboys," http://www.stephen-king.de/interviews/interview6. html. My thanks go to Trina Magi and Patricia Mardeusz, reference librarians at the University of Vermont, for their help in accessing a source for this speech.

2. Stephen King, *Different Seasons*, featuring "Apt Pupil." Movie Tie-In Edition (New York: Signet, 1998), 129. Henceforth, I place within the main text (parenthetical) the page references to King's novella, whose title I likewise continue to place within quotes, so as to distinguish it from the movie *Apt Pupil*.

3. For a model of teaching about the Holocaust that incorporates historical and cultural approaches, as well as reflections on the lessons

and the legacy of the Holocaust, see David Scrase and Wolfgang Mieder (eds), *The Holocaust: Introductory Essays* (Burlington, VT: The Center for Holocaust Studies at the University of Vermont, 1996).

4. In a November 2, 1989, interview, King confirmed that this name choice was deliberate. See Magistrale, *Stephen King: The Second Decade*, 3. By the same token, "Santo Donato" could be understood as a reference to "Thanatos" (Death) as the true patron saint of Todd's hometown.

5. Note, for example, how King employs such sayings as "The early bird catches the worm" (112) and "A shave puts a shine in the morning" (113) as signs of Todd's initial effort to distance himself from the late-rising, unshaven Dussander.

6. King explicitly connects the use of milk to attract the cat with the ruse of the pot of lamb stew in the room Dussander used for prisoner interrogations at the (fictional) Death Camp of Patin where he was commandant after stints at Bergen-Belsen and Auschwitz (157). Within the film, this diabolic means of coaxing information from his starving prisoners is included in the biography of Dussander that Todd reads in the Santo Donato library.

7. Friedrich von Hardenberg, *Novalis Schriften*, edited by Richard Samuel, Hans-Joachim Mähl, and Gerhard Schulz (Stuttgart: Kohlhammer, 1968), 3: 655.

8. "Why are you doing this?" could have been asked of the Nazis even on a pragmatic level, in that they kept the trains running to Auschwitz when the logistics involved undercut their resources at a critical phase of World War II.

9. In a May 31, 2002, interview, King confessed that he could not resist the urge to buy a recent *National Enquirer* issue that featured a story on the Columbine shooters because "I wanted to see the photographs of those two boys lying in a pool of blood." See Magistrale, *Hollywood's Stephen King*, 5.

10. For listings of other reviews of *Apt Pupil*, see *Film Review Annual 1999*, 33–36.

11. My thanks go to Tony Magistrale for his expert editorial guidance and insightful suggestions. Above all, I thank my first German teacher in high school, Rev. Owen Daley S.J. (1929–2007), who opened up a whole world inside and outside the classroom for his pupils and who has served as a model of humane mentoring throughout my teaching career. *Requiescat in pace.*

Chapter 3

Maybe It Shouldn't Be a Party

Kids, Keds, and Death in Stephen King's *Stand By Me* and *Pet Sematary*

Jeffrey A. Weinstock

What connects *Stand By Me* (1986) and *Pet Sematary* (1990) most poignantly—if not most immediately—is the sneaker. In *Stand By Me* (originally published as "The Body" in *Different Seasons* [1982]), four boys venture out of the stagnant town of Castle Rock, Oregon, to view the dead body of an adolescent boy who has been struck and killed by a train and discover that he has been knocked out of his Keds. In what may be considered the most obscene moment in a film that features an epic barf-o-rama, children on a trestle almost run down by a locomotive that makes no apparent attempt even to slow down, and testicle-sucking leeches, Gordie (Wil Wheaton), Chris (River Phoenix), Teddy (Corey Feldman), and Vern (Jerry O'Connell) discover the corpse of Ray Brower sprawled in the brush to one side of the train tracks in his stocking feet. His tennis shoes are nowhere to be found—this is because the train hit Ray Brower with such force that it knocked his Keds into *Pet Sematary* (originally published in 1983, a year after "The Body"). In *Pet Sematary*, it is not a train that is the engine of destruction, but a truck. The son of physician Louis Creed (Dale Midkiff), Gage (Miko Hughes), wanders into the road with its endless parade of semis that runs past their rural Maine home and, like Ray Brower, is knocked out of his diminutive tennis shoes. However, in this "horror" film, rather than the audience being shown Gage's shoeless (dis-Ked-perated?) corpse, the aftermath of the collision is represented instead by a sneaker that lays strewn on the road—the missing sneaker from *Stand By Me*.

Each film arguably crystallizes around the "punctum" of the sneaker and the presence or absence of the sneaker to the viewer condenses each film's attitude toward death and mourning. In *Stand By Me*, the mute presence of the body combined with the fact of the missing sneakers lays bare for the boys—and the viewer—the inevitability of both loss of childhood and loss of life. The corpse of Ray Brower, knocked out of his tennis shoes, prompts the film's protagonist, Gordie Lachance, to mourn the loss of his brother, Dennis (whose name coincidentally rhymes with "tennis," played in the flashback within the flashback by John Cusack), and to confront his own feelings of inadequacy and incompleteness developed from living in the shadow of first his brother's life and then his death. More broadly, as Tony Magistrale asserts, Brower's body symbolizes death on a variety of levels: "The death of their friendly foursome, the death of their summer, and, most importantly, the death of their own childhoods" (*Hollywood's Stephen King*, 38). Beyond even this, however, the body of Ray Brower—a kid knocked out his Keds by a train while picking blueberries—embodies the existentialist angst of living in a world in which accidents occur, things get lost forever, and uneasy ghosts and reanimated corpses emphatically do *not* return from beyond the grave to warn or demand justice or even to antagonize the living and feast upon their brains. What Gordie *Lachance* ultimately has to face is "the chance"—the simple, horrible fact that sometimes accidents happen and people die without reason—and they do not come back.

In contrast to this facticity of haphazard death made manifest by the presentness of the shoeless corpse of Ray Brower, the corpseless shoe that flies in from offscreen at the moment of Gage's death in *Pet Sematary* encapsulates this film's transformation of Chance into Creed as Louis Creed's views on death morph from cynically believing that "we wink out like a candle flame when the wind blows hard" to maintaining that "we go on." By emphasizing the tiny shoe, a potent symbol of childhood, while obscuring the corpse, *Pet Sematary* averts its gaze from death and fixates on a symbol of life thereby instanciating the film's strange cinematic foot fetish in which loss is disavowed. (Death in the film is intriguingly correlated throughout with missing shoes—in addition to Gage being knocked out of his sneakers, when Louis accompanies Victor Pascow [Brad Greenquist] on a late-night jaunt through the woods, he does so barefoot, and when his wife Rachel [Denise Crosby] returns from the grave at the end of the film, she significantly is missing one shoe.) What *Pet Sematary* ultimately evades is the agonizing realization that *Stand By Me* affirms—that chance rather than fate governs the course of human events and that death is final.

This contrast between the two films is deeply ironic and can also be said to speak in a general way to the appeal of horror movies like *Pet Sematary*. It is ironic that *Stand By Me*—a movie directed by Rob Reiner and categorized as "drama" (and not one that most people generally associate with Stephen King)—should confront the reality of death more starkly and potentially more horrifyingly than the very Stephen King–ish horror movie, *Pet Sematary*, in which characters are mutilated and murdered by reanimated corpses. It is arguably the case that, even if what *Pet Sematary* stages is the quintessential gothic theme of "the helplessness of humanity in the face of powers that are both larger than the individual human and committed to his obliteration" (Magistrale, *Hollywood's Stephen King*, 107)—what H. P. Lovecraft would call "Cosmic Horror"—it remains comforting in its assurance that spirit does not simply "wink out" at the moment of death. The resurrections of the cat, Church, along with Gage and Rachel—and most especially the intercession of the "discorporated" Victor Pascow—console one with the knowledge that consciousness persists beyond the moment of death and that the universe is a rule-governed place in which things do not simply happen by chance but for a reason. This suggests ironically that part of the appeal of horror movies in which the laws of reality as we know them are violated and the dead return is both the denial of the finitude of death and the desire to believe that it is fate rather than chance that governs the course of human existence. Thus, at least from this perspective, *Pet Sematary* ultimately emerges as far more comforting in its conclusions than *Stand By Me*'s nihilistic rejection of ghosts, God, and fate.

Maybe It Shouldn't Be a Party:
Stand By Me

There's something eerily appropriate about the fact that "Keds," the name for a brand of children's tennis shoes worn by the dead Ray Brower, can be read as a portmanteau word combining "kids" and "dead" because the whole trajectory of *Stand By Me* consists in a group of kids journeying (in sneakers) toward adulthood by way of the confrontation with death. I believe Arthur Biddle hits the nail on the head when he describes the film as built around an "archetypal rite of passage"—the journey—marking the "transition from one life stage to another" (83). However, the film subverts conventional understandings of this familiar archetype by leading its protagonist and the viewer step-by-step toward the conclusion of the meaninglessness of existence. What Gordie, the film's central protagonist, ultimately must confront and accept is the reality—and finality—of death, as well as the twin realizations that the universe is a chaotic place in which jeeps turn over killing young men and trains hit boys picking blueberries, and that the living must let the dead be dead and focus on the business of life, which the film equates with "standing by" others—caring for family and friends. The film in essence follows a formula that ultimately reveals the meaninglessness of formulas. In the process, it also teaches the viewer how one should accept death, mourn the dead, and conduct the business of living.

In terms of confronting and accepting death, the film in fact takes death as its starting point as an adult Gordie Lachance (Richard Dryfus) contemplates a newspaper report of the death of his childhood friend, Chris Chambers, who, the viewer subsequently learns, died (like Ray Brower) unpredictably of random violence—he was stabbed when trying to break up a fight between two strangers in a fast food restaurant. News of Chris's death prompts Gordie to reflect on the "first time [he] saw a dead human being" and propels him (and the viewer) into the extended flashback that constitutes almost the entire movie detailing his journey, along with Chris, Teddy, and Vern, along the "magic corridor" (King, "The Body," 399) to Ray Brower and adulthood. The scene shifts to 1959 and, to the tune of Ben E. King's "Stand By Me," a young Gordie appears, first in front of a drugstore magazine rack filled with detective and true crime magazines (which foreshadow the boys' own hunt to discover the corpse of a missing adolescent boy) and then playing at being an adult in his clubhouse as he and his friends Chris and Teddy smoke, swear, and play cards.

What the viewer quickly discovers is that each one of these boys in this film about growing up is already missing something or is, on some level, scarred. Chris comes from a family with a bad reputation and is presumed as a result to be "bad" himself—a fact that is exploited by his elementary school teacher when Chris returns stolen milk money only to have his teacher use it not to exonerate him but to purchase a new skirt for herself. Teddy has been physically scarred by his father who held his head to a stove and severely burned one of his ears and is clearly mentally traumatized as well as he is shown in the film to be both war-obsessed and suicidal. Vern, who is not especially bright, more benignly—but also with potent symbolism—has lost a jar of pennies that he buried under his porch and for which he has been searching all summer. Most notably, Gordie himself has been forced to grapple both with the death of his brother in a jeep accident and his parents' neglect that preceded Dennis's accident and has only been accentuated in its aftermath. All of these details work to offset the nostalgic tone of the narration by establishing the town of Castle Rock itself as a kind of "dead world" (Magistrale, *Hollywood's Stephen King*, 40) and, in keeping with much of King's fiction, to unveil the disfunctionality and stultification underlying small-town life. Although the written version of "The Body" is subtitled, "Fall from Innocence," it is clear that these boys in various ways and to varying degrees have already been exposed to corruption and loss *avant la lettre*.

Furthermore, despite the voice-over narration's wistful pronouncement during the junkyard sequence that, "We knew exactly who we were and exactly where we were going," the film's action reveals the boys—especially the film's two central characters, Chris and Gordie—not as focused, self-assured, and complete but instead as identities in flux and engaged in a process of social negotiation and self-creation. Both Gordie and Chris must confront socially constructed senses of themselves as "no good." In Chris's case, what he must grapple with is a discrepancy between the town's expectations of him as someone coming from a "bad family" and his own divergent appraisal of his character, potential, and self-worth. Chris in fact possesses a fairly positive self-image and is shown to be an extremely caring person who bolsters the egos of others (Chris is the character who most frequently touches or puts his arm around the shoulders of others and is variously figured as both a substitute father and a mother figure for Gordie) but who is frustrated by the town's assumptions about him. He assumes that these social expectations will dictate his future course of action—that he will be separated from Gordie in junior high as the latter is slotted into courses intended to prepare him for college—and he has been disillusioned about the moral probity of authority figures as a result of his teacher's cruel opportunism. What the viewer of the film learns at the end is that Chris, in fact, by dint of hard work, managed to overcome social stigmatization, go to college, and become a lawyer—only to end up dead on the floor of a fast food restaurant for no reason other than a desire to play peacemaker.

The damage to Gordie's ego is more profound. While Chris chaffs against the social perception that he is bad as a result of coming from a "bad family," Gordie in fact has accepted the negative appraisals by others as his own truth. Early in the film, Gordie notes that, following the death of his older brother, he had become "the invisible boy" as far as his parents were concerned. However, the film makes it clear that he was always the invisible boy, a distant second best in comparison to his star-athlete brother. During his nightmare in the forest, Gordie dreams of being at the funeral of his brother as his father turns to him and tells him, "It should have been you, Gordon," and, subsequently, just prior to the film's climax in which Gordie fends off Ace and his gang with a gun, the confrontation with Ray Brower's body unleashes a flood of emotions in Gordie as he, in rapid succession, protests his brother's death ("Why did you have to die?"), echoes his father's dream sentiment that it should have been him, and expresses his beliefs that he is "no good" and that his father hates him.

The viewer learns that Gordie, as is the case with Chris, is eventually able to overcome this inferiority complex. At the end of the film, the adult Gordie concludes his recollections and goes outside to play with his son, thus establishing that, not only has Gordie achieved normative adult male sexuality, but that, in contrast to his experience with his own father, he is able to care for and nurture his son. In Gordie's case, clearly, the experience of going to seek Ray Brower's body was not only a turning point in his maturation, but the film also suggests that Gordie, as an author, is able to engage with social issues (such as teenage alienation—the story of "Lard Ass Hogan") and, more broadly, self-creation though creative endeavor. Although Winter quotes King as saying, "The only reason anyone writes stories [. . .] is so they can understand the past and get ready for some future mortality" (107), it is also arguably the case that Gordie's stories—belittled by his father (Marshall Bell) but lauded by his brother and his friends—allow him to sculpt an identity apart from the impressions received from his family and community.

In contrast to Chris and Gordie, Teddy Duchamp (whose last name alludes to an important figure associated with the Dada artistic movement that celebrated irrationality and rejected traditional artistic values) is not so lucky. Unable to accept the reality of his father's abuse and mental illness, within the film Teddy lashes out at those who cast aspersions upon his father, engages in suicidal behavior (standing in front of an oncoming train, only to be pushed from the tracks by Chris), and escapes from his unsatisfactory reality through obsessive engagement with violent war fantasies. What we learn about Teddy at the end of the film is that he was rejected by the military three times, that he floated from odd job to odd job in Castle Rock, and that Gordie believes he spent some time in jail. Only Vern within the film, despite his fear of his older brother, is presented as having an even moderately "normal" or stable home life untouched by domestic violence, alcoholism, or death. The point here is that, rather than having completed identities from the start, it is clear that the boys are instead trying to figure out who they are and where they stand in relation to each other, their families, and the larger community, and the journey to find Ray Brower's body functions as an important turning point in this process of self-discovery. The boys come into being— at least to a certain extent—precisely through the confrontation with death.

The beginnings of this metamorphosis are evident early on in the film, following the junkyard scene. Teddy, who has lost control of himself in response to the taunting by the junkyard attendant, apologizes to the other boys for ruining their "good time." In response, Gordie suggests, "I'm not sure it should be a good time. Going to see a dead kid . . . maybe it shouldn't be a party." This sobering assessment signals a shift from the youthful exuberance of the outing's beginning and suggests a burgeoning awareness of the ethical and existential ramifications of confronting death in the form of the corpse of a boy approximately their own age.

However, the film, despite its message of the omnipresence and inescapability of death—indeed, the shopkeeper who sells Gordie provisions quotes to him from *The Book of Common Prayer*, "In the midst of life, we are in death"—quietly refuses to substitute illusory or supernatural evils for real ones and even cleverly demystifies legend and rumor. Thus, the feared junkyard dog, Chopper, turns out to be a harmless mutt rather than Cujo; Gordie's brother Dennis dies in a jeep accident, but presumably not as a result of the malevolence of a sentient vehicle like Christine; and, perhaps most significantly, the woods in which the kids camp is is not haunted by the ghost of Ray Brower or a Wendigo or a werewolf or any other supernatural entity. There are no Indian burial grounds or vampires with hypnotic stares in this film to confirm that there is more in heaven and earth than is dreamt of in their—and our—philosophy. Instead, what the boys have to contend with is precisely "the natural" in the form of howling coyotes, leeches, the cruelty of other people, and their own traumatic experiences.

Which brings us now to Ray Brower. The discovery of his shoeless body lying in the brush alongside the railroad tracks is the film's pivotal, obscene moment in which the boys confront both the impossibility and the inevitability of death. As Gordie looks down on Ray, he attempts to come to grips with what he sees: "The kid wasn't sick, the kid wasn't sleeping, the kid was dead." This is death stripped of metaphor and meaning. It is not a noble death such as Teddy imagines in his fantasies about his father storming the beaches at Normandy and it is not an exciting or heroic death such as the boys might witness on one of their favorite TV Westerns. Ray Brower was knocked out of his shoes by a train while picking blueberries. He did not commit any crime that warranted death, he does not haunt the woods, and he is not coming back—he is just dead, seemingly for no other reason than for being in the wrong place at the wrong time.

Gordie, the "invisible" boy, looking down on Ray Brower, comes face to face with the meaninglessness that is death. As Biddle put it, "Through the agency of a pair of filthy tennis shoes, Gordie finally is able to transmute death from an abstraction to a concretion and to understand it as a denial of life" (94). Although Magistrale asserts that, for Chris and Gordie, "Ray Brower's mutilated corpse comes to symbolize the dead world of Castle Rock" (*Hollywood's Stephen King*, 40), it is more than this. This corpse of a boy approximately the same age as Gordie forces him to confront the reality of his brother's death and then, as Heldreth observes, to face the prospect of his own (67). Gordie's strange "death drive," his "obsession" (which is the word that Gordie himself uses) with viewing the corpse of Ray Brower, prompts the realization of the "existence of death in life" (Biddle 85) and the realities of accident and loss.

This would be a bleak epiphany indeed were it not for the fact that *Stand By Me* offsets this nihilistic conception of the universe with the countervailing affirmations of positive relationships with others and moments of wonder. First through Gordie's relationship with Chris, and subsequently through the representation of the older Gordie with his own son, the movie shows us that we endow a meaningless universe with significance through caring and nurturing relationships with others. Gordie's magical encounter with the deer that emerges from the forest on the morning that the boys find Ray Brower's corpse and which stands close to him for a few moments before scampering off is the secret story at the heart of Gordie's tale; it is something of which he has never spoken or written before—a rare, wondrous moment of communion with the natural world that reaffirms life in the midst of death.

Ultimately, *Stand By Me* is a film that asks us to stand in Gordie's shoes and to appreciate both the presence of death in life and the wondrousness of life amid mindless destruction. Like Jud Crandall (Fred Gwyne) in *Pet Sematary*, the film advances the position that learning about death is a necessary part of growing up and that death needs to be appreciated as the moment when "pain stops and the good memories begin." What the film rejects entirely is that God or fate governs the course of human existence. Dead is not better in

Stand By Me (although the human heart is certainly stonier); dead is just dead. The job of the living is to let the dead be dead, to mourn the dead even as we live our lives aware that, at any moment, we could be knocked out of our Keds without warning or reason.

Pet Sematary's Foot Fetish

In many respects, *Stand By Me* and *Pet Sematary* are closely linked. Both films stage a confrontation with death and are built around the death of a child—whereas Ray Brower was hit by a train and knocked out of his Keds, Gage Creed gets hit by a truck and is knocked out of his tiny sneakers. In both the films, the primary protagonist, through the intimate confrontation with death, is forced to reconceptualize his understanding of the way the universe works. However, the conclusions at which the films arrive are diametrically opposed: Whereas *Stand By Me* supports an interpretation of the universe as an essentially chaotic place in which human beings endow the world with structure and meaning through relationships and narrative, *Pet Sematary* essentially affirms a Christian conception of the universe in which forces of good and evil war for possession of human souls and in which consciousness persists after physical dissolution. Although *Pet Sematary*, on the one hand, is all about death—it begins in a pet cemetery and subsequently stages or recounts Victor Pascow's death, Church's death, Missy's (Susan Blommaert) death, Gage's death, Rachel's sister Zelda's (Andrew Hubatsek) death, Timmy Baderman's (Peter Stader) death, Jud's dog's death, Jud's death, and ultimately Rachel's death—and the film offers lip service to the idea that "sometimes dead is better" through Jud Crandall's homily on death as being "when the pain stops and the good memories begin," on the other hand, the film enacts a systematic evasion of death by emphasizing that death is not an end. The film arguably begins where *Stand By Me* leaves off—with Louis Creed's rationalistic assessment of the universe—and ends where *Stand By Me* begins—in a universe in which death never really takes place because things happen for a reason and death is not an end but simply a "barrier" separating two states of existence. This conclusion suggests that part of the appeal of "horror" movies like *Pet Sematary*, beneath all the violence and gore, ironically is a comforting affirmation of death as simply a transition, rather than a conclusion.

The existing body of critical literature on *Pet Sematary* is fairly consistent in its appraisal of the film as one enacting a tragic vision in which human beings are manipulated by forces that outstrip human control and punish human beings for overreaching. Magistrale, for example, writes that "[t]he theme of *Pet Sematary* is the helplessness of humanity in the face of powers that are both larger than the individual human and committed to his obliteration" (*Hollywood's Stephen King*, 107). He adds that "*Pet Sematary* is a deeply pessimistic film that highlights the limitations of being human, the malefic design of fate and its consistent pressure to push us toward tragic consequences" (107). Mustazza, attending to the novel, likens *Pet Sematary*'s plot to a Greek tragedy in which fate governs the course of human events and notes that "Like Oedipus, Louis does nothing to cause the tragedy that will grip him" (79–80). In keeping with Mustazza's meditations on Greek tragedy, Strengell (also discussing the novel) interprets *Pet Sematary* as being essentially about "hubris"—Louis Creed is punished for playing God, for transgressing the barrier between life and death that is not meant to be crossed (57).

However, the bleakness of these appraisals is offset by the underlying affirmation of the existence of fate and God. If events are predestined, then human beings are absolved of responsibility; if humans are punished for playing God, then God not only exists but also intervenes in the ordinary course of human affairs; and if death is a barrier not meant to be crossed by the living, then death is not a winking out of consciousness, but simply a transition or transformation. With this in mind, it is clear how the film, despite all surface appearances, can be read as in keeping with Christian values (see King quoted in Winter 134, as well as Strengell 62) and as providing a "temporary escape from the imminent presence of death" (Schroeder 141). Indeed, contra *Stand By Me*, what *Pet Sematary* enacts is the systematic evasion of death.

Like *Stand By Me*, *Pet Sematary* attempts to school the viewer on how to regard death and on appropriate mourning practices. The film begins with a fieldtrip lead by Jud Crandall to the local pet cemetery in which Jud responds to Rachel Creed's concern that the venue's lesson is not appropriate for her young daughter, Ellie (Blaze Berdahl), by noting that "[children] have to learn about death sometime." Ellie grasps the lesson, but resents the inevitability of death and, in reference to the possibility of the death of her cat, Church, indignantly exclaims, "Let God get his own [cat] if he wants one, not mine!" Later, Jud comments that Ellie eventually will "learn what death really is: when pain stops and the good memories begin." All of this leads up to the moment when, following the return of the resurrected Church, the formerly rationalistic doctor professes his belief in an afterlife and acquires, according to Schroeder, "a new sort of faith"

(136). In response to Ellie's inquiry about what happens when one dies, Louis explains that "[s]ome believe that we just wink out like a candle flame when the wind blows hard." When Ellie questions whether he believes this, he responds (following a growl from zombie-Church), "No. I think we go on. Yeah, I have faith in that." Though the film's tagline is "sometimes dead is better," Louis Creed and the viewer come together to appreciate that dead does not necessarily mean gone.

Like *Stand By Me*, *Pet Sematary* focuses on "the ultimate horror of every parent" (Winter 134), the death of a child. As is also the case with Gordie's parents in relation to their son, Dennis, we are shown that Louis's melancholic refusal to accept the deaths of first his son and then his wife is an inappropriate response. As Schroeder asserts, Louis's behavior is a test case for how not to mourn and there is some justification for reading the Wendigo and the physical return of the dead in the movie as "symbolic metaphors for uncontrolled grief and its potential for self and community destruction" (138). However, unlike *Stand By Me*, *Pet Sematary* does not focus on the existential angst of confronting a godless universe, nor does it emphasize the potential fulfillment of nurturing relationships or the power of narrative as a tool for self-creation. Instead, the film interpellates the viewer into a conservative theological framework that asserts that human beings err in overreaching the natural and attempting to play God and that excessive mourning is inappropriate not because death is simply a part of life that needs to be accepted but because death is not the cessation of spirit.

This leads us back to the shoe because, in place of a corpse, *Pet Sematary* asks the viewer to focus on a sneaker in the middle of the road symbolizing Gage's passing—his crossing of the barrier between life and death. In *Stand By Me*, Ray Brower is knocked out of his Keds—his journey is done and he is not going anywhere. Gage, on the other hand, is someplace else—to use Louis's words, he goes on. The sneaker, thus, functions as a sort of fetish object—an object upon which one focuses in order to deny the possibility of loss, of castration, of death. This is *Pet Sematary*'s slight of hand, so to speak—to offer up death only in the end to deny it. Against all appearances, *Stand By Me* finally emerges as the darker of the two films. In a universe governed by chance rather than fate and in which the dead, vengeful or not, do not return, human beings have to make their peace with the inevitability of death in the absence of any kind of consoling belief in an afterlife or divine justice. *Stand By Me*, in essence, puts *Pet Sematary*'s shoe on the other foot.

Chapter 4

The Lonesome Autoerotic Death of Arnie Cunningham in John Carpenter's *Christine*

Philip Simpson

John Carpenter's film adaptation of Stephen King's novel *Christine* (1983) presents us with a lonely teenage boy's sexual awakening literally configured as autoerotic in nature. The plot centers on stereotypically nerdy Arnie Cunningham's fetishistic "love affair" with a demonic 1958 Plymouth Fury named "Christine." The "affair" temporarily transforms Arnie from victimized nerd into charismatic young man. However, the malevolently sentient Christine quickly coerces Arnie into being a willing accomplice to the murder of Arnie's tormentors, further isolates him socially, deforms his personality into a caricature of masculinity, and finally kills him. The socially backward and bullied Arnie is no match for the supernaturally cunning Christine. In a parody of teenage sexual obsession, Arnie forsakes his parents, his best friend, and a real chance at an adult heterosexual relationship to pursue the ultimate in unrequited love. Christine does not return the love she is given, in spite of Arnie's stated belief to the contrary. Rather, she is a vampiric consumer of Arnie's expended energy. Willingly seduced by a demon, Arnie falls prey to his own displaced eroticism. Analysis of what happens to Arnie in the narrative reveals it to be a morality fable, playing out a hysterical male fantasy of loss of identity to a smothering, devouring female force.

In both book and film, the loner Arnie succumbs to the temptation posed by a car specifically gendered as female. Bill Phillips's screenplay adaptation of the novel follows the general plot trajectory and preserves many key scenes, even using some of the book's dialogue verbatim. However, a significant point of departure from the novel is in the nature of evil represented by Christine and the relationship between Christine and Arnie. King's novel strongly suggests that the car's previous owner, Roland LeBay, has somehow animated Christine into monstrous life through the car's absorption of the force of his anger. After LeBay's death, his spirit still controls the car and takes over Arnie as well. Arnie ultimately takes responsibility for the brutal actions committed in his name and dies partially redeemed at the end (Strengell 78; Wiater et al. 312). The film adaptation, by contrast, fully implicates Arnie in Christine's crimes and in fact places him inside Christine as a willing participant during the climactic confrontation with Dennis and Leigh that ends in Arnie's death. In the film adaptation, Arnie may be unduly influenced or even possessed by Christine, but he is fully aware of what is going on. The novel's dream and hallucination sequences are deleted in favor of realism. Arnie revels in the power transferred to him by Christine. The film's Arnie was never "sweet" like the novel's Arnie. The difference in tone, from King's melancholy but ultimately redemptive narrative to Phillips's and Carpenter's pessimistic one, is remarkable.

Although King's source novel sets up the basic narrative conceit of car as mobile haunted house, Carpenter's adaptation strips the narrative of ghosts to its hot-rod essence.[1] The film's opening image of the "V" ornament on Christine's grill, a type of *vagina dentata*, establishes the femaleness of Christine. To the rock 'n' roll strains of George Thorogood's "Bad to the Bone" on the soundtrack, the Christine of Carpenter's film is "born bad" or demonic on a Detroit assembly line (Magistrale, *Hollywood's Stephen King*, 151). According to Anna Powell, "[t]he camera shoots Christine as a diabolical presence from the start as we share the wing mirror's point-of-view of a potential victim on the assembly line" (150). Thus, by beginning the film with such a clear indication that Christine is evil independently of LeBay, Carpenter alters the terms of King's narrative, reduces LeBay to an off-screen presence in the film (Magistrale, *Hollywood's Stephen King*, 150), and removes most of the novel's romantic rivalry between Arnie and Dennis for Leigh's affections. This stripped cinematic narrative is strictly about Arnie and Christine.

Arnie Cunningham is a relatively powerless, lonely boy who thinks buying and owning a car will empower him. From this perspective, then, Arnie is only an exaggerated version of a pathological American codependent relationship with automobiles[2] and, in particular, the male tendency to think of their cars and other purchased machinery of self-empowerment as female, implying that men also often view women as commodities to be bought, sold, or traded. The mercantile view of male/female relationships is a strong thematic component of *Christine*. Early on, the narrative constructs male identity, especially sexuality, in economic terms and illustrates the moral dangers of unreflectively "buying in" to this philosophy, as Arnie does. The film adaptation foregrounds the cost of the autoerotic love affair even more than King's source novel does.

For example, a scene in which Darnell offers Arnie a job working around the garage concludes with a shot of Arnie sitting alone in Christine's cab, lovingly caressing her wheel, as a slow love song plays on the car radio. The car radio, signified in Carpenter's text as the voice of Christine, speaks to Arnie through music, and in this particular scene falsely reassures him of fidelity.[3] In spite of this, Arnie's lowered head and generally weary demeanor suggest something of the toll this unnatural relationship is already costing him. This type of economic reading is encouraged by the juxtaposition of this hauntingly romantic moment with the economic subtext of the business discussion with Darnell. It is also a moment of transition, as the "old" Arnie will in the following scenes give way to the new Arnie, one who sheds his eyeglasses, dresses sharper, seemingly becomes more confident, and gains a girlfriend. However, he has purchased these gains without honest effort. The shortcut fatally corrupts him.

By contrast, Dennis, protected by his empowered status within the social space of the narrative, is relatively immune to Christine's "charms" from the start. He certainly has the potential for corruption through the temptations of sex and cars, as slyly hinted at in Carpenter's directorial choice of 1950s songs that also play on Dennis's car radio. However, Christine chooses the far weaker Arnie and then jealously tries to eliminate his protector, Dennis, through a flexing of supernatural force at a football game, resulting in a terrible injury to Dennis. For the rest of the film, the suddenly demasculinized Dennis is either lying impotently in a hospital bed or hobbling about on crutches. Incapacitated by Christine, Dennis can no longer shield Arnie from sinking even further into madness. When Dennis reenters the narrative later, it is too late for friendship to save Arnie. The limits to Dennis's protective masculine abilities are literalized in Dennis's broken lower body.

Two telling exchanges between Arnie and Dennis, one at the beginning of the film and one toward the end, illustrate the extent to which Arnie and Dennis transform and how their friendship is reinscribed. The exchanges make explicit the linkage between adolescent male sexuality and the empowerment imparted to young men by money, social prominence, and material markers of status—all of which Dennis has and Arnie lacks. The first exchange begins when Dennis is driving Arnie to school, visually establishing Dennis in the active masculine role and Arnie in the passive feminized one. The resulting dialogue between the two boys, in which the experienced Dennis attempts to convince the virginal Arnie that he needs to "get laid" his senior year, displays Dennis's social and sexual superiority to Arnie. When Dennis utilizes a financial metaphor to describe a former sexual partner as a "walking sperm bank" and possible date for Arnie, Arnie replies, "I don't think I have the minimum deposit to open an account, you know what I mean?" Dennis extends the metaphor by telling Arnie that Arnie carries "his life savings between his legs." While undoubtedly overstated and chauvinistic, Dennis's counterarguments to Arnie nevertheless suggest the possibility that sexual energy, properly "invested" with a willing partner, has a restorative and indeed redemptive "life-saving" force. The scene concludes with Arnie's rejection of mutually participatory sexual unions: "I think maybe I'll just beat off." Rather than face the terror that the feminine creates within him, Arnie prefers solitary or autoerotic gratification. Christine will provide the safely sexless solution to his problem of loneliness.

The second exchange occurs just prior to the film's climactic battle between Dennis and Arnie in Darnell's garage. Arnie picks up Dennis to drive him to Arnie's house for their traditional New Year's celebration. The fact that Arnie is driving and Dennis is the passenger is a mirror image of the earlier scene. Now Arnie is clearly in masculine control, while the feminized Dennis is distinctly disempowered both physically (his broken leg) and psychologically (his fear of the supernatural Christine and Arnie's unrepressed anger). During the drive, Arnie taunts Dennis by briefly allowing Christine to drive herself around a dangerous curve, threatens Dennis with death if he is disloyal, and indirectly confesses to murder. The scene illustrates the extent to which Arnie, while still a loner, reverses the direction of the power dynamic with Dennis.

The shift in Arnie's character between the two scenes is so significant because the film initially positions Arnie as significantly handicapped with regard to exercise of male privilege and hence vulnerable to shortcuts or temptations to empowerment. As one of the two central male characters, he is introduced onscreen after Dennis and sharply contrasts with Dennis's self-assurance. Arnie lacks physical power and presence, as visually signified by his thin build, clumsiness, and unstylish clothing and eyeglasses. He is dominated by his mother, Regina, who will not let him leave the driveway to enter Dennis's car without nagging him to keep his lunch cold and, in that most hackneyed of female-as-shrew clichés, to take out the garbage. Most significantly, however, Arnie lacks a car, dooming him to second-class social status in an American high school of the 1970s, and thus priming him for responding to Christine's siren song.[4]

Once Arnie's sexual inexperience and subordinate position to Dennis have been established, the film narrative then propels Arnie and Dennis into the daily high school milieu in which the feminized Arnie is at best ignored and at worst literally besieged and reliant upon masculine Dennis's intervention in events to save him.[5] Helpless even to open a stuck locker without Dennis's help, Arnie remains a marginal figure in the film frame as Dennis interacts with his own friends Chuck and Bemis and flirts with cheerleader Roseanne, whom Dennis, a top player in the sexual competitiveness of high school, will later reject. Even Arnie's future girlfriend, the new transfer Leigh Cabot, does not notice him as she walks down the hall past Dennis, Bemis, and Arnie. Arnie is a nonentity to almost everyone in the school except Dennis and, tragically, Buddy Repperton.

A figure heading for socioeconomic oblivion after high school, Buddy relentlessly bullies the college-bound Arnie. The three-way fight between Arnie, Dennis, and Buddy (another of the story's doomed triangles) in the shop room falls in King's novel shortly after Arnie buys Christine, but Carpenter locates the scene before Christine's entrance. In King's version of the confrontation, Arnie has been emboldened by Christine and stands up fairly well to Buddy. In Carpenter's film, however, Arnie is cowed and needs to be rescued by Dennis and the shop teacher. This narrative shift of a key scene further underscores Arnie's impotence and hence vulnerability to what Christine offers. The confrontation is visually coded as ominously Freudian, as Buddy menaces Arnie with a phallic switchblade, calls him "Cuntingham," and metaphorically castrates him by stabbing his lunch "bag" and releasing a flood of thick white fluid (yogurt that in context here connotes semen) upon which Arnie slips and is helpless before Buddy. Dennis himself is "castrated" when Moochie Welch sneakily grabs his testicles from behind and squeezes, rendering Dennis momentarily helpless. Adding further castrating insult to injury, Buddy crushes Arnie's eyeglasses beneath his boot.

Once the narrative illustrates the extent of Arnie's lack of masculine power in his daily environment, Arnie is primed to meet Christine. He is ready to squander his precious "capital" on the undeserving Christine, who redirects his "life's savings"—not just sexual energy, but money, family attachments, friendship with Dennis, romance with "the prettiest girl in school" Leigh Cabot, and ultimately his life—into a fetishistic and masturbatory relationship with an inhuman but nevertheless female monster.[6] He recognizes immediately that the apparently decrepit Christine, rotting away in LeBay's yard, harbors the potential to rescue Arnie from an adolescent nightmare of power-lessness and victimization by more physically powerful males, such as Buddy Repperton. Christine promises to infuse enough power and charisma into Arnie's life to enable him both to "score" with the pret-tiest girl in the school and to exact vengeance upon Repperton and his gang of toadies. In return, Christine demands uncompromising love and loyalty. The exchange is decidedly banked in Christine's favor by virtue of Arnie's inexperience and need for validation. What chance, then, will Arnie have when Christine swallows him up when he sits behind her wheel?

In fact, ingestion into the body and expulsion from the body becomes a structuring metaphor of the film. The metaphor is introduced in the opening sequence on the assembly line, when capi-talistic machinery squeezes out a fully formed Christine from the raw materials incorporated into the industrial process. Christine, both as a symbol of voracious capitalism and lethal femininity seeking retribu-tion against male entitlement, begins consuming immediately, first by "eating" the fingers of the mechanic who inserts his hand under her hood. The iconography established by the "V" grill ornament and the upraised hood suggests that this mechanic is thoughtlessly inserting his hand into a *vagina dentata*, which then slams shut and crushes or severs (it is unclear as to which) the intruding digits. Having drawn first blood, Christine then "swallows" and suffocates or crushes the line supervisor who insultingly flicks his phallic cigar and dirty ashes onto her plastic-protected, virgin seat upholstery. His body is later dumped out onto the factory floor.

When next we see Christine rusting away in an untended suburban yard 20 years later, the ashes spilled onto her front seat by that hapless line supervisor seem to have metastasized into a filthy cancer that is eating away her entire body. She needs to absorb the life force of a new victim to revitalize her. She has already consumed Roland LeBay and his wife and child, repaying their energy investment by killing all of them with the carbon monoxide excreted by her tailpipe. Christine now begins to ingest Arnie to restore herself to prime condition. Arnie, voluntarily being eaten alive, is in a unique position to comment on this type of sublimely destructive love to Dennis:

> Let me tell you a little something about love, Dennis. It has a voracious appetite. It eats everything—family, friends. It kills me how much it

eats. But I'll tell you something else. You feed it right, and it can be a beautiful thing. And that's what we have. When someone believes in you, you can do anything, anything in the fucking universe. And when you believe right back in that someone, then nobody can stop you then, nobody ever. . . . I'm talking about Christine, man. No shitter ever came between me and Christine.

Arnie's favorite epithet for those who victimize him suggests that those who are ingested by Christine are then rendered into expelled waste.

Scatological references indeed abound in the film, many of them centered on characters and events in Darnell's garage. The garage and attached junkyard are the natural end points of the once-new rolling irons from Detroit. While the garage does serve as the birthing site of the rejuvenated Christine, it is also the place where Dennis and Leigh will dispatch Christine (at least temporarily) with a bulldozer and have her compacted into the cube of iron that will be "dumped" in the junkyard at the end of the film.[7] Darnell's labeling of Christine as a "mechanical asshole" (presumably based on the emission or "farting" of Christine's noxious exhaust fumes when she first pulls into the garage) and a "turd," as well as his own junkyard as a "shit pile," sets the tone for Darnell's garage as being the appropriate setting for the regeneration of the Fury and Arnie's corresponding deterioration. Darnell himself, as a corrupt businessman, represents a defiled "realm of illicit commerce," according to Edward Madden, and "emphatically collapses money, power, and privilege into the language of shit" (148). In his job offer to Arnie, he warns Arnie not to think he had "the gold key to the crapper" and that Arnie does not have "money falling out of his asshole." Darnell describes Roland LeBay in similar excretory terms, as being "mean" enough to "drink ice water and piss ice cubes," thus linking the corrupted setting to the former owner of Christine.

Later in the film, the metaphor will become literal. Buddy Repperton's assault on Christine in Darnell's garage involves, in the words of State Police Detective Junkins, "one of the perpetrators [defecating] on the dashboard," or, in Arnie's earthier statement to his mother, "One of them took a shit on the dashboard of my car, Ma." The fecal imagery persists in several scenes, notably the first interrogation scene between Arnie and Detective Junkins, somewhat reminiscent of the one between Arbogast and Norman Bates in *Psycho*.[8] Junkins is investigating the death of Moochie Welch, one of the suspected vandalizers of Arnie's car. Arnie, responding to

Junkins's comment about defecation and why such an act did not drive Arnie to file a police report, says, "Shit wipes off." Junkins segues, "Moochie Welch kinda got wiped off too. . . . The kid was cut in half, Arnie. They had to scrape his legs up with a shovel." Arnie counters, "Isn't that what you're supposed to do with shit? Scrape it up with a little shovel?"

Having heard the word "shitter" from LeBay's brother at the time of purchasing Christine, Arnie ubiquitously uses the label himself to refer to all of his enemies, not just the late Moochie Welch. On New Year's Eve, ensconced behind the wheel of his car, he proposes a toast to Dennis: "Death to the shitters of the world of 1979." Dennis refuses to toast to that, but asks, "Who are the shitters?" Arnie replies chillingly, "All of them." In the climactic confrontation in Darnell's garage, Arnie screams "Shitters!" at Dennis and Leigh, but moments later is himself expelled from Christine's windshield and fatally impaled on glass as a "reward" for his faith in Christine. The recurrent "shitting" motif ending in Arnie's death focuses viewer attention on the wasteful end product of Arnie's investment into Christine. He receives nothing of benefit for his expenditure. Indeed, he sinks ever deeper into a corruption of the soul, for which the metaphor of choice for both King and Carpenter is "shit." In the sense that "dirty" is an adjective often paired with money, and that economics is so much a subtext of the narrative, the scatological theme also links filth to economic and physical systems of exchange and how blatantly rigged Christine's system truly is. Analogous to a financial scam artist, Christine promises much return on investment but takes from the investor without reciprocity. The excretion or expulsion imagery in the film represents the linear nature of the energy investment; indeed, there is no restorative exchange at all, but only ingestion resulting in polluting effluvia that cannot be escaped. Only Christine, with her supernatural defiance of entropy, can recycle into new generations—as long as there is a supply of energizing victims to draw upon.

Carpenter's film, on the evidence of this obsessive focus on repression and filth, is undoubtedly constructed on a psychoanalytic framework. One of the time-honored strategies of mainstream Hollywood film is to infuse sexuality "in plain sight" through signifiers that suggest sexuality but do not actually portray it. The result is a cinema of sexual fetish. Carpenter embraces this strategy for *Christine*. The film has only one overt semisexual scene: the "petting" session between Arnie and Leigh at the drive-in during a significantly rainy or "wet" night. Carpenter constructs, through careful placement of coded signifiers, nearly every scene in one way or another as sexual in its connotations. Christine rolls off the assembly line with a unique red-and-white paint scheme, signifying from the beginning that she can be both "whore" (symbolized by red) and "virgin" (symbolized by white) to men with the eyes to see her. Christine "castrates" those men who approach her, cutting off digits and reacting murderously to phallic cigars brought into her interior. The car is fetishized as a female-stand in from Arnie's first sight of her, even before he knows to call her "Christine."

Significantly, Arnie's lonely, hungry gaze begins the process of fetishizing the car as female. Eyes figure prominently in the visual grammar of the film, from Arnie's taped spectacles to Christine's magically animated headlights at key "shock" moments. The male gaze begins the cycle of appropriation/victimization. Arnie's gaze and lurid festishization brings Christine to life, or, as Marie Mulvey-Roberts summarizes, "the borders between the animate and the inanimate are broken down by a fetishisation of the feminine" (79). Carpenter's visual aesthetic extends the boundaries of car-fetishization from Arnie to the viewer: "As well as using subjective camera-work for Christine's point-of-view, Carpenter fetishises the car's design with slow, lingering shots of her gleaming chrome and flamboyant tail fins" (151). Thus, in a Hitchcockian flourish, Carpenter implicates the voyeuristic audience itself in Arnie's festishes.[9]

In terms of Arnie's psychosexual neuroses, one cannot overlook the smothering, metaphorically incestuous relationship he has with his mother Regina. Even Regina's name is a not-so-subtle reference to "vagina." Arnie has let himself be dominated by Regina most of his life. The film opens just as matters between mother and son have reached a boiling point, with Arnie's father an ineffectual observer on the sidelines. As Dennis drives Arnie to school, Dennis asks if Arnie and his mother are "having a war." Arnie explains that his upper-class mother is angry and embarrassed that her son is taking shop. Dennis says that she would not think it embarrassing when Arnie fixes his parents' "Volvo" for free. In the context of the rest of this scene, it is tempting to believe that this car make has been carefully chosen for its similarity to the word "vulva." Arnie goes on to describe a heated Scrabble game in which his dad was "blown away early" and he and his mother were "neck and neck" (necking?). However, he loses the game when Regina refuses to accept a triple-word score for his word "fellatio." Thus, the incestuous undertones to Arnie's and Regina's relationship, and the marginal position of the father, are already an entrenched aspect of the Cunningham family dynamics.

The sudden arrival of Christine in his life incites a full-blown struggle between Regina and Christine for possession of Arnie. As a pawn in this struggle, Arnie loathes female force as much as he longs for it to ease his estrangement from society. He wants to be consumed by love and lost in obsession. In psychoanalytic terms, he seeks the womb he has lost. In the nightmare logic of horror film, he of course finds a surrogate womb and literally crawls back into it. His unnatural act is not without consequence. What he does pollutes the entire community, as did Oedipus's crime in Sophocles' play. The monstrous womb, given unholy life by Arnie's act, goes on a rampage until Arnie and his enemies are dead. Suzie Young elaborates, "Arnie's devotion to Christine can be seen partially to conceal and partially to heal a past disappointment: in the place of his real-life phallic mother who is indifferent to his needs, he produces a surrogate—Christine—who is proactive and self-sacrificing in his defence" (131). Young further links this theme to Freud's theory of human development, wherein a male infant's blissful union with the mother is followed by traumatic separation and a later psychic renunciation, or a type of "psychological matricide" (132) and replacement of the mother figure with a female equivalent. Factored into this dynamic, of course, is the developing boy's jealousy of the father who possesses the mother and corresponding desire to kill the father.

This psychological dynamic is heavily emphasized in Carpenter's film. The first night he owns Christine, he yells at his parents but most pointedly at his mother. During Arnie's first visit to Dennis in the hospital, Arnie describes how he stood up to his parents. Arnie then inverts the orthodox understanding of Freudian human development when he psychoanalyzes the origins of his parents' resistance to him: "They just don't want me to grow up, because then they'd have to face growing old. Has it ever occurred to you that part of being a parent is trying to kill your kids?" Later, after Christine is apparently destroyed by Buddy and his gang, Arnie rejects his parents' offer to buy him a new car by coldly telling his mother, "Fuck you." He separates himself from her and the family dining room (it is the last time that Regina appears in the film) to go to his surrogate mother. His father attempts to grab him to go back into the dining room to apologize to his mother; Arnie yells, "Get your mitts off me, mother-fucker!" and seems to be, briefly, on the verge of throttling his own father and literally fulfilling the Oedipal trajectory.

The scene immediately following, located in Darnell's garage, is a turning point in the narrative, wherein Arnie sees for the first time what his car is capable of doing. Isolated from all human contact,

Arnie says to his ruined car, "We'll make it better, huh? They can't hurt us any more, not if we work together. And we'll show those shitters what we can do." Given this pledge of fidelity, Christine spontaneously regenerates her destroyed engine, unveiling for the first time the full range of her supernatural power to Arnie. Enrapt like any virginal heterosexual boy seeing a woman disrobe for the first time, Arnie watches Christine regenerate herself completely to the background accompaniment of the stripper melody "Harlem Nocturne" on the soundtrack.[10] Arnie's displaced Oedipal rage and his lust conflate into one dark force that motivates Christine to drive herself into the night to track down and kill Moochie Welch. Buddy Repperton and the other "shitters" will soon follow.

From that point forward, Arnie, having found a suitable female substitute for his mother and emboldened by his insider's knowledge of Christine's true capabilities, acts invincible. The inner transformation is reflected in Arnie's choice of "uniform." He discards his "nerd" style of dress and begins dressing first as a high-school "yuppie" (collared shirts and sweaters) and then, as his personality turns darker and darker, black shirts and vests. His physical appearance changes as well, first for the better (groomed hair and confident bearing) and then, as Christine vampirically drains him, for the worse (pale face, dark rings around his eyes). He faces down Detective Junkins, looking him in the eyes and lying and evading as necessary, in a series of intense cross-examinations that doubtlessly would have reduced the old Arnie to tears. Yet, for all of this newfound swagger, he cannot help himself from hinting to Dennis what is really happening, perhaps so that someone will recognize what Arnie has accomplished. For example, when Dennis awakens in the hospital to find Arnie visiting him for the first time in weeks, Arnie provides a thinly veiled confession of culpability: "Did you hear about what happened to Moochie?" Dennis then asks what will happen if Buddy Repperton trashes the car again, to which Arnie replies with certain knowledge: "He won't do it again." Prophetically, a few scenes later, Buddy and his friends Richie Trelawney and Don Vandenberg are killed by Christine in an explosive attack on the gas station in which Vandenberg works.

Given Arnie's willing descent into murder, is there any hope at all for his moral redemption and his renunciation of autoeroticism? The Arnie of King's novel is partially redeemed at the eleventh hour by his brief reconnection with Dennis and his final resistance against LeBay. However, Carpenter allows for no such reconciliation between Arnie and Dennis. Arnie is too arrogant, too implicated in the string of killings, to reach out to Dennis. In the context of Carpenter's revision of Arnie's character, it can be inferred that Arnie maintains the relationship more for the enjoyment of seeing his once-powerful friend flat on his back in the hospital than any sense of loyalty or love. The homosocial bond does not hold up. Neither does the heterosexual attraction between Arnie and Leigh. Just before Christine kills Buddy, Arnie does reach out to Leigh once to say he loves her, but her refusal to say the same to Arnie drives him into a profane rage and he hangs up the phone, metaphorically severing the last connection between them.

Arnie at last is so consumed by Christine that he rides with her to Darnell's garage to kill Dennis and Leigh. He sits within her hellishly red cab as she regenerates around him. But now that he has been so consumed, his energy and human connections gone, Christine literally spits him out during a crash into Darnell's office (the site of fecal defilement) and kills him. In Arnie's last scene, he lunges up from the offal of Darnell's office and attempts to draw in Leigh in a last savage embrace. However, it not an attempt to seek comfort while dying—he is trying to kill her. His only tender gesture is reserved for Christine, but it is a gesture that is sexual at the same time. He reaches out a bloody hand to caress the vaginal "V" on her fanged grille and then dies. Christine's headlights fade with his last breath. Thus, Arnie dies alone in a car wreck, truly an autoerotic death. He has not been redeemed at all, and Christine's continuing attack on Dennis and Leigh seems to have been fueled by his consumed life force.

Arnie's bid to empowerment has miserably failed. His enemies are dead, but only at the cost of his own relationships and, eventually, his life. The one true love of his life was a chimera. Christine took from him until the one-sided entropic exchange could no longer be sustained. So, the film's final shot, where Junkins, Leigh, and Dennis watch Christine's apparent disposal in a junkyard, is bleak. In spite of Dennis's and Leigh's survival and Junkins's platitude about them being "heroes," Arnie is lost. Junkins's statement that "[s]ome things can't be helped—some people too" sums up the futility of what Dennis and Leigh have gone through. Arnie never could have been helped. Christine herself, apparently junked but obviously still alive as signified by the slight movement of her grille work, will be back to claim more victims. The landscape of this final scene, strewn with the wreckage of countless automobiles, suggests that Arnie's personal autoerotic tragedy is the tragedy of American's love affair with the automobile.

Notes

1. Conner writes, "The screenplay also resolved the origin of Christine's evil nature. King admits to hedging his bets on just how the demonic car got to be so bad" (73). Robert C. Cumbow finds this unambiguous prologue to be part of Carpenter's storytelling aesthetic: "Arguably, a more gradual recognition of the evil in Christine might have made for more effective horror, but the assumption is that most people going to the movie already know what it's about, and Carpenter, though a sublimely manipulative director, is not one to tease, let alone disappoint, an audience. In *Christine* he goes right for the jugular" (122).

2. Mary Findley explains how this theme structures King's source novel: If contemporary American culture is viewed through the lens of King's car-owner relationship as illustrated in Christine, it is possible to see the detrimental relationships that Americans have with their automobiles. Often unable to pay in full for these mechanized modes of transportation, Americans become slaves to monthly car payments, not to mention the plethora of expenses that go along with car ownership—insurance, maintenance expenses, gasoline, and all too often, with accidents, the expense of hospital bills, as well as physical, emotional, and psychological pain. Car owners are tied to their vehicles by unseen financial chains, but contemporary American existence obscures these disadvantages, and what was once a luxury item has become a necessity as more and more people find the hassle and lack of public transportation prohibitive. (211)

3. Any discussion of *Christine*, either as novel or as film, cannot pass without reference to rock music. King's novel is tied together by epigraphs from the many 1950s rock songs that celebrated cars, speed, sex, and death. The main sections are subtitled "Teenage Car-Songs," "Teenage Love-Songs," and "Teenage Death-Songs." Carpenter is himself a musician who often writes the musical scores for his own films, including the instrumental score for *Christine*. In his selection of rock songs for the film, Carpenter chooses songs that are commentaries upon the action, such as "Boney Maroney" for the scene in which Darnell is crushed by Christine's front seat or "Rock 'n' Roll Is Here to Stay" when the car keeps regenerating in spite of Dennis's and Leigh's crushing of it with the Caterpillar. Cumbow observes that Arnie's contemporaries are given contemporary songs, such as the Rolling Stones' "Beast of Burden," while Christine plays 1950s songs appropriate to the situation. In Carpenter's overall bleak vision, Cumbow maintains that rock music is herein a disruptive force or the dark side of youthful rebellion (125). Leigh is given the last word in the film: "God, I hate rock 'n' roll."

4. Christine does seem to have the ability to lure men into her interior, where they are then at her mercy. The Detroit line worker is compelled to sit in her, and so is Darnell 20 years later. Christine then kills both of

them by squeezing the air out of them. The suffocation imagery is pervasive.

5. John Kenneth Muir comments on this aspect of the film: "*Christine* really seems to exist in the closed off environment of high school, the world of the dominant, athletic male teenager" (116).

6. This aspect of the film is reasonably faithful to King's novel and thus subject to the same criticism that King has taken over the years for what seems to be a persistent gynophobia. From *Carrie* onward, King's fiction has consistently displayed signifiers of what Sylvia Kelso calls "terrifying female processes such as menstruation or giving birth" (267). The monstrous-feminine, as Barbara Creed calls it, pervades King's work. In specific reference to Christine, Kelso calls her a "motorized Belle Dame Sans Merci" (269) and argues that "the basic terror of the novel is the image of a machine out of control, overlaid, by the traditional gynophobic images, with the far more deep-seated terror of a woman out of control" (272). Christine as a strong female signifier is also a terrifying devourer of men. Although some of Christine's past victims have been female, Kelso observes, "in the novel's present its victims are spectacularly and entirely male" (270).

7. In the novel, the anal association is even more explicit: Dennis and Leigh dispatch Christine with a truck that pumps out septic tanks.

8. Of course, Arnie's relationship to his domineering mother also evokes the cinematic memory of Norman Bates and his mother.

9. Robert C. Cumbow explains, "like Hitchcock, Carpenter places the moral burden where it belongs: on the viewer. We *like* Christine, and cheer for her when we see how she boosts the self-esteem of nerdy, ineffectual Arnie, and how she neatly disposes of his enemies without implicating him. It's only as Arnie himself begins to change, his newfound confidence unfolding into arrogance, that we begin to feel we're in too deep" (122; emphasis in the original). In other words, Carpenter creates an experience for the audience not unlike what happens to Arnie. Unlike the novel, mostly told from Dennis's point of view and where Arnie remains a distant figure, we *are* Arnie in the film.

10. Significantly, the audience experiences the visual spectacle of the regeneration along with Arnie and shares Arnie's secret with him. While the other characters struggle with accepting the possibility of the supernatural in the murders of Buddy and the others, the audience and Arnie know it all along. The audience is an accomplice, along with Arnie. Thus, the act of fetishizing through looking uncomfortably bonds the viewer to Arnie. Tony Magistrale maintains that Arnie's culpability in the murders only intensifies the bond "between the car and the boy, as if the two share a lover's secret" (*Hollywood's Stephen King*, 152).

Chapter 5

Tonka Terrors

The Humor and Horror of "Trucks" and *Maximum Overdrive*

Michael A. Arnzen

Who Made Who?

Stephen King's first and only effort in directing a motion picture to date, *Maximum Overdrive* (1986), is considered by many of his readers, reviewers, and film critics alike as an abysmal failure. Reviews of the movie are almost universally negative; some are downright vindictive ("Stephen King's highly publicized run-in with an out-of-control van is an appropriate stanza of poetic justice for directing this particularly fetid chunk of bowl biscuit about machinery gone amok," writes one reviewer at efilmcritic.com). Even King himself is somewhat embarrassed by the movie. When asked in 1991 if he would ever direct again, King said he would like to take a shot at it because *Maximum Overdrive* was "just terrible" and he likened the experience to having "shit on [his] shoes" that he would like to wipe clean (Wood 47).[1]

An aesthetic disappointment in the genre, an embarrassment to the director, and a financial flop for the studio upon its release,[2] *Maximum Overdrive* would seem unworthy of deep critical treatment now, two decades later. Indeed, very little scholarship has been written about the film, despite its rare status in Hollywood cinema history as an adaptation of a previously published work of fiction subsequently both written *and* directed for the screen by its own original author. I find this lack of criticism surprising, if only because of the novelty of such an enterprise in the industry. While the film may not be as remarkable as other adaptations of King's fiction, *Maximum Overdrive*'s failures are precisely what make it an interesting film worth studying, for its flaws put the textual complexities of adaptation into dramatic relief. One of the reasons it may have flopped, for instance, is that King chose to make it a comedy as much as a technohorror story, and audience expectations and desires may have been frustrated. Indeed, because of King's cultural status as one of the most popular horror novelists of all time, *Maximum Overdrive* sheds light on the role of an author/auteur in popular culture like no other work of cinematic art.

Maximum Overdrive was the thirteenth film adapted from Stephen King's work—"a suitable number," as Douglas Winter notes, "to mark the first film directed by the man whose name has become synonymous with modern horror" (181). Loosely based on his short story, "Trucks" (published originally in the 1973 men's magazine *Cavalier*, and later appearing in his 1978 collection, *Night Shift*),[3] *Maximum Overdrive* quite literally provided King with what he called "a crash course in film school" (Wood 47)—and it was released to theaters during the height of his popularity as a horror writer in the mid-1980s.[4] The fact that King, a novelist without any professional experience behind the camera, was given a $10 million budget by the Dino De Laurentiis Company and the artistic freedom to make a movie virtually however he wanted is itself a testament to King's high status in media culture and Hollywood's faith in his creative vision. Granted, King's vocal complaints about the adaptations prior to *Maximum Overdrive*, like Kubrick's treatment of *The Shining*, were a matter of public record (Winter 243), so fan demand (if not King's own artistic drive to correct his image) may have been high. The result of his turn behind the camera, however, is a mixed bag: a film that reflects not only the strengths of Stephen King's imagination and his raw creative passion, but also many of the weaknesses that any rookie film school experiment might generate . . . especially if a neophyte were given a $10 million budget to, quite literally, "blow."

Rarely does Hollywood take such economic risks, but Stephen King's high reputation as author was enough to immediately stamp him as a bankable "auteur"—that is, as a celebrity director, or more accurately, as a singular, dominant creative persona artistically responsible for generating the text. Just as *Psycho* (1960) is rarely considered by the populace as a movie adapted from a great Robert Bloch novel, or as a product of its time, but instead as a classic "Hitchcock" picture, so, too, is *Maximum Overdrive* considered a "Stephen King" picture, a product of "The Master of Terror," through and through. What is odd about this is that King is an *author*, not an *auteur* proper, and yet his role in directing the film is constructed as if he had the same talent and celebrity behind the camera as a Hitchcock—it is, in other words, a vulgar or populist notion of the director as auteur.[5] Everything about the packaging and marketing of *Maximum Overdrive* frames it as the work of King, and the narrative insists to be read as such: from the large marquee trumpeting King's byline in the opening credits to his cameo appearance early in the film, from the dominant image of King in the film poster (holding puppet strings over the actors and trucks that line the very bottom margin) to King's narration of the film's trailer. The auteur's presence is everywhere, suggesting that there is no way to understand the film other than as one man's creation. Indeed, AC/DC's recurring song lyric in the film, "Who Made Who?" constantly reminds the audience of the very idea of authorship. But perhaps one of the reasons that *Maximum Overdrive* failed to live up to its promise is that the function of an author cannot transfer so easily to the cinema because the meanings and successes of a popular film—like all folk art—are as much produced by its collective audience as they are due to the work of any singular progenitor, creator, or auteur.

"Auteur theory" is a popular approach to film studies, but for years critics have rightfully questioned the assumption that a film's "director" can be synonymous with a book's "author." Screenplays are not short stories and there are inherent differences, obviously, between controlling a camera lens over a literal image and manipulating language to conjure an image in the imagination. Films are often the product of studio collaboration than individual acts of creation. In his challenge of auteurism and treatment of the director-as-*litterateur*, Thomas Schatz argues that the quality and artistry of any film is "a melding of institutional forces" and that the "style of a writer, director, star—or even a cinematographer, art director, or costume designer—fuse[s] with the studio's production operations and management structure, its resources and talent pool, its narrative traditions and market strategy" (656). We recognize this when we see the credits roll, yet, as popular audiences we require a storyteller, a singular agent responsible for what we see—and part of this need is constructed by the studio system itself, which seeks to hide their economic motives behind the artist. Thus, the brand name, "Stephen King," serves what Foucault terms an "author-function"—a terminus of meaning, allowing an audience to attribute intention behind, meaning within, and, most importantly, responsibility for a work of art. This is one reason why most reviews of *Maximum Overdrive*, both positive and negative, focus on Stephen King's abilities as a director, rather than on the filmic text itself.

The assumption that one filmmaker—even a writer as crafty as King—is entirely responsible for the end product is, largely, a cultural fantasy. I am not raising the concept of the "author-function" to excuse King for the weaknesses of *Maximum Overdrive*, for many of the choices that contribute to the film—from camera angles to content—obviously bear Stephen King's stamp. Rather, I think the best way to approach the film critically is as an artifact of popular culture, which not only celebrates celebrity but also often mocks the authority of high culture. No matter how "lowbrow" a film it might be, it is nevertheless productive to seek meanings within the culture in which *Maximum Overdrive* is immersed, based in its intertextual references to other films (a lineage of b-movie influences, for instance) and the myriad extratextual influences that inform the text and help to produce its meanings and impact. There is a degree, moreover, to which the overt framing of the film as the artistic enterprise of an adored author-auteur conflicts with the public desire to which the film caters to, especially the desire among the masses to imaginatively disempower the concept of the author (the root of *author*-ity). John Fiske argues that in high culture—the realm of literature—"the veneration of the author-artist is a necessary correlative of the veneration of the text" and acknowledges that this "accords well with the status of the text as a crafted object" (125).[6] But in *popular* culture, "the object of veneration is less the text or artist and more the performer, and the performer . . . exists intertextually." For Fiske, it is more productive to read a movie like *Maximum Overdrive* in terms of its intertextual dynamics, tracing the way it interacts with other popular texts and media, since this is predominantly how mass audiences genuinely "read" a film, despite—or even in rebellion against— the dominant controls of the celebrated author/auteur. "Who made who?" remains an open question, one the audience might ask of the brand name author, as much as they might puzzle over the relationship between the machines and human beings in the plot.

Attack of the Killer "Trucks"

Although many of King's fans and critics find *Maximum Overdrive* dreadful, the film is not entirely damnable as a "gross-out comedy"[7] and it has earned something of a cult status: fifteen years after its release, in 2001, the film evidently had enough commercial appeal to support a wide rerelease of the film on DVD; the film has been parodied, most notably by such popular TV shows as *The Simpsons* (in a 1999 episode called "Maximum Homerdrive")[8]; the soundtrack by heavy metal outfit AC/DC has enjoyed much radio airplay over the past 20 years, and was remastered under the title *Who Made Who* as recent as 2003; there is even a fan site on the Internet solely devoted to the film, called "The Happy Toyz Company" (named after a logo emblazoned on the film's main "villain," the "Green Goblin" truck). Indeed, the film was even *remade* in 1997 by Chris Thomson for the USA cable network, under the property's original literary title, *Trucks*, which credits King's story as the source, but reframes the film's conceit of possession as an "Area 51" alien invasion story (or, what its publicity calls a "close encounter of the machine kind").[9] Given such staying power in the modern imagination and such interest in the property across diverse media, the film is an artifact of popular culture that offers a great deal beyond simply insight into the issues raised by Stephen King.

However, despite the overt camp and lowbrow aesthetics of the film itself, the author's serious narrative message still delivers, and this bears fruitful discussion because the movie's messages are a part of its broader, cultural meanings. In *Hollywood's Stephen King*, Tony Magistrale quite accurately claims, I think, that "*Maximum Overdrive* is King's definitive statement about the destructive potential of machine technology and attendant level of alienation, even as the film has little else to recommend itself as a work of art" (155).

Perhaps what makes King's statement "definitive" is the stark simplicity of its primal allegory, which makes the author-director's stance on technology an unambiguous theme. Like its inspirational text "Trucks," *Maximum Overdrive* is set at an isolated truck stop, the "Dixie Boy," whose redneck occupants find themselves trapped in a battle against sentient 18-wheelers and big rigs—nay, the entire mechanical world—which (under the influence of a comet that has passed near Earth) seems driven, literally, to take over the planet. The film's prologue, starring King in a hilarious, Hitchcockean cameo, encapsulates the story's basic conflict: when a man attempts to make a withdrawal at an ATM, the machine's LED terminal says "you are an asshole" in reply. The machine's protest is hilarious, but what it signifies is obvious enough to explain the remainder of what's to come: the machines are—rudely, impossibly—rebelling against mankind. As the plot develops, we come to learn just how organized—and violent— their rebellion really is, as possessed, driverless trucks progressively break down the microcosm of civilization holed up in the Dixie Boy truck stop, killing anyone who refuses to fuel their engines, ultimately seeking to subordinate and enslave the entire human race.

The source story for this film, "Trucks" is one of many King titles that most critics gather under the respectable umbrella of science fiction dystopia, or more specifically, "technohorror"—that cautionary hybrid genre of science fiction and postmodern horror that depicts runaway machinery and technology spinning dangerously out of man's control. James Egan suggests that King has always been less a writer of the gothic than he is a writer preoccupied with man's loss of control over the machinery he has created under the name of progress. From "The Mangler" to *Christine*, King's career-long preoccupation with "malevolent machines" (142) has constantly raised "interrelated, troubling questions about the power, extent, and validity of science and rationalism in contemporary society" (140). For Egan, "Trucks," in particular, illustrates the fear "of human obsolescence" under the "superior 'species'" of machine, as is illustrated by the written tale's conclusion (143)—which is not as optimistic as the escape to Haven Island dramatized in the film adaptation. Critic Linda Badley suggests that the broader fears about dehumanization dramatized by King's short story, first published in 1973, are a product of its historical-cultural milieu, reflecting the "threat of literal extinction brought on by the fuel shortage of the early seventies . . . personify[ing] the external, corporate evil envisioned by the social and ecological consciences" of that time ("Love and Death," 85). Part of the horror of "Trucks," moreover, stems not merely from King's demonization of the oil industry, but also from the Catch-22 that erupts when the story's narrator considers the alternative: that is, that "turning away from technological advance would be tantamount to turning back the hands of time," and returning to primitive culture out of fear (Davis 72). King's technohorror, ultimately, "mocks the notion of technological 'progress'" through horror that taps into a fear of regression (Egan 150). Though the social allegory of "Trucks" is rel-atively powerful in delivering its cautionary messages about machines and technology, in its cinematic adaptation the humor of such mockery takes center stage.

Indeed, it may very well be the case that *Maximum Overdrive*'s comedic mode muddles the impact of its "technohorror" themes, producing a categorical dissonance that accounts to some extent for the film's poor critical reception. Whereas "Trucks" is a relatively serious and somber dystopia, *Maximum Overdrive*'s hybrid status as horror-comedy complicates audience interpretation and confounds their expectations from "the master of terror"[10]—leaving audiences uncertain whether they should laugh or scream or simply walk out of the theater.

Even the marketing campaign for the movie was rife with mixed messages. In a promotional trailer for the film, for example, King's status as "master of terror" dominates the sales pitch: in the campy sideshow barker tradition of Hitchcock and Castle, King plays up his role as horror auteur, speaking directly to the audience about his role in the upcoming movie and its capability to thrill. After humorously suggesting that other directors have made adaptations of his work that did not quite "do Stephen King right," he then menacingly points at his potential audience on the other side of the camera, and seriously delivers a threat: "I'm going to scare the hell out of you. And that's a promise." But for many, like *New York Times* critic Jon Pareles, that promise was broken: "the movie might be called 'Attack of the Killer Trucks'" he says, comparing the film to the notoriously preposterous b-movie, *Attack of the Killer Tomatoes* (1978)—and concludes that "[King] has taken a promising notion—our dependence on machines—and turned it into one long car-crunch movie."

Putting It in Reverse

Although there may be some class bias latent in his condemnation of "car-crunch" movies, Pareles's point is nonetheless apt: *Maximum Overdrive* is indeed the cinematic equivalent of a demolition derby. In fact, the spectacle of smash-'em-up automobiles may account for the film's appeal to some audiences and its sustained cult following. Demolition derbies, those automobile contests in which skilled drivers ram old, retrofitted cars into one another, are more popular than one might initially assume. Today they are "the largest draw at county fairs outside of top name talent" and they have been entertaining crowds since the mid-1950s (Lowenberg 1).[11] Sometimes called "banger" or "enduro" races, these carnivalesque attractions are inherently violent exhibitions, extreme (and extremely dangerous) battles that pit machine against machine to see who will be the "last one standing"—and these events have many parallels to King's survivalist narrative. Indeed, King may have overtly drawn inspiration from the spectacle and pyrotechnics of the demolition derby when creating his film; the trucks' wanton encirclement of the Dixie Boy is identical to the chaos and thunder evident everywhere in a demolition derby's ring; a number of "junkers" come to life just as derby drivers recycle their cars for the sport; even the excessive number of explosions and car crashes on screen virtually transform the movie theater aisles into a set of bleacher seats at the fairgrounds. But beyond such parallels, I argue that *Maximum Overdrive*, just like the demolition derby, performs a particular kind of cultural work: that is, a popular "rite of reversal," in both its content and its comedic approach to the horror genre.

In "Norm Demolition Derbies: Rites of Reversal in Popular Culture," Robert Jewett and John Lawrence draw on cultural anthropology to posit that "rites of reversal" are performances, rituals, and public events that invoke a topsy-turvy "upside-downing" of normal social hierarchies, in which customary laws are suspended and ordinary behavior is "done backward" to release pent up hostility regarding the oppressions of everyday life (290). Coterminous with Bakhtin's theory of "carnival," rites of reversal are socially sanctioned acts of transgression, or "periodic, cathartic expressions of rebellion against authority," that serve as a sort of cultural safety valve. They are faux rebellions, fictions whose pleasures are momentary and effects fleeting. But, "by letting off steam, such rituals end up reinforcing the very norms which are flaunted and then cheerfully reinstituted at the end of the prescribed festival."

At demolition derbies, audiences vicariously engage in automobile combat but still drive carefully out of the parking lot when the show is over, obeying the law. Following Tom Wolfe, who wrote about the offbeat culture of the demolition derby in his article, "Clean Fun at Riverhead," Jewett and Lawrence see in the event a psychic expression "symbolic of the national consciousness" such that, "with the elimination of direct conflict in modern society, 'Americans have turned to the automobile to satisfy their love of direct aggression'" (291). Inherent in the sublimation of such aggression into "car crunch" rituals like the derby, the authors find a reversal of two dominant cultural norms at work in them: "the sanctity of property and the voluntary acquiescence in traffic regulations" (292).

To claim that King's film dramatizes both of these "norm violations" in *Maximum Overdrive* is beyond obvious; indeed, the possessed tractor trailers and automobiles of the film seem driven *only* to destroy human property and they obey no traffic laws whatsoever. They are vicarious outlaws. When the humans at the truck stop try to outwit the maniacal trucks, the normal "rules" for behavior no longer apply: excessive destruction (like the gleeful elimination of the Green Goblin by bazooka rocket—the climactic moment of the film) seems to become their ultimate aim, well beyond the basic need for survival.

Audiences watch films like *Maximum Overdrive* to see the car crash, to watch the truck explode, and—likewise—to witness the carnage of the mutilated bodies and the breakdown of other fixed structures, like drawbridges and houses. By spectacularly destroying both machines and bodies, King equalizes them. The carnivalesque "rite of reversal," generally, is concerned with degrading the body (and the body politic) in order to liberate. Violence is the great equalizer in this regard. As Fiske asserts, such cultural experiences are like "white-knuckle rides of amusement parks" that invert the relationship of the body to machinery through *jouissance* (82). Fiske cites Tony Bennett's discussion of the amusement park ride in a way that perfectly encapsulates *Maximum Overdrive*'s demolition derby of film: "In releasing the body for pleasure rather than harnessing it for work, part of their appeal may be that they invert the normal relations between people and machinery prevailing in an industrial context" (Fiske 82). The degree to which King succeeds in vicariously engaging his audience in the "white-knuckle" experience of the demolition derby, is the degree to which he is able to "drive" his transgressive themes home.

The comedic absurdity of the film, however, pushes the "reversal" of norms into territory that the physicality and violence of the demolition derby could never approach. In both "Trucks" and *Maximum Overdrive*, what is reversed is not merely the cultural norms that govern everyday life, such as our frustrations with traffic law, but also the implied "natural order" assumed to govern what is, at bottom, an unnatural relationship—the relationship between man and machine. The film makes a mockery of this relationship entirely; if an autonomously driven truck is ludicrous, the rite of reversal that takes place reveals that our autonomous control and mastery over something like a truck is equally something of a wish or fantasy. Thus, the film turns the tables to create a scenario where property wields power over its owner, rendering man a mechanistic object that bends in predictable, programmatic ways under the more powerful machine's will. Given the role of *human* property in this rite of reversal, however, *Maximum Overdrive* and "Trucks" are essentially modern day *slave* narratives of the fantastic.

The subtext of slavery in *Maximum Overdrive* might explain why the majority of the workers at the Dixie Boy are all on parole, hired by the bossy and arrogant Mr Hendershot on the cheap. They are, literally, prisoners of the job, working under a man who sustains and receives power from the industrial complex: he is not only a fuel and oil man, but also stockpiles military weapons in his basement, and is complicit with the trucks to some degree, in their entrapment of the other characters at the truck stop. Thus, the rebellion staged by the trucks projects a reversal of the latent desire for rebellion by workers against not only their oppressive bosses (Mr Hendershot), but also the larger technocratic system of economic or industrial oppression that entraps and enslaves them. Tony Magistrale describes the political unconscious at work here well, when analyzing the correspondences between King's machines and the "capitalist-vampires" of Karl Marx: "King's machines radically invert their original epistemology, blurring the distinctions between slave and owner, exploiter and exploited . . . the anthropomorphized machine is . . . devoid of social conscience, and its only concern is with the perpetuation of its own demonic tyranny through the exploitation of the humans that serve it" (*Hollywood's Stephen King*, 169).

Jewett and Lawrence note that demolition derbies appeal "to lower and middle-class Americans with strongly conformist tendencies" because it offers them a fantasy of power over what they are powerless against, and powerless to change (292). Likewise, the King's "car crunch" picture makes a direct appeal to the lower economic class, in not only it's treatment of redneck heroes at the Dixie Boy (the parolee-cum-diner chef, the toothpick-munching trucker, the grease-besmeared mechanic), but also cinematically stages a sanctioned, collective rebellion of the working class.

King's dystopic short story, "Trucks," raises such issues allegorically, as well, but as a dystopia it lacks the festive, communal elements of the gross-out comedy, and closes with a very different ending. Some critics have called King's *Maximum Overdrive* an exercise in nihilism akin to—and heavily influenced by—the zombie pictures of George Romero, but it might be more fitting to say "Trucks" is more Romero-like in its existential horror than its cinematic adaptation.[12] No rationale is given in "Trucks" for the machine rebellion, and at the story's conclusion there is no unified rebellion, no escape, no human community left whatsoever. The first person narrator progressively finds himself alone, standing at the fuel pump, enslaved by the machines. He speculates that some day in the future, the trucks will die off because "no matter what's happened to them, what mass consciousness we've given them, *they can't reproduce*. In fifty or sixty years they'll be rusting hulks with all menace gone out of them, moveless carcasses for free men to stone and spit at" (142; emphasis in the original). While King specifically mentions "free men," it is a fantasy of freedom deferred, and contingent upon Darwinian regression. "Trucks" is as hopeless as the apocalyptic conclusion of *Night of the Living Dead*.

In the end of the *Maximum Overdrive*, however, King chooses to end in the mode of festivity and social celebration—the typical closure of comedy. The principal characters manage to escape from the Dixie Boy, defeat the Green Goblin, and cheer as they sail *en masse* to the island of Haven. King does not show us any regression to primitive life on the island away from machines[13]; instead, it is as though the allegorically enslaved workers of *Maximum Overdrive* take off on a well-earned vacation. As the camera follows their ship sailing away, we learn through a title screen that the comet that ostensibly has given the machines life has passed. In other words, the world—and the social order—has been restored. The rite of reversal has served its function; the carnival is over and life reverts back to the status quo.

Jack-in-the-Box Comedy

King's adoption of a comic mode, while puzzling to his readers and fans, is nonetheless apt for staging a cinematic "demolition derby" because it encourages a communal pleasure in the funhouse excesses of his plot. While King's "Trucks" is a stronger vehicle for delivering the philosophical themes of this story and personalizing the impact of the narrative, the film itself is far better at realizing the emotional experience of rites of reversal than the written word, because it envelopes the audience's sensorium and encourages a vicarious, collective experience of the event in a social venue (the theater). As William Paul describes horror and comedy, "In no other films are we so aware of other people in the theater because in no other films are they so prompted by the film itself to make their presence known. There is, then, a kind of loss of individuality . . . a loss that brings with it the gain of communal experience, a festive feeling akin to drunkenness" (67). The combination of comedy and horror performs its own "norm demolition derby" through a genre framework, allowing a film like *Maximum Overdrive* to powerfully stage its challenge to authority figures, its inversion of social hierarchies, and its celebration of humanity by encouraging audiences to laugh collectively at not only mechanical oppression, but the oppression of our own bodily mechanisms over our fate, and the concomitant idea of death.

Perhaps one of the elements that saves King's film from being little more than an overblown AC/DC music video is the way its comic playfulness with machines appeals—like many horror films—to our primitive, animistic belief that inanimate objects have a "supernatural" power to move on their own accord, generating an experience of das *Unheimliche*, the Uncanny. What stops the film from succeeding completely in this regard is that it fails to entirely employ cinematic technique in a way that allows us to "surmount" our skeptical disbelief in animism, a prerequisite of the uncanny for Freud (402–403). Although the huge vehicle that rolls beneath the Green Goblin moves rapidly, its smiling mask remains fixed, rigid, and inelastic. Moreover, King's employment of his trucks as "Happy Toyz" ("here comes another load of joy," a slogan says on the side of the Green Goblin) is quite literal—and comes across as a self-indulgent and juvenile play with oversized, remote-controlled Tonka trucks on the author's part.[14] The comedic "knowingness" of the direction—the constant "tongue-in-cheek" approach to the material—allows us to retain a degree of "knowing" ironic distance from the material, refusing to let us suspend disbelief for very long. It is a distance that is *authorial*, reinforced by the dominant presence of the auteur. Some of the best shots in the picture—and the most *unheimlich*—are the point-of-view shots from the inside of any given truck's cab, as the road rapidly rolls beneath the dimmed windshield, the steering wheels turning and the gears shifting "of their own accord." King's film, ultimately, takes a Bergsonian approach to uncanny comedy—in which "the illusion of life" gives us "the distinct impression of a mechanical arrangement" at work in a body, which our collective laughter protests (Bergson 105)—rather than a strictly Freudian one, in which the mere movement of inanimate objects on their own accord raps its knuckles on the doorway of the unconscious and generates existential terror and unsettling uncertainty (Freud 397).

In a telling, early moment during *Maximum Overdrive*, Bill Robinson (Emilio Estevez) sneaks inside the empty cab of the Green Goblin, trying to investigate how the truck has moved (and attacked someone) without the use of an ignition key. He discovers a curtain behind the front seat and—holding the key like a frail weapon—pierces the curtain in case the unknown driver is lurking behind it. Suddenly a jack-in-the-box—apparently one of the "Happy Toyz" in the truck's cargo—springs open, with the Green Goblin's head leering menacingly. This moment not only encapsulates the impetus behind the horror-comedy that King employs in this film for entertainment, but also more broadly serves as an emblem for man's ambiguously scary and laughable relationship to the unpredictability of the machines he creates.

Henri Bergson theorizes the simplest level of comedy as structured off the jack-in-the-box: laughter is generated by the interplay between a soulless mechanism's inflexibly predictable repetition and the uncertain timing (and power) release of repression on a spring. From this simplest of toys, he deduces a remarkably astute theory:

> The comic is that side of a person which reveals his likeness to a thing, that aspect of human events which, through its peculiar inelasticity, conveys the impression of pure mechanism, of automatism, of movement without life. Consequently it expresses an individual or collective

imperfection which calls for an immediate corrective. That corrective is laughter, a social gesture that singles out and represses a special kind of absent-mindedness in men and in events. (117)

This is precisely what King is poking fun at—the absentmindedness in man's reliance on technology—but he does so by "reveal[ing man's] likeness to a thing" through their fantastic reversal in the story's allegory, while also "springing" surprises made possible by the funhouse of cinema on his audience.

One of the disconcerting tensions that remain in *Maximum Overdrive*, however, lurks in the dominating presence of the auteur, "the master of terror" himself, throughout the film. The power of King is never questioned; the only time the hierarchy between creator and audience is "reversed" in the film is in the opening cameo sequence, when King's character attempts to make a withdrawal and is called an "asshole" by the machine. This scene is important because the author's self-deprecating humor within the text reverses the aggrandizement of King by the mass media outside of the text. Indeed, the refusal of cash subtly mocks the notion that the artist is profiting off of the mass media machine.

One thing to note about the scene where Estevez pokes behind the curtain inside the Green Goblin is that this moment not only encapsulates the horror-comedy aesthetic of the film as a whole, but that it also pokes fun at and reveals the position from where those powerful interior point-of-view shots that embody the truck's subjectivity are created. The camera, though always unseen, *is* this jack-in-the-box. In those uncanny point-of-view shots, the implied subjectivity of the viewpoint is at once King's, and the machine's, and ours.

The camera apparatus is itself a technology, the theater itself a sort of mechanism, the media complex itself a technocracy. If there is one machine that is always alive in King's film, but never directly a part of the action, it is the technology of cinema. In *Maximum Overdrive*, both the camera and the auteur behind it remain omnipotent, despite the key jack-in-the-box revelation I have described. Although the comedic crash-up "rites of reversal" throughout *Maximum Overdrive* are effective, their success at satisfying the audience's desire to disempower authority is impeded because the author-function in the film is never, ultimately, questioned, demolished, or reversed in the picture itself.

It was left to King's audience and disappointed film critics everywhere to do that afterward. King has not returned behind the driver's seat ever since.

Notes

An early version of this essay was first presented at the International Conference for the Fantastic in the Arts 28, Ft. Lauderdale, FL (March 2007). I also want to acknowledge the kind research assistance and editorial guidance of Tony Magistrale, Sylvia Kelso, and Rocky Wood.

1. King also sees the studio's compulsory editing of 15 seconds out of the film to meet the MPAA's R-rating standard as part of the reason the film failed. The bloody shoot-out at the Dixie Boy, a moment where a man's "face sort of falls off into his lap," and the last 3 seconds of the scene where a steamroller runs over a little league player were all cut in order to appease the ratings board's concern about "possible deleterious effects on children." See King's discussion of ratings and the import of these moments in "A Postscript to 'Overdrive'" and "The Dreaded X."
2. Wood, Rawsthorne, and Blackburn report that *Maximum Overdrive* "took only $7.4 million" at the box office, failing to earn out its reputed $10 million budget from the Dino De Laurentiis Company, "and was largely regarded as a flop" (195). They also cite the very low member rating (4.3 out of a possible 10) at the Internet Movie Database as a sign of its failure (http://www.imdb.com/title/tt0091499/).
3. Although the film entails a number of differences from the short story—most notably in its coverage of the small town outside the Dixie Boy truck stop—it is still likely that "Trucks" guided King's screenplay; indeed, an early draft of it was first entitled *Trucks* (Wood et al. 193).
4. Twelve years into his career as a best-selling novelist, King's reputation as the so-called Master of Terror was likely at its highpoint. The producers of *Maximum Overdrive* may have banked on the widespread popularity of King's other "living automobile" story, *Christine*, both published by Viking and also adapted by John Carpenter 3 years earlier, in 1983. Moreover, one of King's most successfully adapted works, "The Body" (as *Stand By Me* [Reiner, 1986]) was released on film the very same year as *Maximum Overdrive*. King's best-selling novel, *It*, was also published the same year that *Maximum Overdrive* released, as was the first nonfiction book dedicated to adaptations of King, Jessie Horsting's *Stephen King at the Movies* (NAL, 1986).
5. Auteur theory is in some ways similar to biographical criticism in literature and generally assigns value and meaning to a particular cinematic work based on a historical and/or structural analysis of a body of work by a particular director. In his foundational essay on the term, "Notes on the Auteur Theory in 1962," Andrew Sarris outlines three primary criteria for determining what makes an "auteur": technical competence or technique, a distinguishable personality or style, and a consistent "interior meaning" imbued to the text (586–587).

6. Fiske traces how different journalists catered to different levels of culture in their treatment of Kubrick's adaptation of *The Shining* to illustrate how the author-as-artist is venerated or not: the newspapers centered their comments on Kubrick's auteur signature, whereas the tabloid press talked the movie up as a genre film, comparing it to other popular horror movies (125).

7. This somewhat ambiguous term for the genre (which is sometimes also called "horror-comedy") is employed by William Paul in *Laughing Screaming* to describe those reaction-driven, carnivalesque films that often target teen culture, with the simple aesthetic aim to "make the audience laugh, make the audience scream, make it scream with laughter, make it laugh in terror . . . to stir up the pleasure of pandemonium" (65).

8. There is also a trivial historical connection: Yeardley Smith, the actress who plays Connie in *Maximum Overdrive*, also regularly provides the voice for the animated character named Lisa in *The Simpsons*.

9. This remake is faithful to "Trucks" on many levels beyond title, perhaps because it relocates the technohorror genre-blending away from comedy and into the realm of science fiction, where dystopia has a long tradition. Despite this, the TV version has received lower ratings at imdb.com than *Maximum Overdrive*—"one of the worst ratings of a King adaptation ever . . . only 3.4 out of a possible 10!" (Wood et al. 194). The lower budget may account for this low reception, but one journalistic critic persuasively suggests its "more modest" approach to the scope of the material, its similarity to Hitchcock's *The Birds* (1963), and its attempt to correct and improve upon a flop may make it a stronger film, narratively (Sheib).

10. The headline on the film's theatrical poster reflexively (nay, *tautologically*) employs the term "master" twice: "Stephen King's Masterpiece of Terror Directed by the Master Himself."

11. They also entered mainstream media through television in the 1970s, when the "most watched comedy" of the time, *Happy Days*, dramatized Arthur Fonzarelli's relationship with demolition driver Pinky Tuscadero in various plot threads throughout its second season (Lowenberg 2).

12. Winter, for example, describes *Maximum Overdrive* as "an existential horror-comedy that breeds the surreal side of King's fiction with the 'Living Dead' films of his friend (and *Creepshow* director) George A. Romero" (182).

13. Nor does King show their boat attacked by a possessed Coast Guard boat that fires at them, as was indicated by the screenplay (Wood et al. 194).

14. In one brilliant inside joke that appears in the USA Network remake, *Trucks*, a remote-controlled Tonka truck—no bigger than a shoebox—attacks a person to death in an extended darkly comic scene.

Chapter 6

The Long Dream of Hopeless Sorrow

The Failure of the Communist Myth in Kubrick's *The Shining*

Michael J. Blouin

Yes! tho' that long dream were of hopeless sorrow,
Twere better than the cold reality
Of waking life to him whose heart must be,
And hath been still, upon the lovely earth,
A chaos of deep passion, from his birth.

(Poe 22)

Many critics argue that Stanley Kubrick's 1980 film *The Shining* is about the corruption of the American dream at the hands of its own excesses. Fredric Jameson, in his well-known chapter "Historicism in *The Shining*," wrote that the Overlook Hotel's "old-time turn-of-the-century splendor is undermined by the more meretricious conception of luxury entertained by consumer society" (86). Tony Magistrale agrees in *Hollywood's Stephen King*, stating that the film is a social allegory of a capitalism out of control, an ideology that is no longer capable of distinguishing "work" from "play": "*Play* and *work*, at least as they are defined at the Overlook, are always variable and slippery concepts . . . the concept of *work* is similarly ambiguous, since the most important *work* of the Overlook's caretaker is the *play* of murdering his family" (97). The consensus is a Marxist reading claiming that, in the text, American capitalism asks too much of its subjects and eventually destroys the value of work by replacing it with an excess of play. Jack Torrance is forced into madness because he must slave away without relief or reward. Valdine Clemens echoes these claims in her book *The Return of the Repressed*, arguing that "the Overlook on its lofty mountain peak not only represents the failure of the American Dream since World War II, but it also represents the failure of the original promise of the City on the Hill, the dream of America's puritan forefathers" (190).

The rendition of a corrosive capitalism has thus already been established and exhaustively documented in multiple readings of *The Shining*. Capitalism, however, is not as untenable in this film as scholarship might lead one to believe. I began this essay with an excerpt from Poe's "Dreams" because it expresses that, though the "cold reality" of capitalism may seem "hopeless," the dreams it provides are a way to keep moving forward, to stay sane in the midst of crisis. I propose a radical rereading that (while not completely departing from the popular interpretation of a failed American dream) examines a complementary interpretation: the inclusion of a *Communist myth* in Kubrick's work. I assert that his scope is much broader than previous *Shining* critics have recognized; the film adaptation condemns not only capitalism, but Communism as well. My purpose in this essay is to unmask *The Shining* as a cultural artifact that reveals multiple ideological functions.

To read Stephen King's novel as redemptive in its attitudes toward capitalism and negative toward Communism would be implausible. The novel goes into great detail to demonstrate exactly what it is that haunts the hotel: a section of upper class society that has become obsessed with material wealth to the point of murder. The novel uses a wasp's nest, among other tropes, as a metaphor for white male corruption in capitalist America. Kubrick's well-to-do figures that haunt the Overlook are successful but not necessarily criminal. Unlike King's novel, in Kubrick's film the nontraditional specters are implicated of nothing except possibly drinking too much and engaging in deviant sexual games; surely nothing as unsavory as homicide. The phantom party-goers are attractive, in truth, until Wendy's final revelation. These ghosts function as a seductive agency for Jack, representative of what life *could* look like if Grady the caretaker's work is repeated. This is the illusion of Communism that dissatisfied capitalists in 1921 (the era of the July 4 ball that is replaying itself in the Gold Room) envisioned. No one will be poor because there will exist an equal playing field with equal access to goods, without family responsibilities because *everyone* takes care of *everyone else*. Karl Marx writes in his seminal text from 1848, *The Communist Manifesto*, that in a Communist state "class distinctions have disappeared" (Marx 75).

Jack does not recognize his actions as ideologically inspired, nor does he associate the Overlook's poltergeist with anything political. *The Shining* can thus be read as an American capitalist's nightmare: an infiltration of the system by a hidden Communist power that aims to destroy traditional family values and capture victims that are unaware, swallowing them into its "evil" collective. Jack, tired of dreaming of a better life to no avail, with no sign of wealth or respect in sight, is the ideal target for such a conspiracy.

Fredric Jameson argues that "Jack Nicholson of *The Shining* is possessed neither by evil as such nor by 'the devil' . . . but rather simply by History, by the American past" (90). I suggest that Jack is haunted by something specifically *not* "American" within its own past, by a drive that runs counter to everything America stands for. Much like the post-Vietnam era, the 1920s was a time of increasing nihilism after the horrors of a great war. Many were disenfranchised with global imperialism and the exploitation of the working class. Vladimir Lenin, the Russian leader who blamed World War I on capitalism, rose to high favor during the 1910s and directly after the 1918 armistice. Lenin's Communist ideals offered a political alternative that appeared, at least on the surface, to be honoring the will of the Russian people. Its two promises were, according to Marx, to overthrow the bourgeois and to make goods ultimately accessible to all. Communism subsequently rose in popularity around the world. For devoted functionaries of the American economic structure, Communism became a fantasized threat, demonized and mythologized in numerous forms. Jack seems to be tempted and destroyed by remnants of this same horrific fantasy and thus *The Shining* can be read as a cinematic nightmare in which a capitalist audience watches the myth of its own victimization at the hands of the Communists onscreen.

Jameson goes on to write that *The Shining* shows a "desire for a vanished social hierarchy," and that Jack in particular is "yearning for the certainties and satisfactions of a traditional class system" (97). I do believe that the 1920s holds some appeal and nostalgic effect for Jack with its profligate consumption, but I believe Jack's strongest impulse is to join a larger social movement that *dissolves* the hierarchies that are already established from the moment Jack enters the Overlook. He is willing to give up his own autonomy to become part of a community that will take care of everything for him; he associates with the ghostly masses at the Overlook in order to access the luxurious goods that everyone else seems to have and he has been unable to attain. Jack's distaste for the "traditional" American system is most evident when Danny and his mother are outside of the Overlook, frolicking in the hedge maze and then, later, throwing snowballs at each other. Jack stares off-screen, edited in such a way as to indicate that he is watching his family play, a cruel expression across his face. Wendy jovially taunts her son as they race, "Loser has to keep America clean!" They are never fearful of the maze because they are in it together, fancifully playing, able to escape. Wendy, smiling, calls it "pretty." Jack, meanwhile, is isolated from them, trapped inside his station as father figure. Capitalism, like Communism, makes similar promises of playful ecstasy; for Jack, the promises have yet to be fulfilled and he remains a writer who is lost in the capitalist maze. His faith is shaken; he cannot fantasize about capitalist success without seeing the futility of the act itself. He can embrace the beautiful woman in 237, desire their sexual union, but he always recognizes it as a cruel and mocking masquerade, a sagging corpse underneath. He is suspended between the proletariat and the ruling class, as both an educated writer and a subservient caretaker, and thus cannot see a *way out*; he is unable to escape his worker mindset enough to draw himself fully into the realm of leisure. It is here that he turns to the alluring Communist system, which promises to alleviate his independent burdens and draw him away from work and into the ruling class.

In fairness, then, Jack is not guilty of a "true" Marxist approach. Marx preaches a type of never-ending revolution, in which there is *always* an essential class uprising against the wealthy capitalists. Instead, Jack submits to a degree of what Marx calls "Critical-Utopian" Communism: a postcommunism kind of Communism that can achieve satisfaction, that "deadens the class struggle" and "realise(s) all these castles in the air . . . compelled to appeal to the feelings and purses of the bourgeois" (84). In other words, what was once revolutionary about Communism has become, in *The Shining* at least, simply another attempt at reaching the capitalist dream, a dream that Marx would want no part of, but one that characterized many "Marxist" economies in the twentieth century.

The manipulative leaders of this communal House are speaking not from places of dominance (Grady is still a worker, after all, the caretaker that preceded Jack) but from lowly positions: a bartender (Lloyd) and a butler/caretaker. Jack is swept up by a workers' revolution, albeit one that is striving toward power and wealth more than Marx's ideal community. These ghostly forces at the Overlook want to collaborate with Jack to bring the working class *into* the satisfying world of the elites. It is realistic because Grady and Lloyd are already (on the surface at least) members of the club; they are united with the bourgeois of the Overlook. There is no evidence that Jack is seeking, as some might argue, a degree of separation from the workers or some kind of individual feeling of superiority. He arguably has little ambition but to "get rich quick." Mythological Communism offers this route. In Kubrick's version of this tale, Jack's elementary desire is to flee from the "worker" realm he despises and enter freely into the world of "play" (and consequently, wealth). The revolutionary force that initiates this movement is led not by the debutant specters but by the markedly blue-collar ghosts, the "workers" of the Overlook.

Communism is familiar territory for Kubrick. It seems to be a recurring trope in much of his canon, from 1964's *Dr. Strangelove* to 1987's *Full Metal Jacket*. Kubrick is well aware of the fear that Communists inspire and he explores the concept. *Strangelove* is a film that implicates its audience in much the same way as *The Shining*. The Communists are depicted as living in a "fog shrouded wasteland," possessing a horrifying doomsday device that eventually destroys the world. The myth of the "Ruskies" not only ruins the characters in the film by driving them to outrageous acts (Ripper), but also causes the audience to become suspicious of Communist Russia. The final detonation of the doomsday device creates fear in the viewer of the film, allowing the viewer to fall into the same trap as its gullible characters. What starts as a myth that tempts Jack out of his capitalist depression (ripe with Lenin's attractiveness) ends as a myth of the treachery and evil within this temptation (a product of McCarthyism and the fear of the "Commies" that has persisted throughout American history).

Communism pervades the film not only on a diegetic level but also on an aesthetic one. "The Red Scare" is literally captured by a director who puts great emphasis on color in his films. As the deep red blood pours out of the bright red elevator doors, one might recall Ripper's words from *Strangelove*: "I can no longer sit back and allow communist infiltration, communist indoctrination, communist subversion, and the international communist conspiracy to sap and impurify all of our precious body fluids." The blood that pumps through the veins of this hotel and pours from the lobby elevator is tainted with the political shade of "red," the color that has popularly come to signify the "Ruskie" party. The room is where capitalists tend to congregate, which typifies the spirit of capital (the recently refurbished Gold Room) and is clearly associative of commodity and wealth; at what I argue is the crux of *The Shining*, when Jack follows Grady into the bathroom, the scene is overwhelmed by red. The room that is insistently gold is abandoned in favor of a room that is definitively Communist at the turning point of the film, signifying a major political shift in allegiances for Jack.

The implication of this political shift is initiated by a business transaction gone awry between Jack and Lloyd. Earlier, Jack gets a drink on his credit, maintaining to some degree the capitalist exchange; in other words, his credit allows him to pay for the drinks ("You set 'em up, I'll knock 'em back.") and thus the capitalist system is affirmed. The next time Jack enters the bar, money has materialized within his wallet where it was not at first, as if to draw attention to itself as the only medium of commercial exchange. Yet, here the system is dismantled; Lloyd coyly remarks that there is no charge.

"No charge?" Jack is skeptical, bewildered at the thought.
"Your money's no good here," Lloyd confirms.

Jack is caught off guard and displays a rare moment of doubt. He counters that he is the kind of guy who likes to know who's buying his drinks, to which Lloyd reassures: "It's not a matter that concerns you, Mr. Torrance." The exchange of money is rejected and the American dollar as a commodity loses its authority. In its place, Jack can achieve parity within the ostentatious crowd. He can get all of the drinks and respect he wants, without "paying" with the very almighty dollar that has eluded him. Marx assures us that "there can be no wage-labor when there is no longer any capital" (70). This Communist manipulative promise is revealed as Grady glorifies Jack's newfound position by telling him: "You're the important one, sir." All he has to do is join the House and he will receive all of the benefits that come with communal membership. This change ominously appears on the television that Wendy and Danny are watching earlier in the film, as if the impending Communist forces within the hotel are trying to influence them as well. They are watching the film *The Summer of '42* in which a young man, who has recently done a service for a young woman, is offered payment and *refuses it*. Instead, he accepts donuts and coffee and her good company. *Community* is favored over *payment* to the individual worker and the individual is rewarded with necessities and amiable conversation. Money as a commodity loses its importance.

Communism seeks to reveal the emptiness of all capitalist products, not just material but ideological as well. Capitalism is guilty of glorifying the family the same way it glorifies money and wealth. Stuart Ullman, the manager who embodies the capitalist ideology saturating the Overlook, advocates the family unit as an essential ingredient to the system. A "traditional" family allows for a man to work and a woman to take care of the home while they both raise a child to continue the process. Ullman is perpetuating capitalism's family values and trying to inculcate the Torrances. He is always concerned with the well-being of Jack's family, asking if they are content with the situation. If the family is satisfied in their measly servant's quarters, then the system maintains control. After all, of all the grand places in the hotel, he places the Torrances in a "very nicely self-contained" space. It is, as he says, "very cozy for a family." They even have their own station wagon in the form of a Sno-Cat.

For Danny and his mother, this iconic family unit is strong. While Communism is urging Jack to address the oppressive and hollow nature of this system, his family remains loyal to it. They rely on each other to survive, pumping their own meaning into what Marx labeled "the bourgeois clap-trap . . . the hallowed co-relation of parent and child" that he found to be "disgusting" (71). Their belief in a mother and son's *duty* to one another demonstrates that they believe *meaning is still possible* despite being overwhelmed by capitalist commodities. This answers the question Jameson poses: "how to project the illusion that things still happen, that events exist, that there are still stories to tell, in a situation in which the uniqueness and the irrevocability of private destinies and of individuality itself seems to have evaporated?" (89). He argues that the only connection (and even this, he claims, is tenuous) within *The Shining* is between Danny and the black community; I find that Danny's bond with his mother trumps all.

Terrible carnage appears in the film when this privatized family unit is attacked by the invasive entity that possesses Jack.[1] Friedrich Engels discusses the removal of value for the family in a Communist system in his *The Origin of the Family*: "With the transfer of the means of production into common ownership, the single family ceases to be the economic unit of society. Private housekeeping is transformed into a social industry. The care and education of the children becomes a public affair" (139). Indeed, Grady is "interested" in Danny and his talent and he dictates to Jack exactly how the child (and his wife) should be dealt with. It is a communal matter. If family values are what Ullman pushes on the Torrances, Grady insists on a revolution against this ideological practice. There is no sympathy or need to preserve the family for economic stability; instead, it must be ruthlessly chopped into pieces and neatly stacked in one of the wings. Marx's battle cry echoes through the halls of the Overlook: "Abolish the family!" (71). Surely this taps into the American paranoia of the Communist threat where leftists were historically painted in such a fashion (look no further than Ripper's theories in *Strangelove* of the Communist poisoning the water supply) as to make a heartless massacre of the family plausible. The Communist myth in *The Shining* undermines whatever capitalism holds dear (e.g., the exchange of money, the family).

Yet, capitalism cannot be so easily defeated. It allows its subjects an *illusion* of autonomy with playthings that Communism does not recognize. Commodities are capable of being claimed, signifying whatever the subject desires and helping to create a fantasy world. What Communism dismisses as materialist kitsch that holds no real value outside of a capitalist economy can actually represent and promote the essential act of dreaming (evident in Danny's Apollo 11 and Mickey Mouse sweaters, advocating the dreams of a star-gazing nation). This pastiche reveals not only the fakeness but also the *appealing imagination* of American culture. It demonstrates how subjects of capitalism, in infantile delight, can take reproducible objects devoid of any actual value (e.g., Danny's toy trucks, the images on the screen) and use them to *play*, to fantasize and create meaning. An artificial image of a space shuttle can embody a nation's hope, it's nostalgic affinity for past achievements, and, most importantly, it's aspirations of boundless mobility. One can *play* astronaut, join the collective that feels warmly about such noble ventures, and feel as if maybe there is meaning and movement within what Communists label a cold and sterile simulacrum. Wendy and Danny cling to what is pastiche because it is more tolerable than the alternative: The Communist myth that seeks to eradicate their union and remove the value from all capitalist products, wherein money and media are revealed to be devoid of any meaning. In this film, television best demonstrates the *usefulness* of these materials.

Television is famous for commodity advertisements and advocating certain capitalist values. From the beginning of the film, Wendy and Danny bask in what Homer Simpson calls "the warm re-assuring glow" of this increasingly central element in the family unit. While providing an escape from the grim reality of an abusive husband/ father, it also provides Danny with useful knowledge. James Hala writes in his essay "Kubrick's *The Shining*: The Specters and the Critics": "Danny learns a lot from television" (209). He learns about the survival of the fittest concept from a documentary on cannibalism, and he learns how to "run, run, run" from the Road Runner cartoons; both of these televised messages help him to avoid being destroyed by Jack in the final scenes of the film. A weather report for Colorado projected through the television triggers a "shining" vision in Dick Hallorann and prompts him to fly to the Overlook and indirectly save the day. Thus, television, while despised by many as a tool for capitalist consumerism, actually works largely *to improve* the besieged lives of the characters in this film (and, by extension, thwart the forces that are at work in the hotel). *The Simpsons* parody "The Shinning" insists that catastrophe is avoided only because of television.

Capitalism *must* be maintained to a degree because it promotes whatever is necessary for sanity in a world full of hierarchies, of inescapable "haves and have-nots": the freedom to dream. Danny can aspire to "keep America clean" (in multiple senses of the word) and Wendy is allowed to believe that she can actually save Danny from the brooding world he briefly retreats to ("Danny, wake up!"). Fantasy, yes, but they can at least find beauty in the "boring" world of *work* and manage to *play* with each other, uniting against the adult world of responsibility.

Unfortunately, Jack's projections are fragments of this very past, of an illusion with a predetermined, tragic end. Jack's dream of Communism is itself a form of self-destruction; it is to dream of an ending to dreams, one that inevitably concludes with paralysis. When he unknowingly accepts Communism, Jack's cultural vocabulary (a product of capitalism) ceases to reach for meaning. He converses first in a nonsensical string of popular catchphrases and then in unintelligible grunts and howls. Without the ability to fantasize (specifically, the ability to compose any kind of creative thought or independent ambition), Jack is left with nowhere to run, frozen in space and time; he is like Sisyphus without the "play" of the rock. *The Communist Manifesto*, similar to the American dream, promises fulfillment that, in reality, is impossible.

Grady's Lenin–esque campaign full of utopian promises that are predicated on necessary violence ultimately reveals a Stalin-esque dictatorship; the fantasy of Communism cannot make good on its promise of equality and the will of the masses. Grady is just as demanding of Jack as Ullman and the capitalists. The assurance of "independence" (the July 4 celebration is featured, after all) is revealed to be hiding a fascist underbelly, the truth of Communist governments that often promise equal opportunity and humanism but guise a dictator. Jack can have all of the drinks he wants, but only because he receives them under "orders from the house," as Lloyd affably puts it. Mihalio Markovic, in response to the *Manifesto*, highlights this contradiction: "Experience has shown how easy it is for a small group within a class to manipulate the power of the whole class and to manipulate the vast majority of the class. Marx could not have foreseen Stalinism" (Marx 162). Grady and Ullman are actually not so different. Jack's final fantasy, which he achieves at the hands of Communist temptation, turns out to be nothing more than an inversion of his nightmare of menial status. In reaction to the *Manifesto*, Wagner and Strauss note "the question then arises whether there is any guarantee that, as a result [of Communism], exploitation will be eliminated" (Marx 153). Real freedom is a myth that neither political ideology, capitalism nor Marxism, has realized. Jack inevitably fails in both, snared in their harsh realities of limitation; he is at the end frozen and immobile, a caricature in the simulacrum he incorrectly thought he could transcend. His demise mirrors that of unsuccessful Communist and capitalist states. Their stagnation is representative of his own.

Note

1. Interestingly, one of Communism's most infamous groups, started by Abimael Guzman in Peru in the late 1960s, was called "The Shining Path." It is a militaristic sect that gained momentum in the years building up to 1980 (the year Kubrick's *The Shining* was released). It promoted violence against any oppressive capitalist establishment that stood in its way. One might surmise that the path that leads Jack to an axe-wielding disassembly of the capitalist unit in the film is shadowed closely by that of this brutal Communist alliance.

Chapter 7

The Prisoner, the Pen, and the Number One Fan

Misery as a Prison Film

Mary Findley

> There is a justice higher than that of man. I will be judged by him.
>
> *Misery*, 1990

While much has been written about *The Shawshank Redemption* (1994) and *The Green Mile* (1999), two prison films that stick out as anomalies in Stephen King's cinematic landscape and often garner shocked responses such as, "*That's* a King film?" or "Stephen King wrote that?" from self-professed antihorror fans, no critical analysis currently exists that posits the film *Misery* in it's rightful place: as one of King's prison movies. Although set in a semi-comfortable rural farmhouse in Colorado, a far cry from the stagnant walls of Shawshank Prison or cell block E on Death Row with the infamous green mile, *Misery's* main character, novelist Paul Sheldon, is an innocent man unjustly sentenced to a life of solitary confinement with no one to rely on but his cruel and irrational jailer, Annie Wilkes. Like Andy Dufresne of *The Shawshank Redemption* and John Coffey of *The Green Mile*, Paul Sheldon must somehow find redemption in the face of extraordinarily cruel circumstances and seemingly insurmountable obstacles. These circumstances and obstacles, along with his inner resolve to free himself from his unjust imprisonment and his eventual personal growth as a result of this experience, place *Misery* as the first of King's prison film trilogy.

The critical analysis that does exist on what might easily be considered King's own personal nightmare, being held captive by a deranged fan hell-bent on controlling his creative power, focuses mostly on gender issues, as is evidenced by Kathleen Lant's article "The Rape of Constant Reader: Stephen King's Construction of the Female Reader and Violation of the Female Body in *Misery*," sexual symbolism, as discussed in Natalie Schroeder's article "Stephen King's *Misery*: Freudian Sexual Symbolism and the Battle of the Sexes," and the reader/writer relationship. *Misery* has even been touted as "a thinly veiled self-examination of his fans, his writing, and his genre work" by Gary Hoppenstand and Ray Browne (13). In addition, criticism has largely focused on the novel, with only Tony Magistrale's *Hollywood's Stephen King* undertaking a critical analysis of Rob Reiner's phenomenal film adaptation for which Kathy Bates won the 1990 Best Actress Oscar.

What is even more interesting, however, is the fact that nearly all of the existing criticism uses specific language that warrants a closer examination of *Misery* within the context of a prison narrative or prison film. For example, in the article "Stephen King's *Misery*: Freudian Sexual Symbolism and the Battle of the Sexes," Natalie Schroeder states, "At the beginning of *Misery*, Paul Sheldon regains consciousness to learn gradually that he is the victim of a car wreck and that he has been saved and *imprisoned* by Annie Wilkes" ("Stephen King's *Misery*," 137; emphasis in the original). In "The Rape of the Constant Reader," Kathleen Margaret Lant states that Paul Sheldon is "the *prisoner* of Annie Wilkes" (94), clearly creating the idea of Paul as prisoner and Annie as his jailer. Hoppenstand and Browne contend that "King's novel chronicles Annie's continued *imprisonment* and torture of Paul as she forces him to revise his despised character, Misery, and write a new adventure for her" (14), and Magistrale states, "Without his craft, Paul Sheldon could not have survived his *sentence as a prisoner* in Annie Wilke's haunted farmhouse" (*Hollywood's Stephen King*, 70; emphasis mine). While following their own scholarly discourse in relationship to the novel or film, one thing clearly emerges here: the language and subtext of this scholarship indicates that, perhaps, *Misery* should really be examined through a different critical lens.

Much like Andy Dufresne in *The Shawshank Redemption*, who foolishly positioned himself outside of the house of his adulterous wife and her lover who were later found murdered, and John Coffey in *The Green Mile*, who chose to cradle two dead girls and cry that he "tried to take it back" as search teams approached, Paul Sheldon also makes a critical error that sets his life in a downward spiral. His decision to drive his ill-equipped '65 Ford Mustang in the Colorado mountains during a snowstorm proves to be a fatal mistake whose implications alter the course of his life. His inability to handle the slippery snow-laden roads result in a devastating accident that sentences him to the enslavement of his physical injuries and to a life imprisoned by Annie Wilkes. The latter is his crazed number one fan who pulls him from his cold metal coffin, breathes life back into him (much like a Death Row inmate nursed back to health in order to live out his or her sentence), and takes him back to her farmhouse where, unbeknownst to him, his prison sentence begins.

From the start, Reiner visually sets up the idea that Sheldon is housed in a veritable prison. Wilkes's spare bedroom, which doubles as Sheldon's makeshift hospital room, is devoid of anything remotely comforting and homey. There are no pictures on the walls, there is no carpeting, no furniture other than an end table or two and the single hospital-like bed, no television, no radio, no computer, no color present anywhere in the room; there is nothing but the bare necessities and an inlaid shelf that, curiously enough, holds extra rolls of toilet paper and other stock items typically found in a prison cell. Aligning the audience with Sheldon's point of view, Reiner continues creating a visual prison for the audience. Pulled into Sheldon's mental state of haze and drug-induced confusion, a strange blurred image slowly pulls into focus as he wakes from a state of unconsciousness. The image, the audience realizes, is that of a shadow cast on a sterile white wall by light coming through a window; a shadow that, curiously enough, resembles a barred window, an obscure and symbolic prison looming in both the cinematic foreground and in Paul Sheldon's future. A booming voice, that of Annie Wilkes proclaiming that she is his number one fan, pulls Sheldon from his unconscious stupor and into the reality of his situation: he is bedridden, helpless, confined, and at the mercy of this total stranger who also happens to be a registered nurse. At first, he is grateful for what appears to be a sincere effort to save his life, but his vociferous gratefulness quickly turns to silent fear as he soon discovers the mental instability of his nurse who later acts as his jailer.

This concern escalates, and his true predicament, that of a prisoner sentenced to solitary confinement with only a mentally and emotionally unstable, Jekyll-and-Hyde personality to rely on, becomes extremely clear to both Sheldon and the audience when Wilkes enters Sheldon's bedroom, her face half framed in the dark shadows of the night (visually creating the Jekyll-and-Hyde dichotomy), and subjects him to a raging tirade after finishing the recently released *Misery's Child*, the last of the Misery books. Distraught, out of control, and gripped by fury because Sheldon has killed off her favorite character, Wilkes unleashes her vehemence, smashing objects around the room in a tirade before she verbally hands down his sentence, asserting her merciless control over his life. This scene is perhaps one of the most visually symbolic and important scenes in the entire film. Judge Wilkes dictates his sentence and closes the door while the innocent and stunned Paul Sheldon feels the weight of his sentence pressing down upon him. Once the door closes, the camera angle shifts to a long side-shot of Sheldon in bed. He is illuminated by moonlight drifting through the window and this time the image and the picture are clear. Shadowy bars cast by the windowpanes envelope him and illuminate his dire situation. In the next shot the audience is again aligned with Sheldon's point of view as he looks out, this time through what appears to be a barred window, as Annie's vehicle pulls out of the driveway. In contemplation over what to do next, he glances at the door. The camera angle reveals vertical slats, once again resembling prison bars, then the shot switches back to Sheldon in bed, this time framed in front of vertical bars that make up the headboard behind him. The consistent use of prison imagery here shows that he is symbolically barred in, and his desperate attempt to escape, by falling to the floor and pulling himself along by one arm, results in excruciating pain as would be the result of any prisoner's desperate and unplanned attempt at escape. As he slinks closer to the door, the audience is once again positioned with his point of view and the looming door, pinstriped wallpaper, and vertical slats on the nearby shelf further confirm the feeling of entrapment and imprisonment. As he reaches up for the doorknob, he confirms what the audience already suspects. The door is locked. The symbolic prison has clanked shut around him and he is left with only the echo of his thoughts to fulfill the long, lonely hours in his cell.

Up until this point in the film, Annie's power over Paul has been felt and alluded to, but not visibly or physically forced. Her declaration that she has not told anyone about him, however, changes the power dynamic and puts Sheldon in a precarious position. With all personal power stripped, he will now have no choice but to bend to the will of his jailer, even when it compromises his sense of personal integrity and his belief in what is right and wrong. Much like Andy Dufresne, an innocent man who previously walked the straight and narrow and is forced to keep corrupt accounting books in prison, something that clearly goes against his personal sense of integrity and truth, Sheldon, who knows his latest manuscript is a true representation of his personal truth as a writer, is forced to burn it and engage in resurrecting Misery, the character he had finally put behind him. This goes completely against his sense of personal truth, integrity, and the authentic voice of his writing, but, like Dufresne, he cannot move forward and cannot move on, until he first surrenders his will and engages his own personal suffering. A similar activity is paralleled in *The Green Mile* when John Coffey is taken from Death Row in the middle of the night and asked to heal the brain tumor of the warden's wife. Although Coffey's childish innocence makes him eager to go for a ride and causes him to delight in seeing the stars in the night sky, he is still given little choice in the matter. He is forced to use his gift, possibly to his own detriment, in order to help someone else. Sheldon, Dufresne, and Coffey all sacrifice their own needs and want to satisfy the needs and wants of someone else; they do so, not willingly, but because they have to. Their lives depend on it.

All three of King's prison films—*The Shawshank Redemption*, *The Green Mile*, and *Misery*—share an important theme: personal redemption. All three characters must redeem or win back their freedom and come to terms with their definition of truth. Andy must find a way to manipulate the very system and people that put him in prison in order to free himself, both physically and spiritually. John Coffey must find a way, jailed and sitting on Death Row, to free himself from the constant torment, pain, and responsibility that comes with his gift to heal others, a gift that causes him great anguish because he feels and experiences the pain of others. Paul Sheldon must find a way to use his writing, the very thing that ultimately attracted Annie and caused her to imprison him, in order to free himself both physically and spiritually. It is this theme of redemption, of freeing oneself both physically and spiritually despite the mounting odds, that links these three films together as cinematic siblings. To understand *Misery*'s proper place in the King film canon, it is necessary to consider it in context with these other films.

While other interpretations of *Misery*, both the novel and the film, certainly hold merit, they tend to focus on isolated aspects, microcosms within the story, and not on the story as a whole. Lant asserts that "the true horror . . . resides in King's own view of the creative process and, primarily, in the sexual roles he imposes upon that process," with creativity being a male prerogative and readership being a female prerogative that can "usurp the creative process" and "threaten the artist's autonomy and his masculinity" ("The Rape," 90). Although her essay touches on the prison theme, its true direction is in pursuing the microcosm of male/female sexual roles, even though the article has been set up to beg the question of whether King himself is entrapped and imprisoned by his own celebrity. She states, "He is a victim of his own celebrity status. King is a household name, a contemporary figure of popular culture . . . King can no longer attend conventions or book fairs; he is so heavily in demand that he finds himself threatened physically by the affection of his fans" ("The Rape," 90). By positing Paul Sheldon as a shadow double for King himself, and focusing on Sheldon's imprisonment as a result of his celebrity status, the theme of imprisonment enters into the forefront of her argument.

Additionally, King positions Paul Sheldon as a prisoner when discussing where the idea for the novel originated. In his book *On Writing*, he states,

> In the early 1980s, my wife and I went to London on a combined business/pleasure trip. I fell asleep on the plane and had a dream about a popular writer (it may or may not have been me, but it sure to God wasn't James Caan) who fell into the clutches of a psychotic fan living on a farm somewhere out in the back of the beyond. The fan was a woman isolated by her growing paranoia. She kept some livestock in the barn, including her pet pig, Misery. The pig was named after the continuing main character in the writer's best-selling bodice-rippers. My clearest memory of this dream upon waking was something the woman said to the writer, who had a broken leg and was being kept *prisoner* in the back bedroom. I wrote it on an American Airlines cocktail napkin so I wouldn't forget it, then put it in my pocket. (165; emphasis in the original)

King, again, refers to Sheldon as a prisoner a little further on: "By the time I had finished that first Brown's Hotel session, in which Paul Sheldon wakes up to find himself Annie Wilke's *prisoner*, I thought I knew what was going to happen" (167). He also uses this opportunity to discuss the idea of redemption that, I assert, ties *Misery* thematically to *The Shawshank Redemption* and *The Green Mile*: "Paul Sheldon turned out to be a good deal more resourceful than I initially thought, and his efforts to play Scheherazade and save his life gave me a chance to say some things about the redemptive power of writing that I had long felt but never articulated" (168).

As previously mentioned, all three protagonists—Sheldon, Dufresne, and Coffey—have gifts that are exploited by their jailers. Dufresne's gift is with accounting and bookkeeping, Coffey's gift surrounds the act of healing, and Paul's ability to write all, in one way or another, keep them alive. Coffey's gift keeps him alive in a figurative sense, maintaining his hope and belief in that which is good, alive despite being faced with daily evidence to the contrary, such as the irrational and cruel behavior displayed by Percy. Andy's and Paul's gifts, however, keep them alive in a literal sense. As long as they are both useful to their respective jailers and continue to provide them with some sense of emotional or financial fulfillment, their security remains intact. Their usefulness and their ability to prostitute their individual gifts buy them time, time to live and time to hatch an escape plan. Paul realizes quickly, however, that any attempt at physical escape is out of the question for two reasons: his body, though on the mend, is still incapacitated, and Annie, whose physical strength and bulk far outweigh Paul's, will either directly or indirectly foil any attempt he makes to escape. His plan to drug Annie with an overdose of Novril, either to kill her off or to buy him time to escape, for example, is foiled by her clumsiness at an impromptu dinner in her dining room to celebrate *Misery's Return*. His second plan, to stab her with a butcher knife hidden in his sling, is also foiled when she realizes he has been out of his bedroom-cell. As punishment for his rebellion, and to insure his physical compliance with his imprisonment, she ties him to the bed and smashes both of his ankles with a sledgehammer, an act she calls "hobbling," all the while proclaiming her love for him. The prevalence of Annie's use of violence against Paul mirrors the violence experienced or seen by both Dufrense and Coffey. Dufrense experiences violence from other inmates and also from the warden, who hands out stints in solitary confinement as a way to break Dufrense's spirit; Coffey is forever tormented by the violent behavior of his jailer, Percy, towards others on the cellblock.

The passage of time in this film, as is common with prison films, is noted by the changing of seasons that occurs outside of Paul's window. Deep winter melts slowly into spring, spring blooms into summer. Paul, busily trying to ward off Annie's sporadic propensity toward violence, undertakes the task of bringing Misery back to life at her demand. Annie's meticulous attention to detail and insistence on perfection, however, reminds him that he cannot cheat. He cannot get his characters (or himself) out of their predicaments dishonestly. He must stay true to the story and find a way to bring Misery back from the dead. As a parallel, he soon realizes he must also stay true to the larger game that has become his life. Like Andy, he must defy his own personal integrity in order to play by the rules created and dictated by his jailer. Paul's challenge, much like Andy's, is to intellectually outsmart his jailer opponent by using the very thing she is forcing him to do (write) to defeat her in the end. Though both were innocent men when they entered into confinement, Paul and Andy have no choice but to turn to criminal activities in order to free themselves from the injustice imposed upon them. The environment in which they are forced to perform, an environment of criminal activity, is the only playing field they have.

Gaining physical strength by lifting the old Royal typewriter he is forced to write with, and gaining mental and emotional strength by figuring out a way to outsmart Annie at her own game, Sheldon quietly acquiesces to his sentence and goes along with the daily routine laid out before him. Everything is structured and repetitive: his conversations with Annie, his writing schedule, his meals (which arrive on cafeteria trays with equally divided portions), his sleep schedule, and even his bodily functions. He urinates on cue into a plastic jug while Annie waits, a further testament to the fact that, like a prisoner, he has lost any sense of privacy. Even Paul's thoughts are open for review as Annie reads each chapter of *Misery's Return*. It is through this act of writing, however, that Paul regains the strength and spiritual resolve to win back his freedom. She can control his physical activity, his schedule, his food, his work, even his bodily functions, but she cannot control his imagination. Though she believes she can control his writing, she merely dictates that it occurs. His mind, the wellspring that feeds his writing, can be played with, but never controlled. She can make him act in defiance of whom and what he knows himself to be, but she cannot make him accept this as his personal truth. Just as Andy and Coffey are controlled and forced into actions that compromise their personal choice and integrity, their minds and their hearts, those areas wherein exists the essence of who they really are, remain indomitable. Andy commits fraud and becomes a criminal in order to secure his freedom, but not because he *is* a criminal. It is because he was *not* a criminal that he could secure his freedom and be redeemed from the rotten hand life had dealt him. Because John Coffey was not a murderer, he willingly goes to his death with the assurance that his pain will finally be over and he will be at peace in a better place. It is because Paul Sheldon was *not* the murderer Annie contended he was for killing Misery, that he could murder Wilkes with the very instrument she forced upon him, and later tell his agent, "In some way, Annie Wilkes, that whole experience helped me." Having lived through their own personal hells, having everything stripped from them, having no foreseeable way out of their cruel predicaments, Paul Sheldon, Andy Dufresne, and John Coffey all found redemption and emerged stronger than the circumstances that once imprisoned them.

The parallels between *The Shawshank Redemption* and *The Green Mile*, both of which were directed by Frank Darabont, are more obvious than any parallels that include *Misery*, but this is largely because of Darabont's creative consistency in both films. For example, both of Darabont's films are narrated and told as flashbacks. *The Shawshank Redemption* is narrated by Red, played by Morgan Freeman, and *The Green Mile* is narrated by Paul Edgecomb, played by Tom Hanks. Both films also posit the main characters as easily identifiable victims, almost childlike in their behavior at times. These characters are lovable, likeable, and seem almost sweetly innocent. The audience sides with them immediately and wants them to emerge victorious in the end. King even refers to *The Green Mile* as "the first R-rated Hallmark Hall of Fame production," and goes on to say that "for a story that is set on death row, it has a really feel good, praise-the-human-condition sentiment to it" (Magistrale, *Hollywood's Stephen King*, 13). It is this same "feel good, praise-the-human-condition sentiment" that audiences have come to expect from King's prison films and it is also what makes both *Shawshank* and *The Green Mile* stick out as anomalies on Stephen King's cinematic landscape. This sentiment of good feeling is clearly missing from *Misery* and is a key reason why it has not been looked at in the same scholarly light. Whether the audience even likes Paul Sheldon at the beginning of the film is up for debate. A successful, popular novelist disgruntled with the very writing that has brought him fame, fortune, and opportunity is a far cry from the likes of Andy Dufresne or John Coffey, making it difficult for the audience, at first, to understand or side with Sheldon. An audience can perhaps sympathize with his physical predicament and with the extent of his injuries, but his personality does not have the obvious innocence, likeability, or redeeming qualities necessary to win it over. As a matter of fact, Annie Wilkes is the more likable character at the start of the film, and it isn't until her mental instability and violence position her as the antagonistic monster that the audience's allegiance begins to align with Sheldon. Even at that point, however, the audience is pulled into feeling sorry for Annie at times as "she may be viewed as an unfortunate victim of her own mental illness, as she exhibits nearly textbook symptoms of a manic depressive personality" (Magistrale, *Hollywood's Stephen King*, 65). This is not the case with Warden Norton, who forces Andy into his criminal bookkeeping activity, or Percy Wetmore, the cruel jailer in *The Green Mile*. These characters have no logical or physical excuse for their erratic and cruel behavior and the audience's disgust at their behavior is established from the start. Andy Dufresne and John Coffey are clearly victims and pawns in the hands of these monsters, and the audience wants justice. In *Misery*, the audience wonders whether, perhaps, Paul Sheldon deserves a bit of what he gets at the start. Perhaps his smugness at the very living that brought him fame and fortune will turn to humbleness when he realizes how quickly it can all be taken away.

Another reason *Misery* is overlooked as a prison film is the absence of the feel-good sentiment at the film's end. In *The Shawshank Redemption* the audience rejoices with Andy's freedom and Red's ability to join him for a blissful future at the ocean's edge. The sunny beach, the blue water, the ocean breeze all wash over the audience and cleanse any residual feelings of angst leftover from Dufresne's prison days. In *The Green Mile* John Coffey's death, though difficult and heart wrenching to watch, means that he is finally at rest, while Paul Edgecomb, the last of the green mile wardens to survive, carries part of Coffey's gift into the future, living years beyond his normal life span. Though it is possible to view Edgecomb's seeming immortality in a negative light, he is nevertheless the bearer of Coffey's love and light into the future. At the end of *Misery*, however, there is little to rejoice about. Even though Paul Sheldon has regained his freedom and reclaimed his literary career with a novel that is not part of the Misery series, the ghost of Annie Wilkes still lingers near. This ghost, it seems, or the memory of what happened to him during his imprisonment, is not a positive influence over Paul, but a threatening cloud of doom that lingers dangerously near. The last scene in the film is a testament to Annie's haunting presence. Sheldon, peacefully sitting with his agent, starts to squirm and move forward in his chair when he believes he sees the threatening likeness of Annie Wilkes wheeling a cart to the table. Though he remains calm, a trick he mastered to survive his time in Annie's imprisonment, his body language clearly shows his discomfort, even after the apparition transforms into a harmless waitress who professes that she is his "number one fan." It is a chilling reminder that Paul may still not be completely safe from Annie's grasp. Even though she is dead, her influence lingers.

Thanks in part to Frank Darabont's creative style and narrative referencing, King's film audience has come to expect a certain formulaic structure and emotional sentiment from his prison films. *Misery* does not operate within such a recognizable structure. Nonetheless, although Rob Reiner's film adaptation of Stephen King's novel *Misery* was released in 1990, four years before the release of *The Shawshank Redemption* and nine years before the release of *The Green Mile*, his film is the first of King's prison movies.

Chapter 8

Redemption through the Feminine in *The Shawshank Redemption*; Or, Why Rita Hayworth's Name Belongs in the Title

Tony Magistrale

> *I have always looked on disobedience toward the oppressive as the only way to use the miracle of having been born.*
>
> Fallaci 13

*T*he *Shawshank Redemption* (1994) revolves around men in prison—their interpersonal friendships and conflicts, their coping mechanisms in adjusting to "all the time in the world," and their adaptability to lives that exclude freedom of movement. Perhaps less obvious, but nevertheless central to the film's plot, the men in Shawshank are also forced to reconsider their relationships to women. There are only three or four "living females" who appear in this two-and-a-half hour movie, and they occupy cameo roles: Andy's wife, who opens the film in a torrid embrace with her adulterous lover just before they are both murdered; the two landladies who unlock the door to the same apartment Red and Brooks will share; and the sole woman who is a member of Red's third parole board when his petition is finally approved. None of these women is present in her respective mise-en-scene for very long.

At first glance, the loss of contact with women in *The Shawshank Redemption* seems designed to be part of the punishment that the inmates must endure; moreover, it is easy and natural for viewers to enter a celluloid microcosm devoid of women because the film's men are so interesting to observe. Yet, despite the obvious male-centeredness of this filmic text, sounds and images of women haunt its perimeters—from the posters of the three Hollywood starlets that mark the decades of Andy Dufresne's term while also hiding his escape tunnel; to the two sopranos whose duet from Mozart's *The Marriage of Figaro* graces the prison yard with feminine song; to the rock wall in a Buxton hayfield where Andy made love and asked his wife to marry him and, later, serves as a reference point for Red to reconnect with Andy; to the film's final shot on the beach at Zihuatanejo, the Mexican town on the Pacific Ocean whose native name in Nahuatl "Cihualtan" means "the place of women." Furthermore, in the course of the movie, Dufresne becomes more and more "feminized," sympathetic to and affiliated with feminine oppression, images, and gendered behavior; women in *The Shawshank Redemption*, particularly through their artistic representations that undermine patriarchal authority, are inextricably connected to Andy's quest for redemption.

The earliest constructions of femininity and sexuality in this film, however, are reflective of the traumatized perspective that accompanies Andy to jail. "A bitter argument" with his wife over her infidelity precipitates a series of events that result in the murders of her and her lover and the false conviction of Andy as their killer. During the first few years of his incarceration at Shawshank, a gang of rapists nicknamed The Sisters beset Andy. Andy's duplicitous wife and The Sisters share at least this in common: They begin the film's concern with exploring and subverting traditional definitions of femininity.

In the opening courtroom scene and flashback, we learn that Andy's wife behaves in a highly aggressive manner, especially as a female in the 1940s; she initiates the desire for a divorce, she walks out on the security of a bourgeois home and husband to cohabit with her golf-pro lover, and her sexual hunger is palpable as she paws at her lover's clothes in his bedroom. As an indirect consequence of her actions, Andy's life is turned upside down: He is abruptly severed from his job as a successful bank vice president, thrown into a small stone cell, and forced to live the next 20 years of his life "in the path of the tornado." The Sisters entrap Andy in secluded corners of the prison basement laundry and in an isolated projection booth and physically assault him. The image of woman as sexual predator and The Sisters as a perversion of the feminine dominate the first two years of Andy's imprisonment and the first third of the movie; as Red notes, "Every so often, Andy would show up with fresh bruises. The Sisters kept after him . . . I also believe that if things had gone on that way, this place would have got the best of him." The despair over his wife's infidelity (which years later remains fresh enough in Andy's mind so that when he offers tax help to Captain Hadley on the prison roof, his questions unconsciously betray a strong self-referential prejudice,

"Do you trust your wife? Do you think she would go behind your back, try to hamstring you?"), his false conviction for her death, and the constant physical assault by Bogs and The Sisters combine to push Andy toward the "institutionalized" state of death-in-life that eventually destroys Brooks Hatlen. Andy begins this film at a point where he is wary of both the feminine and the sexual; in the intervening years that follow, however, he reintegrates with the anima as a result of his own "feminization" at Shawshank and an eventual willingness to accept responsibility for his wife's actions and death. He rediscovers reason to hope—and it is important to note that Andy's personal rebirth commences with Rita Hayworth and the movie *Gilda*.

Stephen King included Hayworth's name in the original title of the novella on which this film is based—"Rita Hayworth and Shawshank Redemption"—but he chose not to reference her most famous movie, *Gilda* (see Kermode 36–37). Although her name is excluded in the title of Frank Darabont's 1994 film adaptation, the movie's references to *Gilda* are both appropriate and metatextual. *Gilda* was released in 1946; Red informs us that Andy arrives at Shawshank in 1947. Thus, it is likely that Dufresne would have been acquainted with this film, and perhaps even viewed it prior to the three occasions in the same month that he watches it when incarcerated. *Gilda*, therefore, represents a part of his life that extends beyond the walls of Shawshank, and Rita Hayworth serves as his first symbol of hope in a place where hope is sometimes viewed as "a dangerous thing." As referenced in the movie *Gilda* and later as a wall poster in his prison cell, Rita Hayworth offers Andy a reminder of feminine beauty, a defiant trope, and a literal and imaginative passageway out of Shawshank prison.

The inmates' euphoric admiration for Hayworth's character in *Gilda*, in addition to the obvious sexual titillation it affords, is further developed on a subliminal level because of the social condition that connects them: mutual incarceration. The image of Gilda as a "caged canary," which is how she is introduced by her husband in the opening of the scene that appears in *Shawshank*, mirrors the convicts' caged, imprisoned status. Although she appears on screen very much unrestrained—and self-confident in the awareness of the sexuality she exudes—Gilda is a beautiful bird entrapped in a patriarchal power struggle. The linking of Gilda with Andy is more than just a reflection of the latter's visual appreciation of a sexualized woman, the surface level on which her image is enjoyed by Red and the rest of the excited inmates. Hayworth's character poses a more direct and intimate parallel to Andy himself. *Gilda* is a text that is frequently associated with film noir, and Hayworth plays the role of the classic femme fatale: a mysterious, difficult-to-control woman who is not easily seduced by men. Dufresne's wife is likewise a femme fatale who rebels against the strictures of a traditionally patriarchal marriage to a banker, and thus maintains a connection to Gilda that Andy will come to acknowledge in the course of his "gender rehabilitation" in Shawshank prison. Like Andy, Gilda is herself one of Red's "exotic birds" whose "feathers are just too bright" trapped in a cage constructed by males who seek simultaneously to exploit and punish her. As Mark Kermode notes in his book on *The Shawshank Redemption*, "[t]he strangely sexual bond . . . homosocial if not homosexual—in which Hayworth becomes a commodified property, passed between the two male leads, also seems particularly significant" (37).

While *Gilda* is being screened in the background for the convicts in the audience—featuring Hayworth encountering her ex-lover and new husband in the same room for the first time together—The Sisters force Andy into the projection room where Bogs insists that Andy is "gonna swallow what I give you to swallow." Dufresne feigns capitulation to this command, only to then use a film reel—a literal piece of *Gilda* itself—as a weapon against the men who would seek his sexual violation. At this moment, *Gilda* becomes a simulacrum of Andy's sexualization; the two films are intertextually connected when Hayworth's character confronts a gendered tension on screen at the exact moment that Andy encounters the predatory Sisters.

Eventually overcome by them, Andy is forced to his knees. From this position, Darabont sets up a reverse-shot conversation in which Andy, in acerbic language that parallels Gilda's own background dialogue with her former lover, gains control over Bogs, despite his inferior positioning. As the viewer is presented with alternating medium and close-ups of Dufresne and Bogs, the latter is shot against a completely black background. The darkness in the frame behind him reflects the darkness that engulfs Bog's psyche. In contrast, Andy's mise-en-scene includes several silver film reels of *Gilda*; they are stacked on the table behind him and appear illuminated within a cool blue light. Compared with the dark dankness that occupies the rest of the room, the movie reels appear clean and fresh, suffused in blue light. Like Hayworth's resplendent hair and face throughout *Gilda*, the film canisters project a nearly angelic presence. (The silver-blue glow of the movie reels foreshadows the color of the sky and ocean at the end of the *Shawshank*; further, it might also suggest the color of the "exotic birds" to which Red later alludes in constructing metaphors that connect the "soaring voices" of the duet in the prison yard to the flight of his absent friend.) *Gilda*'s film canisters—

symbolic of art, mystery, and imagination, as well as a steely resistance, all qualities that apply equally to both Andy and Gilda—are positioned behind Dufresne, while the primitive Bogs, immersed in darkness and totally indifferent to *Gilda*'s allure, threatens to put "all eight inches of this steel [knife] in [Andy's] ear" if he fails to perform fellatio.

Gilda's sharp-tongued commentary and her independent behavior, both directed at her male suitors, are paralleled in Andy's attitude toward Bogs in this scene. Although outnumbered by The Sisters and in danger of violation—sexual as well as penetration via the knife— Andy disarms his male assailants verbally. In film noir, the femme fatale possesses an array of weapons: her facial beauty, accented by heavy make-up, and her tight clothing and requisite stiletto-heeled pumps all serve to phallicize her image even as it becomes a fetishized object of the male gaze. Janey Place posits that the strength of the noir woman is expressed "by her dominance in composition, angle, camera movement and lighting. She is overwhelmingly the compositional focus . . . ambition expressed metaphorically in her freedom of movement and visual dominance" (54–56). Her outward appearance is further empowered by her aggressive attitude and combative language in the company of men she seldom respects. Thus, Dufresne is again linked to Gilda when he baffles the appropriately named Bogs linguistically, taunting him with his book knowledge of the bite-reflex, and completing his verbal comeuppance by asking, "You even know how to *read*, you ignorant fuck?" Although severely beaten as a consequence of his refusal to comply with his assailants' demand, Andy stands up to Bogs and The Sisters in a way that is highly suggestive of Gilda's assertiveness in the face of patriarchal dominance. In his discussion of *Gilda* as film noir text, Richard Dyer argues that Hayworth's singing and dancing emerge as a source of "defiance, not just of a trapped wife against her husband, but of a woman against the male system" (119). Similarly, Deborah Jermyn notes that the territory of film noir features "feisty women, female deception, fear of women, [and] the 'threat' of female sexuality" (159). Like the unruly femme fatale in noir who resists relegation to passivity, Andy assumes many of her characteristics first in his struggle against Bogs and The Sisters—who, in spite of their name, are "bull queers [that] take by force" and thus represent the masculine and patriarchal at its worst—and, later, in his involvement with the authority of Warden Norton.

As the film takes us deeper into Andy's life at Shawshank, his acts of hegemonic rebellion are subtly but increasingly affiliated with feminine representation and resistance. In arguably the most famous scene in *The Shawshank Redemption*, Andy defies the prison authorities long enough to share the gift of music with his fellow inmates. Instead of being gratefully humbled when his request for books and records is so generously answered by the state legislature, their arrival encourages Andy to push the envelope in an act of insolence. Using the prison public address system, Dufresne fills the prison yard with the music of two sopranos, "beautiful birds that flapped into our drab little cage," as Red calls them. The stunned silence that freezes convicts and guards alike is as much about hearing song emitted through the rusted loudspeakers in the prison yard—long accustomed to issuing the dry commands of a bureaucratic penal system—as it is the introduction of the feminine into this exclusively masculine domain. As in the earlier identification the film makes between Andy and *Gilda*, the duet of the two females is aligned with Dufresne in an act of institutional subversion. When the warden reacts with such fury to this seemingly innocuous stunt, it is because he perceives it correctly as the most defiant moment in the entire film. Indeed, to pull it off Andy commandeers and sequesters himself in the prison supervisor's office—an incredibly brazen act in itself—and then proceeds to lock one of the more amicable guards at Shawshank in the bathroom, refusing to let him out. In doing so, Dufresne also disobeys the command to assemble the books and records and "get all this stuff out of here . . . before the warden comes back."

Red's acknowledgment that he has "no idea to this day what those two Italian ladies were singing about" is certainly shared by the rest of the prison population (note that the guard Andy locks in the bathroom is reading a *Jughead* comic book, not a Mozart biography), Warden Norton included. Andy, on the other hand, knows exactly what this duet is about; he selects it deliberately from all the other musical recordings available in the box. In choosing an excerpt from Act 3 of Mozart's *The Marriage of Figaro* (1786), we see another example of Andy's identification with art as a vehicle for personal liberation: "For the briefest of moments," Red informs us, "every man at Shawshank felt free." Just as important, the duet is also sung by women and concerns the troubles women share in a world dominated by men—and it is on this level, as in *Gilda*, that we witness Andy again establishing an intimate bond with feminine independence and acts of subversion against male authority. The sopranos are a chambermaid (Susanna) and her mistress (Countess Almaviva). They are plotting a scheme to chasten as well as win back the amorous attention of Count Almaviva, the countess's wayward husband who has lost sexual interest in his wife and is currently focused on seducing the younger Susanna. The duet creates an obvious self-referential plot that mirrors Andy's own situation: a spouse's betrayal. But the music also goes on to outline a plan of action that empowers the women by altering a condition that is frustrating to them both. In this way, their scheming is an act of defiance against the patriarchal authority of the count and the ancient privileged custom of *le droit du seigneur*, whereby a lord possesses the right to sleep with any of his domestics.

The rebellious plot that the two women hatch in song needs to be viewed as paralleling and possibly even inspiring Dufresne's decision to subvert the warden's power in not only refusing to "turn it [the music] off," but also by actually increasing the volume of the recording all the while smiling and staring directly into the warden's face, a clear indication that the latter's fury is providing Andy with great amusement. This forces Norton, who is surrounded by a phalanx of uniformed guards, to break through the plate glass of his own office door. Just before Captain Hadley does so, he taps on the glass with his nightstick and notes, "You're mine now, Dufresne." In a context other than this particular prison film, where we watch Andy struggle to avoid sexual possession at the hands of The Sisters, Hadley's remark might not appear so ominous. But we also recall that earlier in the film the captain used this same nightstick to murder the "fresh fish." Red later informs us that "Andy received two weeks in the hole for that little stunt." Even after the operatic women are silenced, Andy still hears their music resonating in his head as he spends time "in the hole," yet another feminized image frequently associated with Andy, and one that serves to contrast Hadley's phallic stick. The reimposition of penal authority at the conclusion of the scene underscores the gap that exists between the masculine world—with its constant threat of violent penetration and intimidating language—and the feminine realm of enchanting beauty that disguises a subversive design. Moreover, it clearly suggests as well that Dufresne's allegiances are once more with defiant women "in the hole," rather than with the men who would silence them.

The elimination of Bogs and The Sisters from Dufresne's life coincides with another hole that Andy will employ in his escape from Shawshank. Not coincidentally, the posters of the Hollywood starlets with the word "Mother" etched on the wall just above their heads provide cover for the mouth of the tunnel—a tight, vagina-like canal that facilitates Andy's rebirth into the world—and continue to shift the film's orientation toward an emphasis on identification with the feminine as Andy's sole inspiration and means for expressing defiant action. The posters in Andy's cell belie a seditious intent, and not merely because they hide the opening of the escape tunnel. When the warden notices the picture of Rita Hayworth at his first meeting with Andy during the cell toss, he comments, "I can't say I approve of this." Later in the film, after Andy is reported missing from his cell, the warden's consternation is directed at the photograph of Raquel Welch, "that cupcake on the wall," and Dufresne's escape route is only then discovered after the enraged Norton throws a carved rock through the paper that secrets it. The poster featuring Welch is a movie still from *One Million Years B.C.* (1966), another film that, like *Gilda*, creates a cinematic reference point to Dufresne's situation. In *One Million Years*, Caveman Tumak is a rebel figure banished by his own father from a savage, phallocentric tribe. After days of wandering alone, he is rescued and nursed back to health by several female members of another tribe, including Loana (Welch's character) who falls in love with Tumak. Thus, Andy's final defiant moment in *Shawshank* is again associated with and ultimately enabled by female artistic representation; Loana/Welch's filmic character and her photograph in Andy's cell that hides the completed escape tunnel, aligned as they are with acts of blatant patriarchal subversion, undermine male authority systems in both the movies. In this context it is ironically appropriate that the warden indicts "Miss Fuzzy Britches" for a role in Andy's disappearance even prior to discovering the tunnel, recognizing that Welch and Defresne are bound together in a "damn conspiracy and everyone's in on it, including her."

Norton's dismissal of the women on Dufrense's wall is informed by a prudish misogyny that is distinguished from the candid eroticism of the sexualized poster art. The warden's religious zealotry, of course, is a hypocritical mask to hide his secular avarice and illegal schemes; his character is far more morally debased than the "pornographic" photographs he decries. In fact, because all three actresses are so intimately tied to Andy and the magic of the movies, projected as they are up on the wall of Andy's cell, their provocative poses appear less immoral than mystical, less promiscuous than majestic. Kermode enriches this point in his insistence that "Andy's ultimate escape, in which he will *literally* step through a movie poster to freedom, suggests that the escapist possibilities of the medium are powerful enough to transcend physically reality. Perhaps *this* is the true 'religious' message at the heart of *The Shawshank Redemption*" (38; emphasis in the original). On one occasion, Andy is even pictured gazing up adoringly at Marilyn Monroe's long legs and billowing skirt, as though she had somehow been elevated to the level of iconic status. Indeed she has:

Her poster guards the portal for Andy's escape as her hands block access to the glorious secrets behind her skirt.

That the warden so clearly dislikes the posters of the women supports their role as subversive symbols in an authoritarian male domain and thereby links them directly to Andy himself. Indeed, Andy is as much an object of the "male gaze" in Shawshank prison as Rita Hayworth, Marilyn Monroe, and Raquel Welch became sexualized objects on a larger screen. But Dufresne's bond with these women involves more than simply reversing the gendered focus of sexual objectification (Neale 14–15). Rather, Andy rises to the level of celebrity status during his tenure at Shawshank. The warden is totally dependent on his money-laundering skills, and the convicts talk about him, especially after his escape, with the same tone of awe and reverence with which men—and women—responded to Rita Hayworth in the 1940s, or still use when discussing Marilyn Monroe today. In each of these examples, the "myths" surrounding these individual celebrities, particularly Hayworth and Monroe, became somehow larger than life, just as Andy's history became part of the folklore of Shawshank.

As the starlet posters (and the secret they maintain) are an incitement to Andy—literal and figurative—of life beyond the stonewalls of the prison, the wall safe in Norton's office (which is likewise linked to *his* destiny) maintains its own hidden secret behind his wife's crocheted religious sampler, "His Judgement Cometh and that Right Soon . . ." This foreboding prognostication, produced by a woman and her church group whose levels of fear and repression are meant to contrast sharply with the cinematic women of Andy's wall art, points the way to Norton's fate as Andy's poster girls simultaneously inspire and disguise his own. However, while Andy finds redemptive freedom through the birth canal behind the female adornments on his wall, the safe in Norton's office is anything but "safe" as its contents produce the warden's doom. These respective holes (as well as the feminine art that conceals them) in the walls of Shawshank prison become apt metaphors for each of the men who revisit them nightly. Andy's tunnel is the start of a "visionary" pipeline that extends all the way "down there" to Mexico, while the depth of Norton's small and shallow repository is, in contrast, as terribly finite as suicide.

Shawshank owes as much to the gothic narrative as it does to prison dramas that precede it. Incarcerated in a gray, stone, castle-like fortress that Kermode describes as "one part cathedral, two parts Castle Frankenstein" (18), the Shawshank penitentiary is honeycombed with the requisite gothic genre's secret corners, cells, and passageways. Andy's combination of innocence—the "only innocent man in Shawshank"—and refined demeanor—an educated bank vice president incarcerated with hardened felons—link him to the persecuted yet intrepid gothic maiden who is besieged by various hypermasculine monsters that are a sexual and psychological threat. Thus, Andy's "feminization" is psychological and physical, and it helps to bond him further to the female figures with whom he is aligned at critical points throughout the film. Ironically, these women are, in turn, "masculinized" within the contexts of their cultural eras and artistic personae; their collective conduct is noteworthy because it challenges gendered definitions of what it means to be female. From the fierce sexual independence evinced by Dufresne's wife, to the plotting sopranos from *Figaro*, to the movie stars staring down from his wall, these self-confident women model for Andy the "doubleness of space" that Eve Sedgwick suggests is a major convention of the gothic established by the deconstruction of gender boundaries and the blurring of traditional behavior norms (20). Andy stands apart from the other inmates at Shawshank because he integrates feminine traits into his personality, especially since the women who are referenced in this film employ their femininity as a means for asserting themselves against the male power arrangements they respectively encounter. Confronted in prison with his own experience of patriarchal abuse, Dufrense certainly empathizes with the oppression of women even as his own effort to undermine masculine authority at Shawshank indicates that he also aligns himself with their subversive energies.

Andy's feminine face and body (when he first notices Andy, Red calls him a "tall drink of water") and eccentric personality are compelling features that both prison inmates and authorities find impossible to resist. Andy draws the entire prison population to him— out of a desire to befriend him, or to exploit his intellect, or to possess him sexually. Like the traditional gothic heroine in literature and film, Andy is under personal siege and must constantly protect himself against masculine intrusions that endanger his integrity and personal code of conduct. The film reveals him to be, if not the exclusive then at least, the primary target of The Sisters' violent sexual lust. Once freed from their oppression, however, he becomes the warden's "bitch," made to prostitute his business acumen for Norton's illegal schemes: "A convicted murderer who provides solid financial planning is a nice pet to have." To ensure Dufresne's continued cooperation in his criminal operations, Norton relies on sexual intimidation that once again assigns Andy to a feminine role: "I'll pull you out of that one bunk Hilton and cast you down with the sodomites. You'll think you were fucked by a train." The warden's threat of course is an explicit reference to rape, the means by which desperate men always exert emotional as well as physical dominance over women.

Within the prison culture itself, Andy is a teacher, friend, and nurturer to a degree that would have been considered "feminine" during the 1940s and beyond. He designs and maintains the Shawshank library and is responsible for tutoring several convicts, enabling them to attain high school equivalency diplomas. Andy emerges as a highly stable resource that dispenses kindly advice; throughout most of this film, his character is best defined as an aid to others. In effect, Andy becomes the surrogate mother all these inmates should have had in their misguided lives. He cares deeply for the people he loves, and he assumes the risks that love entails. Like many mothers supporting their children, Dufresne also retains a psychic toughness in the face of severe adversarial conditions. The injustices of the legal system that put him in Shawshank continue in the treatment he receives as a convict, but Andy never does surrender to self-pity or despair. Each time he emerges from progressively longer stints in solitary confinement, for example, he comes out with a clearer sense of purpose—more defiant and resolute.

Perhaps this is the reason Red is sent to the same rock wall in Buxton that holds so much meaning for Andy's marriage; it is a test for measuring the degree to which both men have changed. In bringing Red to this place, Andy demonstrates that he is again willing to trust. As well, he shows a willingness to risk failure once more. Although his marriage may have ended prematurely, Dufresne hopes that his friendship with Red will not; although he failed to appreciate love when he had it before, he hopes he has now learned to communicate its value to Red. The scale of Andy's shaping influence is confirmed as early as when Red is still a prisoner facing his last parole board. In marked contrast to his subservient posturing in front of earlier officials, the black man becomes an extension of Dufresne, appropriating his assertive persona before a board whose enlarged degree of sympathy toward Red's plight and attitude is signaled through the significant inclusion of a female officer. When presented parole opportunities on two earlier occasions, each time Red relied on the same inauthentic cant: "I can honestly say I'm a changed man." Only after he is gone, however, does the memory of Andy's influence help to change Red into a man capable of speaking his mind honestly in the face of authority. The degree of Red's insolence in front of the third parole board is again reminiscent of Rita Hayworth's linguistic aggressiveness in *Gilda*, but it might also remind us of Andy's defiant wife. Additionally, the scene takes us back to *Figaro* as well, insofar as the relationship between Red and Andy parallels that of the countess and Susanna. Susanna and Andy inspire a rebellious "hope" to individuals who occupy subordinate positions in institutional prisons— Red, who has spent 40 years "asking permission to piss," and Mozart's Countess Almaviva, trapped in the "prison" that is her marriage to the count.

In the end, Andy's redemption is more about recognizing and transforming the limitations of his former self that contributed to the destruction of his marriage than it is about escaping the stone of Shawshank for the sand of Zihuatanejo. He endures incarceration at Shawshank to learn this about his marriage and his wife: "I didn't pull the trigger, but I drove her away. And that's why she died, because of me, the way I am." In the film's opening scene, Andy reveals something of the way he was, pictured brooding inside an automobile "entrapped" in a stereotypical masculinity that isolates him in a state of clench-fisted despair. His response to his wife's infidelity appears about to verge into violence, he resorts to heavy drinking alone as a consequence of her sexual betrayal, and his only means of expression is limited to a loaded gun. This portrait of a humiliated man enduring a private hell contrasts with the highly developed social and communicative role Andy takes on while at Shawshank.

Like Dostoevski's personal transformation as a result of his years spent in a Siberian gulag, Dufresne's own suffering—the loss of his marriage and his freedom, and the various punishments he endures as a convict at Shawshank—has opened him more profoundly to the sufferings of others. During his long prison term, the masculine stoniness he brought to his marriage and the stereotypical male-gendered response we see him exhibit in the film's opening montage undergo a kind of geological breakdown. Andy comes to empathize with his wife's marital situation and, through his identification with her and the film's other self-empowered representations of the feminine, becomes a better man. Dufresne's gradual acceptance of his complicity in his wife's infidelity and death is the best explanation for his reparative efforts to express his feelings toward the prisoners he comes to love, Red in particular. One of the most satisfying aspects of this movie is watching a man evolve through contact with the feminine; that this occurs in a male prison narrative that is nearly womanless makes *Shawshank* all the more remarkable a film. Dufresne's rehabilitation consists of changing the "hard man, closed book" his wife "complained about all the time" into a person who empathizes with what it means to be an oppressed woman. Ironically, the film comes full circle when Andy Dufresne follows the seditious example set by his own wife: He abandons an unsatisfying relationship in an oppressive institution to "get busy living" on the shores of Zihuatanejo, "the place of women."

Acknowledgments

The author is indebted to Dennis Mahoney, Brian Kent, Kathy FitzGerald, and Matthew Muller who were tremendously insightful in supplying commentary to multiple drafts of this chapter.

Chapter 9

Christian Martyr or Grateful Slave?

The Magical Negro as Uncle Tom in Frank Darabont's *The Green Mile*

Brian Kent

"In the beginning, there was Uncle Tom." So writes Donald Bogle concerning the representation of blacks in American cinema (3). Bogle comments specifically on the first black character in the movies (albeit one played by a white actor in blackface), the title role in a 1903 version of Harriet Beecher Stowe's *Uncle Tom's Cabin*. But Bogle's statement resonates, as well, with the ubiquitousness of the "Tom" portrayal throughout the history of cinema—that of the saintly, self-sacrificing black man whose primary concern in life is the well-being of his white masters, even when that concern translates into suffering for Tom himself, for his family, or for African Americans in general. One assumes, of course, that since the era of the civil rights movement and the concomitant awareness of how such images of African Americans in film foster pernicious racial stereotyping, the Uncle Tom character would necessarily go the way of blackface minstrelsy itself. After all, as Linda Williams emphasizes in *Playing the Race Card: Melodramas of Black and White from Uncle Tom to O.J. Simpson*, "the 'Tom lens,' for all its romantic racialist sympathy for the suffering African, is undeniably white supremacist and deeply violent" (xv–xvi).

Film critics and scholars have begun to wonder recently, however, whether the "Tom lens" has, in fact, become historical artifact or simply been nuanced to appear in different guises with the same underlying (intentional or not) white supremacist orientation. Such critical wonder has zeroed in most aggressively on the recurring role of the saintly black with supernatural powers who uses these powers exclusively for the benefit of white people, often white people who are complete strangers. This "magical Negro" operates as a secondary character in films that foreground the concerns and behavior of their primary white characters. Krin Gabbard, who published a 2004 book-length treatment of this phenomenon entitled *Black Magic: White Hollywood and African American Culture*, explains in his introduction that "African Americans often appear in films for no other reason than to help white people reaffirm their own superiority. . . . [Because] white culture has assigned black culture a central role in its own self-definition while simultaneously marginalizing or erasing black people, the films that perpetuate this project often resort to what I have called magic" (6).

Awareness of the self-defining sleight of hand at work in representations of the magical Negro hit a critical flashpoint in 1999–2000 with the appearance of three frontline Hollywood productions in which a black male with supernatural powers puts those powers at the service of the films' primary white characters. *Family Man* stars Nicholas Cage and Don Cheadle in a reconfiguring of Frank Capra's *It's a Wonderful Life*, where Cheadle's angel intervenes in the life of Cage's character to reveal its spiritual emptiness. In *The Legend of Bagger Vance*, Will Smith plays a magical caddy in 1930s Georgia who essentially appears out of nowhere to help Matt Damon's character rediscover his golf swing and, in the process, win back the heart of his ex-girlfriend Charlize Theron. The most commercially successful of the three, *The Green Mile*, tells the story of Tom Hanks's Death Row prison guard in 1930s Louisiana whose life is transformed by his encounter with a gigantic black inmate played by the relatively unknown actor Michael Clarke Duncan. Duncan's John Coffey is falsely convicted of the rape and murder of two young white girls and displays Christ-like attributes as he awaits and eventually endures his execution.

This trio of black angels may be benevolent and wise because of a richness of spirit, but their spiritual wealth seems engendered more out of white need for self-affirmation than out of the joys and sorrows of black life itself. The situation is reminiscent of slave characters from nineteenth-century American literature whose devotion to their white masters supersedes the suffering they endure at the hands of those same masters, thus affirming for more liberally minded white readers that the evil slavery represented was not inherent to what it meant to *be* white in the United States. Stowe's Uncle Tom became the iconic representative of that self-affirming process.

Frank Darabont's *The Green Mile* offers an especially telling example of the relationship between the magical Negro and what Williams calls the Tom lens, given the obvious Christian implications evident in the physical and mental suffering of its miracle-working John Coffey. The level of pacifism and submissiveness in John Coffey's behavior has even led Tania Modleski to claim that Coffey "makes Uncle Tom look like Stokely Charmichael." What is particularly unnerving about the behavior of such characters is that the concerns and condition of the African American communities from which these magical Negroes emerge are set aside in favor of exercising supernatural powers on behalf of the white characters who represent the very social and political structure that oppresses them. Spike Lee brought this point of view into memorable focus in a 2001 *Cineaste* interview as he examined the mind-boggling discrepancies between fantasy and reality in *The Legend of Bagger Vance*. "Why," he wondered, "isn't [Bagger] using [his magical abilities] to try and stop some of the other brothers from being lynched and castrated? Why is he fucking around with Matt Damon and trying to teach him a golf swing? I don't understand this! That is insane. What world was that?! Please tell me."

One might easily wonder the same things about the 1930s, Depression-era Louisiana prison setting of *The Green Mile*, and why Coffey does not use his powers to address, most obviously, the inordinate numbers of blacks imprisoned and executed at the film's Cold Mountain prison. Lee mentions *The Green Mile* specifically also, particularly Coffey's desire to die rather than save even his own life: "In the end Tom Hanks offers to set him free, but guess what? He'd rather die with Tom Hanks looking on. Get the fuck outta here! That's that old grateful slave shit."

I would like to address "that old grateful slave shit" as a dimension of John Coffey's character in *The Green Mile* and as a manifestation of the larger Hollywood phenomenon of the magical Negro. To do so, I wish to return to the nineteenth-century literary heyday of the Uncle Tom persona and examine key elements in the Uncle Tom dynamic as it appeared in three of the most well-known slave characters created by white authors: Uncle Tom, of course, from Stowe's *Uncle Tom's Cabin*; Huck Finn's traveling companion Jim, from Mark Twain's *Adventures of Huckleberry Finn*; and Uncle Remus, the central storytelling figure in Joel Chandler Harris's *Tales of Uncle Remus*. If, as Linda Williams asserts, melodrama is "the fundamental mode by which American mass culture has 'talked to itself' about the enduring moral dilemma of race" (xiv) and if such a "conversation" can only be carried on through extremes, since "melodrama cannot tell the story of the middle ground" (307), then what does the melodramatic treatment of John Coffey's character ultimately reveal to us about the enduring moral dilemma of race?

"What a Thing 't Is to Be a Christian!"

When interviewer Tony Magistrale asked Stephen King, author of the novel that is the basis for Darabont's *The Green Mile*, what he thought of Spike Lee's objection to the character of Coffey, King did not mince words. "It's complete bullshit," he responded, defending Coffey's behavior as consistent with that of a Christ figure, black or white: "Christ figures are supposed to do good to them that revile you, to turn the other cheek to those who strike you. By doing good for white people . . . he is basically exhibiting his saintliness" (13–14). King's remark strikes a particularly resonant Uncle Tom note with regard to Stowe's original character. Whatever defense might be mounted to counter the charges of racial denigration inherent to Uncle Tom must rest on Stowe's overall Christian vision and the way in which that vision serves as the basis for recognizing the humanity of African Americans and thus the moral depravity of slavery. Tom's Christ-like self-sacrifice is the symbolic heart at the center of Stowe's Christian ethos.

When George Shelby shows up at the point of Tom's death, a death attributable to the vicious whipping inflicted upon him by Simon Legree, Tom tells his young master, "O, Mas'r George, ye're too late. The Lord's bought me, and is going to take me home—*and I long to go* [emphasis mine]. Heaven is better than Kintuck" (451–52). The parallel to the scene where Coffey responds to Paul Edgecomb's offer to let him escape is unmistakable. In speaking of his impending execution, Coffey insists, "I want to go," because he is tired of the pain and loneliness, tired of people being ugly to one another, tired of the suffering he feels so intensely. Death offers the sanctuary of heavenly bliss.

With his last breaths, Stowe's Uncle Tom speaks of love and forgiveness, even for the despicable Legree, as he tells George, "'He an't done me no real harm—only opened the gate of the kingdom for me; that's all! . . . Give my love to Mas'r, and dear good Missis, and every-body in the place! Ye don't know! 'Pears like I loves them all! I loves every creatur' everywhar!—it's nothing *but* love! O, Mas'r George! what a thing 't is to be a Christian!" (452; emphasis in the original). Tom's vehement projection of Christian love allows Stowe's white readers the self-satisfaction that comes with recognizing Tom's obvious moral righteousness, thereby assuaging any misgivings they might feel about his awful fate, and their own culpability in it.

Objections to John Coffey in *The Green Mile*, beginning with Spike Lee's, often center on the way Coffey's execution for a crime he did not commit is presented in a manner that nonetheless allows audience-members to feel righteous about his death. After all, the reasoning apparently goes, Edgecomb and his cohorts are merely opening the gate of the kingdom for Coffey, offering him the solace of dying for their sins and achieving his heavenly reward. The guards themselves are all suitably transformed by Coffey's loving presence, Paul Edgecomb and Brutus "Brutal" Howell even deciding to no longer participate in executions. But what of the larger political and social structure that is responsible for so much of the ugliness that transpires every day, especially as it is directed at African Americans like John Coffey?

The tension between viewing Coffey's behavior as a pacifist surrender to an unjust status quo and seeing in it the Christian reward of moral nobility and heavenly salvation is where the link between the nineteenth-century figure of Uncle Tom and the twentieth-century figure of John Coffey resonates most distinctly. When confronted with the agonizing fate of Uncle Tom and the role slavery plays in it, nineteenth-century readers were naturally left in a position of gaging their own responsibility for doing something about the evils perpetrated by slavery, a seemingly insurmountable dilemma. The work of melodrama is to evoke emotional response, in the case of Uncle Tom to get readers to *feel* sympathy for Tom's plight. That sympathy becomes the basis for the larger Christian sympathy that puts them in harmony with the great interests of humanity, which, in Stowe's view, is the primary action required of them.

A similar process appears to be at work in responding to the obvious injustice of Coffey's death in *The Green Mile*, but even more so in responding to the suffering that he must bear for the sins of others. The emotional trajectory of the film elicits our sympathy for what Coffey must endure at the same time that it makes us feel that Coffey is a good and noble figure and so what happens to him is also ultimately a necessary thing—evident, of course, in the consequences of his death for the white guards who carry out his punishment. But, as Kim D. Hester-Williams makes clear in her analysis of the physical suffering Coffey undergoes as a result of his individual acts of healing throughout the film, as well as his final, ultimate act of self-sacrifice: "Elevating Coffey to the divine status of Savior allows the spectator to dismiss his suffering, especially since he suffers for the 'good' of others; he saves those who *can* [emphasis in the original] be saved. They are not, presumably, as he is, economically or socially dispensable."

Coffey's intervention into the lives of the white characters surrounding him at the Cold Mountain prison represents an obvious attempt to demonstrate the power of Christian love to combat the "darkness" that informs so much of human experience and that is so evident in the men that make their way to the Green Mile. But whether Stephen King likes it or not, by making Coffey a black man he also introduces an inevitable symbolic undercurrent of racial forgiveness into the story, of white and black coming together in the miraculous embrace of Christian love. The film, however, offers no acknowledgment of race whatsoever in this process, as though it is only natural that an innocent black man condemned to death would use the occasion of his unjust execution as the means for the physical and moral healing of his white brethren. It is this absence that accounts for comments like *Nation* reviewer Stuart Klawans's that Coffey dies "in the name of a race love that is little better than hate" (35).

"I Knowed He Was White Inside"

According to Eric Lott, with Stowe's creation of Uncle Tom, "we are already on our way to the gentle, childlike, self-sacrificing, essentially *aesthetic* slave Mark Twain created in Jim" (33; emphasis in the original). The nature of Jim's characterization as it is projected through Huck's and Jim's travels and burgeoning friendship has, of course, been subject to intense critical debate. The ending of *Huckleberry Finn*, in particular, offers considerable flexibility in identifying the nature of Twain's own attitude and intent when it comes to the matter of race. After Tom gets shot as part of the escape from the Phelps plantation, Jim refuses to leave him behind while Huck and Jim make their getaway. Huck's response is both ambiguous and revealing: "I knowed he was white inside" (290). Later, of course, a doctor arrives to tend Tom's wound and Jim comes out from hiding to help, knowing it will mean certain capture and return to slavery, as well as punishment for escaping in the first place.

Despite Huck's progress in recognizing Jim's goodness and humanity during their journey down the river, at the end of the novel he still privileges whiteness in the way he perceives those characteristics in Jim. Rather than seeing Jim's behavior as a manifestation of his individual being, and recognizing that such qualities can occur in a human being irrespective of race, Huck sees Jim's goodness as a reflection of his ability to act like a white person, establishing whiteness as the norm by which all such attributes are measured. A good deal of critical debate on the novel centers on whether this represents Twain's complex understanding of the difficulties Huck still faces in overcoming racist ideas in American society, or is, in fact, a reflection of Twain's own ambivalent attitudes about race.

A similar confusion about the privileged position of whiteness operates in *The Green Mile*. Although the film offers no real glimpse into the racial attitudes of the guards as they might pertain to their new inmate (except, of course, for the clearly racist archvillain Percy Wetmore), historical precedent would suggest that feelings about race would play into the guards' initial perceptions of the newest member of E Block. But Coffey establishes his humanity in the guards' eyes by tending to sick whites, much as Jim tends to Tom. In fact, in Stephen King's novel, when the guards are walking Coffey back to the truck after his miraculous cure of Melinda Moores's brain tumor, they head off into the bushes to urinate, leaving Coffey alone by the truck, free to run off if he has a mind to. Paul Edgecomb realizes this mistake as he makes his way back from the bushes and figures Coffey may, indeed, be gone, that he may have "just lit out for the territories, like Huck and Jim on the Big Muddy" (Bk 5, p. 87). But in true Jim fashion, Coffey remains, because he still has work to do on behalf of the community of white guards as they prepare him for his own execution.

Given the complete absence of an African American community or culture in *The Green Mile*, one might legitimately wonder whether, after the guards witness the saintly and miraculous behavior of John Coffey and then observe the noble manner in which he meets his death, they think to themselves, "I knowed he was white inside." Heather J. Hicks wonders, along these lines, whether "black characters must be assigned saint-like goodness to counteract the racism white audiences automatically direct toward a black character on screen. That is, for white audiences, a saintly black character is the moral equivalent of a 'normal' white character" (28). King's text might inadvertently add some credence to such an observation in the way it conceives of the goodness that emanates from John Coffey as "something white."

To be fair, King has developed a pattern of references to good and evil throughout his fiction in which he pits the powers of white and black forces in constant struggle. Whiteness, in this respect, is not conceived within racial terms. But in this novel where the author continually impresses upon readers the imposing black presence of John Coffey's body, the language is nevertheless striking. One might also argue that these words come from Paul Edgecomb—"That's how

I think of it," the narrator says—and that King thus purposely invests this conception of whiteness into his character's understanding of Coffey to complicate the racial dynamics at work. But King himself has stated that the only reason he decided to make Coffey a black character is that the moment he was discovered with the two dead white girls in his arms his blackness guaranteed that he would be executed. The spiritual dimension of his character, however, "had nothing to do with black or white." Edgecomb is the novel's heroic protagonist and shows no signs of wrestling with racial issues as part of the moral transformation he undergoes, suggesting that his understanding of the good spirit within Coffey as "something white" does not complicate our heroic view of him. This is emblematic of the way Darabont's film refuses to engage the racial issues inherent in John Coffey being black.

If nothing in *The Green Mile* overtly suggests the privileging of white sensibility or culture over black (which is only noticeable by its absence in the film), a viewer can nonetheless come away from the film feeling that what really triumphs is the normality and power of whiteness. Despite the central presence of Coffey in *The Green Mile*, only the white characters surrounding him are allowed to develop and grow as human beings. He is an expedient for that growth and development. In *Black Magic*, Krin Gabbard warns that filmmakers "must stop thinking about whiteness as 'normal'" because that message fosters the belief in blackness as the other, the outsider, the transgressor in what is conceived to be a white realm of existence. Such a belief may not be spoken in so many words, but, as Gabbard also warns, "ideology works best when it is unnoticed" (15).

At the end of *Huckleberry Finn*, after Tom makes it clear that Jim has been granted his freedom by Miss Watson, one might think that Jim would recognize and resent the way in which Tom has jeopardized Jim's life and freedom for "the *adventure* of it" (303; emphasis in the original). Not so. He is content with the $40 Tom gives him for "being prisoner for us so patient, and doing it up so good" (306). Earlier, at the Phelps plantation when Tom reveals to Jim his baroque plan for effecting Jim's escape, Jim quite rightly sees that it makes no sense, "but he allowed [Huck and Tom] was white folks and knowed better than him; so he was satisfied" (262). At that moment, readers can feel the sting of Twain's barbed irony. Yet, when confronted at the end with Jim's happy acquiescence to the evil way he has been manipulated by Tom Sawyer, some of the sting of that earlier moment turns into a disquiet over Twain's possible complicity in what white folks are allowed at the expense of black. The fact that John Coffey goes to his death in the electric chair for a crime he did not commit with the final words, "I'm sorry for what I am," engenders a similar disquiet with regard to the makers of *The Green Mile*.

"Look Like Hit's a Mighty Onwrong"

In *The Intent to Live: Achieving Your True Potential as an Actor*, acting coach Larry Moss describes the work he did to prepare Michael Clarke Duncan for the role of John Coffey in *The Green Mile*. When discussing the choices actors make in the roles they play, Moss advises that "no actor should ever play a racial stereotype" (271). Yet, in assessing Coffey's character, as played by Duncan in the film, Heather J. Hicks declares that it is "an amalgam of racist stereotypes" (37). Clearly, differing perceptions of intent are at work in the two views.

The dynamics of intent and effect with regard to white-authored texts about black characters are on rich display in Joel Chandler Harris's famous creation of Uncle Remus from the nineteenth century. Harris's stories rely on the presentation, through Uncle Remus, of an array of ingenuous, creative, and hugely entertaining tales from a rich tradition of African and African American folklore involving the exploits of Brer Rabbit, Brer Fox, and a host of other animals and quasihuman figures. The tales are fraught with the kind of double meanings that appear to make Uncle Remus's relationship to slavery problematic, as when Remus tries to comfort the boy who questions the injustice at work in one tale's outcome: "'Dat w'at make I say w'at I duz, honey. In dis worril, lots er fokes is gotter suffer fer udder fokes sins. Look like hit's mighty onwrong; but hit's des dat away. Tribbalashun seem like she's a waitin' roun' de cornder fer ter ketch one en all un us, honey'" (102).

Despite such seemingly subversive elements, was the primary effect of the entire fictional configuration Harris created simply to reconfirm already deeply embedded attitudes his reading audience shared with regard to African Americans? "Harris was the first to pay careful tribute to the great complexity of inherited African American folklore," writes Eric J. Sundquist. "Even so, he came perilously close to perpetuating the sentiment that blacks were indeed closer to the animal kingdom or, at the least, savage in their naturally determined behavior. Part of Harris's popularity, an unavoidable dissonance between intention and effect, no doubt came from such an identification in the minds of many white readers" (341).

The dissonance Sundquist speaks of can be instructive in considering *The Green Mile* when it comes to the film's apparent attempt to eliminate racial considerations as a primary dynamic in John Coffey's Christ-like interactions with his executioners. During an exchange in Magistrale's interview with Stephen King concerning what the former saw as the obvious racial implications of Coffey's character despite King's assurance that his conception of Coffey had nothing to do with black or white, King suggested that Magistrale's response demonstrated an "imaginative failing" because it could not accept the idea of a black Christ without bringing historical racial dynamics into the equation. Darabont's *The Green Mile* adopts a similar attitude, assuming as a backdrop for the story, a spiritually and imaginatively inspired racial parity that makes commenting on historical social reality superfluous. As racially enlightened as this may appear to be, the end result can leave one agreeing with *New Yorker* reviewer David Denby that "*The Green Mile* is a fantasy of taming the black giant, passing itself off as liberal humanism." The grandiosity of the film's illusions, Denby continues, actually shows the filmmakers treating their audience "like a bunch of tent-show suckers" and exuding "a tinge of bizarre and unnecessary self-congratulation" (103).

The word "unnecessary" in Denby's critique strikes me as especially suggestive, since contained within Darabont's film is a story that wants to be told. It involves the suffering John Coffey has endured during his lifetime and how he passes the burden of that suffering onto Paul Edgecomb before he dies. In keeping with the universal dimension of Coffey's Christ persona, the cause or nature of that suffering is never more specifically defined than the sins of the world, of people being ugly to one another, every day, all over the world. Coffey cannot even remember where he received the scars that so prominently mark his body. All of which lends a degree of irony to acting coach Larry Moss's description of helping Michael Clarke Duncan to create a very detailed back story for the character as motivation for his performance. The story included Coffey having been beaten so often and coming so close to being lynched, "that when he was taken into the room with a bunch of white men, he knew the blows were coming. He had to overcome his terror and his certainty that there would be a beating, which he did by trying to keep things peaceful." Coffey's imagined biography went on to detail his parents being lynched when he was a baby and being brought up by his maternal grandmother. Moss also mentions that "the back story was especially alive in Michael because he had personally experienced police brutality in his childhood" (138). In other words, in bringing the character of Coffey to life on screen, Moss and Duncan created a very specific racial context for his suffering, a context the film itself presents not at all. In the words of the character

Hammersmith, in fact, it was "like [Coffey] dropped out of the sky" (as, apparently, saviors are wont to do).

In the Magistrale interview, King stated that "whatever past [Coffey] has is completely lost, and that's crucial to the story" (14). One might wonder why. The dramatic emphasis provided by the frame through which Paul Edgecomb presents his story concerns the older Edgecomb communicating the physical and emotional effects of his encounter with John Coffey. In King's words, Edgecomb has been "inoculated with life" as a result of whatever Coffey passed on to him while giving him the vision of William Wharton's guilt in the death of the two girls. The inoculation means Edgecomb will live much longer than most human beings do, consequently suffering the kind of recognition and sorrow that pained Coffey so. The nature of that suffering, beyond the specific grief of seeing loved ones continually die, remains a universalized awareness of people being ugly to one another, every day, all over the world. Edgecomb claims it is his punishment for "letting John Coffey ride the lightning."

In an intriguing analysis of the film's conclusion, Heather J. Hicks argues that although *The Green Mile* appears to present "harmonious and cooperative race relations," the sense of suffering that Coffey passes on to Edgecomb actually reveals Coffey's character to be a trickster figure, one intent upon making Edgecomb cognizant of what it means to be black in Louisiana in the 1930s. The ending, therefore, shows "white masculinity beset." Whiteness itself becomes a tenuous construction for Paul Edgecomb, given what he now knows about the reality of black existence. Thus, the Magical African American Friend, in Hicks's view, "may indeed be good mojo" (52). But her argument would be bolstered if the sense of suffering that Coffey imparts to Edgecomb had a more definite sense of the African American experience that ultimately forms the basis for it. What if the beatings, the lynchings, the brutality that formed the back story for Coffey's characterization were more specifically realized in Edgecomb's understanding of why he must be punished for letting Coffey ride the lightning? What if the suffering that Edgecomb endures were the specific emotional trauma induced in Coffey by all these events? It might, indeed, lead Edgecomb to a more tenuous understanding of what whiteness means, especially within the larger context of human suffering universalized by Coffey's statement about how people treat one another every day, all over the world.

King might well respond to such musings with something akin to, "[t]hat's all fine and dandy, but that's not the book I wrote." Yet, I think there are undeveloped suggestions of just this type of conception in the serialized novel that did not find their way into Darabont's script at all. In Book V, for example, when Edgecomb explains to Brutal his awareness of what Coffey really meant when he was discovered with the two dead girls in his arms and could only weep and moan, "I couldn't help it. I tried to take it back, but it was too late." His captors, of course, interpret this as an admission of his guilt. But, as King writes, "[t]hey heard what he was saying in a way that would agree with what they were seeing, and what they were seeing was black" (21–22). By the end of the film, especially as a result of the vision imparted to him by Coffey, one might naturally assume that Edgecomb "sees black" in a fundamentally different way. Consequently, he sees white differently as well. How, exactly, that transformation occurs for him is not, however, undertaken by King in the novel, or by Darabont in the film. This unrealized dimension might ultimately make more valuable and effective the film's *intention* with regard to the racial dynamics suggested by Coffey's fate, as opposed to the bizarre and self-congratulating *effect* of *The Green Mile* in its current form.

"Why, These Angels . . . Just Like Up in Heaven"

One of the most disconcerting moments in *The Green Mile* occurs as Coffey sits mesmerized by the dancing and singing of Fred Astaire and Ginger Rogers in the film *Top Hat*, shortly before being executed. He whispers to himself, "Why, these angels . . . just like up in heaven." The scene epitomizes the manner in which whiteness serves as the cultural default for *The Green Mile* and highlights the echoes of an Uncle Tom sensibility at work in Coffey's character.

In *Playing the Race Card*, Linda Williams asks, "Why, in an era in which the figure of the Tom has been so thoroughly discredited by blacks and whites alike, such a Tom-like hero has been resuscitated in the exaggerated body of a black giant." She then surmises that Coffey's reconfigured Tom scenario "is necessary to perform melodrama's moral legibility," allowing the film to "safely re-enact all the worst anti-Tom scenarios of the paranoid white racist imagination, apparently in order to disavow them" (303). The question to ask of Frank Darabont's *The Green Mile* is, Does the film accomplish such disavowal? Its intention, no doubt, is to transcend all such questions and motivations about race with a larger, more universal message about Christian suffering and love. But, even if effective in this regard, what if the unintended effect of that transcendence is a false view of historical social reality? A possible answer to that question may be suggested by the film's mass appeal, particularly for white audiences, which may indicate that historical reality is secondary to a desire to believe that the pain endured by blacks is *not* racially specific, that in their suffering they are "just like us"—needing to overcome *universal* human suffering through Christian redemption. Such a conception conveniently eliminates racism as a fundamental element of white people's contribution to that suffering

Williams's discussion of the post–civil war "Tommer" stage shows indicates that they "served the purpose of humanizing whites in their own eyes by claiming fellow feeling with a nostalgicized way of life associated with slavery" (86). Does *The Green Mile*, then, offer a post–civil rights parallel in which whites are humanized in their own eyes by projecting a nostalgicized way of life associated with race relations in the South in the 1930s? Is the enduring moral dilemma posed by *The Green Mile* and its echoes of white-inspired slave characters from the past that whites desperately want to see themselves as better than their history and even their own actions reveal them to be? In this respect, one can understand Spike Lee's contention that when he saw *The Green Mile* he knew Michael Clarke Duncan would get an Academy Award nomination, since "the Academy just loves roles like that because it makes them feel so liberal" (205).

On some level, Harriet Beecher Stowe, Mark Twain, and Joel Chandler Harris probably felt a similar liberal self-satisfaction in their manifestations of the Tom character, since their creations served the necessary purpose within the immediate context and aftermath of slavery of convincing a white supremacist society that African Americans were indeed fully human. One can, of course, argue the point about the degree to which supremacist beliefs still operate in American society, despite the fantasy offered by the recent magical Negro films. Such arguments certainly surfaced in response to *The Green Mile*, suggesting to filmmakers in general that they recognize and dispense with, once and for all, "that grateful slave shit." When and if Spike Lee finds the financing he needs to make his already scripted *Spike Lee's Huckleberry Finn*, it should be instructive to see how Jim will appear through the eyes of a black filmmaker keenly attuned to both the destructive capabilities of the "Tom lens" and to twenty-first-century racial politics.

Chapter 10

White Soul

The "Magical Negro" in the Films of Stephen King

Sarah Nilsen

In the film version of Stephen King's *The Green Mile*, the magical Negro character, John Coffey, unjustly charged with committing a horrific interracial crime (the rape and murder of two white girls) is offered a final request before his execution for the brutal crimes of the real perpetrator: a white man. Revealing that he "ain't never seen me a flicker show," Coffey asks to see a movie. We then watch him transfixed, mouth agape, staring in awe at Fred Astaire singing, "Heaven, I'm in heaven" and dancing in the "Cheek to Cheek" number from *Top Hat*. This cinematic image of ecstatic heterosexual union makes Coffey murmur, "Angels, just like up in heaven."

Top Hat appears to offer the viewer a utopian vision of dominant culture through the heterosexual union of a white couple. But this image is mediated through the Christ-like eyes of Coffey who, in the film we are watching, has suffered the pains inflicted upon him by a racist society. King explained that Coffey, "who is obviously a Christ figure" is black "because his color makes certain that he will fry . . . Christ figures are supposed to do good to them that revile you, to turn the other cheek to those who strike you. By doing good for white people—and particularly the wife of the warden, the man who is going to put Coffey to death—he is basically exhibiting his saintliness" (Magistrale, *Hollywood's Stephen King*, 14). Are we to assume that Coffey is joyfully imagining his triumphant union with these white "angels" up in heaven after his unjust and brutal execution? What possible visual pleasure can cinema offer to those in the audience who stand outside of the dominant order? This chapter examines the way in which King has frequently returned to the figure of the magical Negro in his films in order to secure white masculinity and appease white guilt. As Linda Williams states, "What is striking in *The Green Mile* . . . is the remarkable extent to which the establishment of white virtue rests upon a paradoxical administration of pain and death to the black body so that white people may weep" ("Melodrama in Black and White," 20).

Charges of racism in the films of Stephen King entered into public discourse with the release of *The Green Mile*. As the film theorist Tania Modleski wrote in her essay "In Hollywood, Racist Stereotypes Can Still Earn Oscar Nominations," "films like this one enable white people to indulge their most prurient and fearful imaginings about African-Americans and have their dread symbolically exorcised, all the while allowing them to feel good about a black man's dying to preserve the status quo" (B10). Spike Lee made the film a center of his attack on mainstream media while touring with his just-released film, *Bamboozled*, a film about racism in the media. Speaking to students at Yale, he attacked King's creation of a "magical, mystical Negro." "They're still doing the same old thing," he argued, "recycling the noble savage and the happy slave" (Lee 1). Considering the paucity of nonwhite characters in King's cinematic universe, it is significant that when dominant African American characters do appear in *The Shining*, *The Stand*, *The Talisman*, and *The Green Mile*, they embody the stereotype of the magical Negro. King's work has become so associated with this figure that the *Wikipedia* entry for the "Magical Negro" lists his characters as emblematic of this stereotype.

Though several commentators have discussed the characteristics of the magical Negro as a racial archetype, there has been little consideration of the cultural and psychological significance of this representation. The films of Stephen King, therefore, provide an opportunity to theorize the constructed meaning of the magical Negro across the multiple axes of power that John Fiske has shown "crisscross our daily lives and the identities and relations that we form and re-form as we move through them" (*Media Matters*, 65). The analysis of how the figure of the magical Negro functions along the axes of race, gender, and sexuality reveals how "they are not so much stable social categories as axes of power along which strategies are deployed and tactics practiced: they are terrains of struggle" (*Media Matters*, 67). In the films of Stephen King, the magical Negro is a figure that is mobilized in a variety of axial relations in order to secure white masculinity.

In many ways the magical Negro is a monstrous creation. Characterized by a lack of history and a lack of any connection to a family or the community, he, and the character is typically a black male, has magical powers that mark him as otherworldly. His initial appearance disrupts the social order and yet his primary purpose within the narrative is to selflessly use his powers to save a white man. The lineage of the magical Negro in Hollywood films can be traced back to Sidney Poitier and his role in *The Defiant Ones* (1958). Released soon after the conflagration that was ignited surrounding desegregation in Little Rock, Arkansas, the film directly takes on the issue of race as a social problem told from a white, liberal point of view. K. Anthony Appiah called Poitier's character a saint and asked whether

> the Saint draws on the tradition of the superior virtue of the oppressed? Is there, in fact, somewhere in the Saint's background a theodicy that draws on the Christian notion that suffering is ennobling? So that the black person who represents underserved suffering in the American imagination can also, therefore, represent moral nobility? Does the Saint exist to address the guilt of white audiences, afraid that black people are angry at them, wanting to be forgiven, seeking a black person who is not only admirable and lovable, but who loves white people back? (Appiah 83)

Linkages can be made between the appearance of the magical Negro in films and times of social unrest and racial discord. These magical figures can be seen to function then as a means to appease the social anxiety of the dominant group by counteracting the racism that white audiences normally have toward black characters within mainstream films. "For white audiences, a saintly black character is the moral equivalent of a 'normal' white character" (Hicks 28).

One of the predominant explanations about racism in film tends to be culturalist, emphasizing how the racialized Other provides identity for the nonracialized white subject. In his famous explanation of orientalist racism, Edward Said explains that "the Orient helped to define Europe (or the West) as its contrasting idea, image, personality, experience. Yet none of this Orient is merely imaginative" (1–2). Following this argument, racism is linked to the nature of the social order and the identities produced within that order. The racism, then, of the individual subject under white supremacy partakes of the racism of the society as a whole. These individuals are socially constructed by a racist cultural orientation. A culturalist approach would help address the question of why the magical Negro exists in the work of Stephen King. In her article, "Reading King Darkly: Issues of Race in Stephen King's Novels," Samantha Figliola does take such an approach in her analysis of Stephen King's construction of race in his novels. Figliola argues that King has "drawn his black characters from a complex web of political and literary sources" including the work of Faulkner and especially the *Adventures of Huckleberry Finn*. I would also add the work of Leslie Fiedler, in particular *Love and Death in the American Novel* (1960), which King directly cites as an influence in interviews. Figliola provides these sources to argue that "while King does gravitate to certain 'types' of black heroes—primarily to nurturers—he does so consciously rather than through ignorance of bigotry" (143).

King's upbringing in the overwhelmingly white state of Maine is provided as the explanation for his lack of actual exposure to the black community. According to his own recollection, his time as a student in the late 1960s at the University of Maine in Orono was a formative period for his dawning realization of the issue of racism. In a 1984 interview, King stated that his understanding of race was primarily derived through television coverage. "Watts was going up in flames, and . . . Martin Luther King had been shot . . . At that time, college campuses were in revolt—utter revolt" (Beahm 46). King's recollection of those events typify the dominant ideological constructions of the civil rights movement by the late 1960s in which nonviolent political action had become replaced with images of social disorder and violence erupting from within the black community. According to King's American literature professor, King had also read Eldridge Cleaver's *Soul on Ice* and had decided that he was going to write about "white soul" (Figliola 145). In a 1983 interview with *Playboy*, King admitted his difficulty in developing believable black characters. He described both Hallorann in *The Shining* and Mother Abigail in *The Stand* as "cardboard caricatures of superblack heroes, viewed through rose-tinted glasses of white-liberal guilt" (Underwood and Miller 46).

What explains King's compulsion then to keep returning to the magical Negro? When challenged in an interview with Tony Magistrale about Spike Lee's attack on King's use of the magical Negro, King responded that "I am not surprised that this is Spike's reaction. It's a knee jerk reaction of a man who sees everything in terms of his race" (*Hollywood's Stephen King*, 14). King's denial of racial awareness belies the fact that he utilizes the magical Negro as a device to secure white masculinity against the threat of otherness, and, like Lee, he, too, sees everything in terms of his own race.

A multiaxial analysis of the magical Negro and gender and sexuality will reveal the manner in which race has been mobilized in King's films. As Fiske argues, "[g]ender difference is experienced and operationalized differently within different racial and class formations, and the differences are magnified when applied in interracial and interclass relations" (66). First, the magical Negro's existence is directly linked to a crisis of masculinity resulting from the declining economic status of the white protagonist. This crisis is seen most explicitly in *The Shining* (1980). Released during the waning years of the Carter administration, the power of white masculinity had suffered significantly because of the losses of the Vietnam War and the impeachment of Nixon. Additionally, the perceived successes of the women's and civil rights movements challenged the stability of white male identity. With the transformation from a manufacturing to a service economy, working and middle-class white men experienced a significant alteration of their work lives. Donna Haraway has described this transformation as a "feminization of work" in which "work is being defined as both literally male and female and feminized, whether performed by men and women. To be feminized means to be made extremely vulnerable; able to be disassembled, reassembled, exploited as a reserve force; seen less as workers than as servers; subjected to time arrangements on and off the paid job that make a mockery of a limited work day; leading to an existence that always borders on being obscene, out of place, and reducible to sex" (Haraway 166).

Reduced to the feminine role of the caretaker after losing his job as a teacher, Jack Torrance struggles to fit into a changing social order. The character of Jack draws on King's own work experiences in which he suffered through a series of hellish jobs, including work at a commercial laundry, while attempting to become a writer and support his young family. Unable to function within the new workforce, strapped down by familial demands, emasculated by the patriarchal forefathers that haunt the Overlook, Jack's only viable response to his feminization as a male is the turn toward physical force and violence. As he obsessively reiterates, "All work and no play makes Jack a dull boy." In *The Green Mile*, the daily job of the prison guards is as caregivers to the prisoners. When Edgecomb lectures Percy for scaring the prisoners, the latter responds that they are not running a "cradle school." Occurring during the Depression, when jobs are scarce, the male guards are forced to "play a domestic role in relation to their infantilized prisoners" (Hicks 39). Work is the formative social force in King's cinematic world that directly shapes the male protagonists' subjectivity and ties them to the social order.

In comparison, the magical Negro characters are not defined by their relation to the workplace or family. Rather than shaped by the same social pressures that define white masculinity, their subjectivity is dependent upon innate special magical powers endowed by nature.

These powers are necessarily linked to their race, and also lead to their death. What would appear to be a special gift, the ability to see the future or the past, is, in fact, an unbearable burden because it forces these characters to look at the horrors of a society from which they are excluded. Rather than being able to use their powers to liberate themselves or their community, in fact, these characters are often sacrificed in order to sustain the white social order. Hallorann has inherited from his grandmother the ability to shine, a term King admitted was a "pejorative word for 'Black'" (Underwood 125). His first appearance occurs when the Torrances arrive to take over care of the hotel. Hallorann's presence is easily overlooked by Delbert Grady who views him as a "nigger cook," doubly removed from the imperatives of white masculinity. His ability to shine, though, is immediately recognized by Danny, thus equating those powers with something childlike, pre-Oedipal and beyond the Symbolic. He immediately offers up his powers to protect Danny and his family against the supernatural forces of the hotel, which during all his years at the hotel have never troubled him. Apparently, Danny is a much greater threat to the legacy of castrating masculine forces inhabiting the hotel than Hallorann had ever been, and it is Danny's power that the hotel is most interested in subsuming. Called back to the hotel by Danny, when Hallorann does arrive he is easily killed by Jack, since he was either unable to shine his own death or because he was willing to sacrifice himself in order to help Danny survive.

During the making of the film, Kubrick had suggested an ending in which Hallorann returns and kills the family. But this idea had to be dismissed because the powers of the magical Negro must be used for the protection—and not the destruction—of white society. As Patricia Hill Collins has argued, "[a]s the 'Others' of society who can never really belong, strangers threaten the moral and social order. But they are simultaneously essential for its survival because those individuals who stand at the margins of society clarify its boundaries. African-American women [and men], by not belonging, emphasize the significance of belonging" (Collins 68).

John Coffey in *The Green Mile* has no prior identity before his appearance at the prison for the crime he is accused of committing. King states that "as far as using his powers to help his race, he has no family; he's a total loner. Whatever past he has is completely lost, and that's crucial to the story" (Magistrale, *Hollywood's Stephen King*, 14). When asked where his powers came from, Coffey responds, "Don't know much of anything. Never had." Coffey also only uses his powers to save others and right the wrongs in an otherwise decent and ordered society. He has not been able to protect himself from the scars that he carries and he cannot save himself from own execution. His powers force him to carry within himself the legacy of racism in this country, and his scars are literal signifiers of this legacy.

We are meant to feel relief when Coffey asks for his own death. When Edgecomb asks Coffey to expunge him of his responsibility in killing one of God's miracles, Coffey responds, "Tell God, the Father, it was a kindness you done. I want it to be over and done with." White people are comforted in his death because his suffering will end— not American racism, just Coffey's stake in it. As Nöel Carroll has explained about King's work, "the horror story can be conceptualized as a symbolic defense of a culture's standards of normality; the genre employs the abnormal, only for the purpose of showing it vanquished by the forces of the normal. The abnormal is allowed center stage solely as a foil to the cultural order, which will ultimately be vindicated by the end of the fiction" (*The Philosophy of Horror*, 199).

Another key axial relationship in King's use of the magical Negro as a narrative trope is the alignment of race and femininity because of their mutual powerful and different sexuality. When asked about his inability to create believable women, King admitted that "it is proba- bly the most justifiable" of all the criticisms leveled against him and equated it with his difficulty in handling black characters (Underwood 47). King cited Leslie Fiedler's *Love and Death in the American Novel* as confirming the manner in which he depicted women in his own work as "either bitches or zeroes. There's no in between, no real women" (Underwood 94). The sexual potency of both the female and magical Negro characters in *The Shining* and *The Green Mile* are directly linked with the white male protagonist's own impotence and castration anxiety. King's 1983 interview with *Playboy* is particularly revelatory in explaining why impotence is a key aspect of King's construction of white masculinity. When asked if there was any "bogeymen hiding in [his] libido," King responded "the only sexual problem that [I've] had was more functional. Some years ago, [I've] suffered from periodic impotence, and that's no fun, believe me" (Underwood 45).

The casting of Rebecca De Mornay as Wendy in the television miniseries of *The Shining* (1997) indicates King's intention to create a sexually provocative and powerful female protagonist. In the scene titled, "Caretaking Required," Wendy, clad in white silk lingerie, forcefully seduces Jack, cooing, "I've got something for you, if you want it." She, too, like the hotel, could "use some caretaking." When Jack attempts to thwart her efforts, she brings up his prior difficulties with impotency when he had been drinking. "You're not drinking anymore," Wendy taunts, "but all your old drinking habits are back." Emasculated, Jack succumbs to her demands, leading to Jack's resumption of drinking and his murderous pursuit of Wendy and Danny. When given the choice between Wendy in silk lingerie or a drinking session with the Overlook's spirits in the bar, Jack prefers the hangover over the sex.

The choice of both Scatman Crothers and Melvin Van Peebles as Halloran is also telling and relates to King's admission that his black characters were based on "superblack heroes." Both Crothers and Van Peebles played "superblack heroes" in the blaxploitation films of the 1970s that celebrated the hypersexuality of black masculinity. Halloran's identity is primarily defined by his magical powers, until we are taken, in the Kubrick film, into the private sanctum of his bedroom. There, unexpectedly, hang two paintings of nude black women that overwhelm the scene, emphasizing Halloran's overt sexuality. In the television miniseries, Van Peebles is literally dressed as a pimp in a velvet red suit and he drives a convertible Cadillac. In both adaptations of the novel, Halloran returns in order to align himself with Wendy against Jack. In the film version, this alignment leads to the butchering of Halloran after he supplies Wendy and Danny with the snowcat so that they can flee the hotel; while in the television version, though severely wounded, he is able to help Wendy and Danny flee the hotel. As Williams shows, "the power and potency of the monster body . . . should not be interpreted as an eruption of the normally repressed animal sexuality of the civilized male (the monster as double for the male viewer and characters in the film), but as the feared power and potency of a different kind of sexuality (the monster as double for the women)" ("When a Woman Looks," 20).

Impotence is also a problem for Edgecomb in *The Green Mile* because of a urinary infection. When Coffey first arrives at the Green Mile, Edgecomb is in the bathroom hunched over in pain. An ongoing motif in the film is Edgecomb grabbing his crotch in pain or straining to urinate. His cure at the hands of Coffey creates an exceptional potency on his part that is not normal for him. Able to have sex with his wife four times that night, he later admits to Coffey that his wife was pleased, thanks to him, "several times." Coffey's black sexual potency becomes tied directly to the monstrous feminine in his encounter with the warden's wife. Because of a brain tumor she has become a "foul-mouthed" harridan whose sexual crudity has made her into an embarrassing pariah in the community. When Coffey arrives, under the cover of night to help cure her, the guards and the warden stand around powerless and unknowing in the face of Coffey's power and dominance. Coffey's first vision of the wife is the illicit gaze of the black rapist through the crack of the door. Sprawled across the bed, with her nightgown up over her thighs, the wife encounters Coffey's eye and cries, "Don't come near me, pig fucker." As Coffey leans over her intimately, enacting the most feared act of miscegenation, he sucks part of her into himself in an interracial kiss. After this highly sexualized exchange, she acknowledges their commonality, "I dreamed of you," she reveals. "I dreamed you were wandering in the dark and so was I. And we found each other in the dark." As Linda Williams states, "Coffey's miracles entail repeated, ritualistic, prophylactic enactments of interracial sexual threats that ultimately function to master white fear and paranoia" ("Melodrama in Black and White," 18). Those enactments of these interracial sexual threats are what lead to our acceptance of Coffey's execution as a necessary kindness. "This would help explain the often vindictive destruction of the monster in the horror film and the fact that this destruction generates the frequent sympathy of the women characters, who seem to sense the extent to which the monster's death is an exorcism of the power of their own sexuality" (Williams, "Melodrama in Black and White," 23–24).

The most striking axial relation fuctioning in the construction of the magical Negro in King's films is a homosexual one. King uses the magical Negro to represent a natural form of interracial homosocial bonding in contrast to more homophobic renderings of predatory homosexuality. The clearest filmic rendering of this relationship can be found in *The Shawshank Redemption*, *The Shining*, and *The Green Mile*. In *The Shawshank Redemption*, the seemingly platonic love relationship between Andy and Red is juxtaposed with the most horrific images of gay rape. The homoerotic implications of the relationship between Red and Andy are seemingly neutralized through the cinematic fantasy of Rita Hayworth. Significantly, in a scene that is reminiscent of Coffey's first experience of cinema as an introduction to heteronormative sexuality, Andy also is aligned with straight, white desire through the cinematic image of Rita Hayworth. This image coincides with a homosexual assault from The Sisters. As Eve Kosofsky Sedgwick has written, the path of heterosexual desire is deeply homosocial, for even within the heterosexual circuit, "we are in the presence . . . of a desire to consolidate partnership with authoritative males in and through the bodies of females. . . . Men's heterosexual relationships . . . have as their raison d'etre an ultimate bonding between men" (*Between Men*, 38).

The central argument about the homoerotic interracial bond as a narrative device and its influence on King can again be traced to Fiedler's *Love and Death in the American Novel*. In Fiedler's linking of Negro and Native American characters and homosexuality as intertwined in white male bonding narratives of the American literary tradition, Fiedler constructs a "developmental narrative of sexual desire that locates the homoerotic in an imaginary, presymbolic realm, while casting the heterosexual on the side of uncontested Law, a formulation that reiterates the cultural compulsion toward maintaining heterosexuality as a simultaneously compulsory and natural psychic development" (Wiegman, "Fiedler and Sons," 49). In *The Shining*, Danny and Hallorann are bonded together because of their supernatural abilities. Their unity against the patriarchal order of the hotel leads to Jack's violent unrest and the awakening of what Pauline Kael described as "a hideous debauch when Wendy sees two figures in the bedroom—one of them, wearing a dog costume, who looks up at her while . . . still bent over the genitals of a man in evening clothes" (4). Jack then is posed, as he struggles under the demands of heterosexuality, between the homosocial bonds of Danny and Hallorann, and the horror of homosexual perversity.

Similarly, in *The Green Mile*, the homosocial bond shared by Coffey and Edgecomb deflects any of the possibilities of homosexual rape implied by Coffey's initial grabbing of Edgecomb's crotch. Later in the film, in a parallel scene, homosexual desire becomes equated with something perverse and sadistic as Billy the Kid grabs Percy and, while groping him, whispers in his ear that he is soft like a girl, and that he wants to fuck his asshole. Immediately before Percy shoots Billy the Kid, he again taunts him by saying, "Want to suck my dick." The homosocial bond then between both Danny and Hallorann and Coffey and Edgecomb is a friendship dependent on the necessary sacrifice of the magical Negro so that white masculinity can be sustained, simultaneously negating homosexual desire. As Wiegman argues, "Fiedler's redefinition of the U.S. literary landscape simultaneously reads and encodes the transformation of the historic agency of African American protest into a sentimental male bonding relation. Such sentimentalization emerges as the definitive mark of white masculine subjectivity, integrating both 'Negro and homosexual' as thematic concerns while negating their subjective personalities as components not only of the category of 'man,' but of 'America' as well" ("Fiedler and Sons," 52).

One of King's most fantastic cinematic renderings of the magical Negro occurs in the Michael Jackson short film, *Ghosts*. Cowritten with Stephen King and shot in 1997 with the special effects wizard, Stan Winston, the 35-minute film cost over $15 million, more than any other Jackson video. King wrote the first screenplay in 1993 but the production was shelved because of allegations against Jackson of sexual misconduct with children. Set in the mythical town of Normal Valley where, as the population sign says, "Nice Regular People" live, all the male children have been supposedly frightened by the local magical Negro, Maestro (Jackson), who inhabits a haunted castle on the hill. The white mayor (also played by Jackson in white face) arrives with parents and children in tow in order to expel the Maestro from their town.

The multiaxial alignments that occur in this film are particularly fraught with tension because of the casting of Michael Jackson as not only the magical Negro but also as the character of emasculated, white masculinity in the figure of the mayor. Corpulent, sweating, dressed in a monochromatic grey suit and wearing glasses, the mayor, caretaker of Normal Valley, is powerless in even persuading the group of suburban parents he leads to help him cast out the monster in their town. Lacking the physical force or charisma of white masculinity, he resorts to childish taunts, such as "Back to the circus, you freak," to threaten the Maestro. The alignment of white masculinity with feminization and repression is counteracted by the monstrous potency of the magical Negro. The Maestro reveals his horrific powers by pulling open his mouth to expose a massive phallic tongue. Through the use of special effects, the Maestro and "his family" of ghouls perform, while the Maestro continues to morph into a variety of forms, culminating with his transformation into a dancing skeleton moonwalking for the watching audience of children and parents. The Maestro is then sucked into the mayor's body, and, as in *The Green Mile*, the magical Negro provides the fantastic image of white male repression unleashed. The mayor, still bloated and bland, begins to dance, like Michael Jackson, repeatedly grabbing his crotch and thrusting his hips toward the children and parents. Once the Maestro leaves the mayor's body though, he returns to his previous state and continues his effort to expel the Maestro. But his powers have been fully depleted and he eventually leaves the castle alone.

The real axial relation that drives this narrative is the one between the Maestro and the boys. At the end of the film, it is the boys who want the Maestro to stay and the boys who put on the Maestro's mask. The innocence of this interracial, homosocial bond, which, as previously mentioned, appears in other Stephen King films, becomes problematic when considered within the context of pedophilia. King, in his column for *Entertainment Weekly*, defends Jackson by asking "whether this is a country where a peculiar person such as Michael Jackson can get a fair shake and be considered innocent until proven guilty . . . or is this just a twenty-first century American barnyard where we all feel free to turn on the moonwalking rooster . . . and peck it to death?" ("You Don't Know Jackson," 80).

A multiaxial reading of the magical Negro in the films of Stephen King illustrates how this racialized trope is a manifestation of troubled white masculinity that functions to maintain the dominant order while appeasing white liberal guilt. How, then, does the magical Negro help to answer charges of racism in King's films? K. Anthony Appiah's own attempt to read race in our culture is instructive in helping to answer this question: "If the film reflects a racist or homophobic culture," he argues, "then what's wrong is that the culture is racist or homophobic: the film's just a symptom and boycotting is like blowing the smoke when we should be dousing the fire. If a film reinforces racism, then what's wrong is that it makes the culture more racist than it would have been otherwise" (85).

Chapter 11

Reaganomics, Cocaine, and Race

David Cronenberg's Off-Kilter America and *The Dead Zone*

Sarah E. Turner

Although John Smith, no middle initial, was long dead and in his grave before the first hip-hop single hit the charts, Nelson George's comments regarding the ubiquitous nature of crack and cocaine in the black community—and the inability or refusal by the rest of the country to adequately address this issue—provide an interesting lens through which to consider David Cronenberg's 1983 film *The Dead Zone*. "During the eight years of Reagan's presidency, the ripple effect of crack flowed through all the social service agencies of our country—welfare, child care, Medicaid, you name the area of concern and crack's impact could be felt in it" (George 41). While King's 1979 novel ends with the posthumous voice of Smith asking Sarah whether she was still using that "wicked cocaine"—that oft-repeated drug reference is entirely absent from the film. Highlighted instead are pictures of Ronald Reagan, who both haunts the perimeters of the film in framed photographs and in the character of Greg Stillson.[1] Within the pages of the novel, John Smith's numerous references and allusions to Sarah's cocaine habit serve to locate the text firmly in the Reagan years, and yet, the film lacks such a contextualization—while there are visual reminders of Reagan's presidency, not to mention the character of Greg Stillson, the focus on drugs is noticeably absent. While it might be argued that this is simply Cronenberg's decision to focus on other aspects of the novel, it is interesting to consider this lack in light of the omnipresence of snow in the film.

William Beard writes of Cronenberg's dominant sensibility of "resignation, sadness, an undertone of grief and a dedication to isolation and impotence" common across the body of his work but most prevalent in *The Dead Zone* ("Anatomy," 177). And yet, Cronenberg's vision of King's text reflects not the desolation of the human heart but instead a pessimistic commentary on the state of racial relations and tensions in America in 1983. Judith Halberstam defines gothic fiction as "a technology of subjectivity, one which produces the deviant subjectivities opposite which the normal, the healthy, and the *pure* can be known" (emphasis mine) (2). Thus, the monster is positioned as deviant, as outside the status quo or hegemonic culture (which, in this country, is white), abnormal to the norms of whiteness, impure as measured against the purity of whiteness. John Smith's otherness, then, is not simply linked to his freakish and often terrifying second sight; his otherness is made monstrous because his subjectivity is defined as racialized Other. His monstrous body is not the body found in King's novel—scarred both from the accident and then the various surgeries that attempted to return Smith to a kind of normalcy. Indeed, in the novel, characters comment frequently upon the visibility and the impact of those scars: "there was a hideous Frankenstein scar running up out of his coat collar to just under his jaw" (*The Dead Zone*, 360) "and those scars running up and down his neck" (357). Instead, his filmic body signifies a sense of otherness, monstrous because of what it is not. "Monsters have to be everything the human is not, and, in producing the negative of human, [gothic] novels make way for the invention of human as white, male, middle class, and heterosexual" (Halberstam 22).

As representative of this "normative heterosexuality," Greg Stillson and Frank Dodd subvert easy definitions of the "monster," at the same time reversing the binary oppositions of white/black and good/evil, an inversion that underscores Cronenberg's *Dead Zone* as a critique of American race relations. It may seem odd to argue that Cronenberg's vision of *The Dead Zone* can be read as a commentary on American racism and racial relations, given the complete absence of racial otherness in the film's 105 minutes, save for the brief shot of an Asian American man in the band that plays outside at the Stillson rally in the latter part of the film.[2] However, it is the very absence of color, reified through the construction of John Smith as monstrous other, that forces the viewer to consider the question of race and what that absence suggests.

Noticeably present because of their absence is both the novel's joking reference to Sarah's cocaine habit and anyone who is not a member of the hegemonic culture. Granted, the film is set in an unnamed New England locale, of which Maine and Vermont are the whitest in the country, but the movie's omnipresent whiteness—the milk that pours out of the truck when John Smith's Volkswagen collides with it; the ubiquitous snow that provides the backdrop for many of the shots; the white picket fences and window casings that frame Smith and place him, time and time again, outside the scene or the crowd—all of these referential points remind the viewer that the opposite, blackness, is noticeably and deliberately absent.[3] In this way, seeing Smith frequently outside the action, voyeuristically taking part but not actually active himself, underscores the reading of this text that posits him as representational of otherness/blackness.

The opening shots of the movie dwell lovingly on white picket fences and idyllic New England homes and yet, slowly, the idyllic shots are overshadowed or "blacked" out by what appear initially to be random black shapes, first triangular and then more abstract, that slowly obfuscate the scene. Eventually, these blacked-out spaces join together to form the title of the film and all but obscure the anonymous solitary figure walking along a rural road. The figure is indistinguishable—neither black nor white, just solitary—but the juxtaposition of the obfuscating black shapes and the idealized white images call to mind a set of binary oppositions that situate black *against* white, other against dominant.

In his book-length study of Cronenberg's canon, William Beard makes much of the milk truck that Smith collides with, connecting the milk to mothers, maternity, and, in a sense, emasculation. He also questions why viewers need to know it was a milk truck, and not some other kind of truck (lumber comes to mind, given the New England locale) (*Artist as Monster*, 172–73). Ultimately, however, it is specifically the whiteness of the milk that subsumes Smith and his car that is inherent to the underlying racial message of the text—whiteness attacks him, almost takes his life, and plunges him into the role of Other/blackness that he assumes.

This would explain, then, Cronenberg's decision to open the film with John Smith reading Edgar Allan Poe's "The Raven" to his middle-school students, a decision that is both intriguing and troubling in that he sets a tone of racial intolerance from the opening shots.[4] Although much has been said about the parallels between John Smith and the narrator of the poem, and the obvious references and fanatical brooding on the embodiment of Poe's Lenore in the figure of Sarah, there is another, much "darker" reading of Cronenberg's decision to reference Poe. Poe's poem, albeit about lost love and questionable sanity, also reflects Poe's truly American gothic side in its fear of blackness and by extension, black characters and imagery.

Missing from Cronenberg's interpretation of King's book are black characters[5]; instead, he constructs for his viewers a primary character who is positioned as "Other" and then marginalized as a result. Leper-like, people are afraid of John Smith and are unwilling to touch him, to take his hand. There is an interesting parallel between the figure of John Smith and that of John Coffey in *The Green Mile*—in that both men are sideshow freaks who are destined to die—no one can or is willing to save them. In a sense, that is why, King argues, it is neces-sary that Coffey is a black man. But in this case, although John Smith, as played by Christopher Walken, is clearly white, he is constructed as racial Other after the accident that gives him his "second sight."

In an interview between King and Magistrale in *Hollywood's Stephen King*, the latter questions King's construction of Coffey as a black man, a question that seems to affront King:

TM: Does John Coffey have to be black? What happens to the film's meaning if he is a white character?

SK: In most cases you can cast a character in either race. Morgan Freeman in *Shawshank* could have been cast as a white man. But in the case of John Coffey, he's supposed to be black because that puts him in a situation where the minute he gets caught with those two little blond girls in his arms, he's a doomed man.

TM: . . . If John Coffey is a Christ figure, he's also a *black* Christ; his suffering, it seems to me, becomes all the more profound because he is black and a victim of wounds that are particular to his racial history.

SK: I think your answer represents an imaginative failing on your part. (14–15)

Is it then possible also to picture John Smith as a *black* Christ figure? Or as the original *black* Christ figure, John Coffey's antecedent, as this film predates *The Green Mile* by 16 years (1983/1999). To paraphrase Magistrale, what would happen to *The Dead Zone* if Morgan Freeman had been cast as John Smith, a character whose very name suggests he is both every man and no man in particular? On many levels, it would be impossible to cast a black actor in this role as that would undermine the construction of John Smith, monstrous Other to the hegemonic culture, when he emerges from the coma. John Smith must be white because he is "every man" and every man in America is, as per the status quo, white; that realization in itself suggests a problematic reality regarding race relations in the United States.

Chris Rodley outlines Cronenberg's fascination with the "breakdown of social order" in the introduction to *Cronenberg on Cronenberg* (xvii).

Perhaps, Rodley suggests, it is Cronenberg's Canadianess that enables him to comment so subtly and yet so successfully on American culture in this filmic text. Rodley goes on to note, "*The Dead Zone* marks the beginning of a much more personalized, claustrophobic, interiorized and affecting cinema for Cronenberg" (xx). This personalized and claustrophobic cinema resonates with references to American gothic, especially southern gothic—the interiority and the fear of blackness. Never does the viewer see Smith looking at himself; although framed frequently throughout the film by windows and door frames, absent are mirrors or a sense that Smith has actually seen what others see in him, namely, his otherness. Instead, viewers are given frequent images of Hydes to his Dr Jekyll in the figures of Dodd and Stillson—both in person and in the looming election posters, billboards, and buttons— monsters in their own right, as white and wicked inversions of John's savior-like status as black Christ.

Late in the film, John Smith confronts Sam Weizak with a question regarding history and the ability to change it. Smith asks Weizak if he would kill Hitler if he could go back in time, armed with the knowledge of history and hindsight. Weizak's response is that as a man of science and medicine, who loves people, he most certainly would kill Hitler. This response not only solidifies Smith's intention to kill Greg Stillson, the latter linked to Hitler throughout the film, but even more important to this reading of the text, it also raises the specter of Stillson's Armageddon as a racial war, not a nuclear war. Hitler's genocide of the Jews, gypsies, homosexuals, and the disabled is reenvisioned in Stillson's warped mind as a genocide against all those not white—specifically those in America he sees as causing unemployment and inflation: blacks and other minorities. While Stillson is careful in his campaign rhetoric to avoid any direct references to those outside of the hegemonic culture, it is clear that Stillson is referring to blacks and other minorities as the root cause for his rhetorical question, "what has happened to this country?" Stillson's campaign is most appropriately read as a white-supremacist campaign to "clean up America" evidenced through the complete absence of anyone not white at the various rallies and town meetings he holds.[6]

There is only one direct reference to America's black population, made at the end of Stillson's visit with Chris's father, Roger Stuart, when Stillson jokingly refers to his opponent's practice of "buying black votes in the ghetto." Into this xenophobic exchange steps John Smith and Stillson presses a campaign button into his hand in passing. In the previous scene, just after meeting Chris's father, the camera frames John in the door of his home as he looks out at the oversized campaign billboard of Stillson directly facing his home. Stillson is once again framed, this time by the television screen in the Stuarts' home, as John and Roger watch Stillson speaking of unemployment in America. The parallels between Stillson as politician-actor and Reagan as actor-politician cannot be overlooked. Jonathan Crane argues, "[M]aybe Cronenberg is a conservative at heart, but, if so, it would be hard to identify any latter-day conservative tougher on things as they are than the author of [this] film" (65). Crane's comment suggests that earlier readings of this film have perhaps misread or underread Cronenberg's intentions in that his seemingly conservative nature is instead a harsh criticism on the Reagan years, the rise of the conservative right, and the institutionalized racism suggested both by the group of *white* men to whom Stillson announces "the missiles are flying" in Smith's vision and by the conspiracy theory that connected the CIA to the rising crack epidemic in the inner cities of America. Nelson George's comments on "police impotence in cleaning neighborhood of drug trafficking and our government's failure in drug interdiction (or complicity in the trade) produced cynicism and alienation that made Nancy Reagan's 'Just Say No' campaign a joke" (42) make the absence of an antidrug campaign in Stillson's platform all the more salient.

Chris Rodley informs us that "ironically, [Jeffrey] Boam had completed his first draft of *The Dead Zone* for Lorimar the day Ronald Reagan was elected President" (113). Cronenberg talks about the various other scripts for *The Dead Zone*, including one written by King himself, that he rejected because of their tendency to focus on the grotesque, the shock value; instead, he chose Boam's text because of its focus on John Smith—his character and his story.[7] Rodley's use of the term "ironic" must be read through the lens of Crane's recognition of Cronenberg as a conservative with a conscience—the presence literally and metaphorically of Reagan in the text—through photographs as well as Greg Stillson's character (113–114). The most notable example of this takes place in the office of Mr Brenner, editor of the local newspaper. With Reagan's head shot looming over his shoulder, Stillson disenfranchises Brenner and undermines his freedom of speech through intimidation and blackmail.

In the Peter Morris biography of Cronenberg, the director relates a fascinating anecdote about a man who, in commenting on Cronenberg's Canadianness, says "the fact that you make your films in Canada makes them even more eerie and dreamlike, because it's like America, but it's not. The streets look American, but they're not, and the accents are American, but not quite. Everything's a little off kilter;

it's a sort of dream like image of America" (106). *The Dead Zone* was filmed in Niagara-on-the-Lake, a small town south of Toronto, Canada, which, even in 1983, was racially diverse, certainly much more so than Maine or New Hampshire, and yet the crowd scenes and classrooms are uniformly white. Cronenberg, it seems, must have gone out of his way to ensure that no one outside the parameters of the hegemonic culture was captured by the gaze of his camera. Why? The verisimilitude of his construction of America seems questionable. King does not specify in his text that the crowds or students are uniformly white, just that often they are working-class mill hands and students. The description of Cronenberg's America as "a little off kilter" illustrates the sophistication and complexity of his vision; his America, thus, may not deal directly with drug epidemics and racism, but these issues haunt the film's perimeters, much like the image of Reagan. With this in mind, Stillson's political platform is intriguing because, while he does focus on unemployment and inflation, he makes no mention whatsoever of the "ripple effect of crack" or the looming specter of middle-class drug use (George 41).

In trying to define this film, and arguing that *The Dead Zone* represents a shift away from the horror films of Cronenberg's earlier work, Magistrale argues that this film does not reflect Cronenberg's tendency toward what James Verniere has labeled a "kind of cinema of pathology in which the ultimate horror is the horror of a diseased psyche" (*Hollywood's Stephen King*, 124). However, the diseased psyche is exactly what this film attacks: the diseased psyche of an America in which racism and racial intolerance are still rampant. Magistrale describes John Smith's ability to "view certain trenchant past and future events that are connected to *any* person with whom he comes into direct personal contact" (emphasis mine), but this is not true (119). Smith is shown taking his mother's hand both shortly after he emerges from what she describes as a "trance" and again at her deathbed, and in neither instance do visions or psychic reactions take place. The same is true when Smith has contact with his father, Weizak, and Sarah; he hugs and touches his father on several occasions without repercussions, and, beyond the initial moment of contact with Weizak where he "sees" his mother, John is able to shake hands or be touched by the doctor without a vision. Moreover, he has sex with Sarah—perhaps the ultimate in "direct personal contact"—and yet never in the film does he have visions of Sarah or events connected to her life.

I argue that this absence of psychic visions is the consequence of the ability of those intimate with John and his life precoma to still see him as he was, before he was constructed as John Smith, monstrous Other. Although Weizak was not familiar with the "precoma" John Smith, the fact that he is a Polish Jew who immigrated to this country allows him to also see the man as he was. With the exception of Chris, it is only those who perceive and ultimately shun the John Smith reborn as Other who "benefit" from his visions. Each person who is the recipient or focus of his visions (with the exception of Sam Weizak) views Smith with distaste, animosity, distrust, or out and out hatred—Mrs. Dodd calls him a "devil sent from hell" and the television reporter calls him a "fucking freak" after Smith "sees" the reporter's dead drug-addicted sister Terry; even the nurse whose house is burning shuns him after her daughter is saved. There is reluctance on the part of many to have any physical contact with him, as if they might be tainted as a result. Sheriff Bannerman seemingly goes against his better judgment in seeking John out and, when confronted with the possibility that his own deputy might be responsible for all the killings, turns his anger and frustration on John and banishes him from Dodd's home. Roger Stuart also banishes Smith from his home and from his son Chris in a scene reminiscent of "whites only signs" and locales. Smith's first physical contact with Greg Stillson, at an outdoor rally, and his subsequent banishment from that public place at the hands of Stillson's goon Sonny, suggests that for a black man in America, public spaces are equated with white spaces.

William Beard spends much time discussing the repression he sees as central to the film and to John Smith's character; it is this belief in sexual repression that forms the mainstay for his assertion that Dodd is Smith's alter ego (*Artist as Monster*, 194). However, it is not exactly a sexual repression that keeps Smith from consummating his desires for Sarah; they do have one brief sexual encounter that must be read as "taboo" not because it is an act of adultery but because it is an act of interracial coupling. He "can't" have Sarah and, therefore, she must be married before he comes out of his coma because the American gothic tale that this text really mirrors will not allow the possibility of miscegenation (think of Faulkner's *Absalom! Absalom!* and the death of Charles Bon at the hands of Henry Sutpen). Smith is not the emasculated figure denying his sexuality because of some deep-seated Freudian repressions and longings *à la Psycho*, as Beard would argue; instead, his is a repression out of self-preservation. He is cognizant that the "normality" he seeks, a normality dictated by the dominant ideology around him—family, home, relationships—is denied to him because he is constructed as monster ("Anatomy," 171).

In an interview with Chris Rodley, Cronenberg talks about why the movie version completely rewrites the novel's scene with Chuck Chatsworth. Instead of a high-school formal after-party and lightning-induced fire that kills 90 of his classmates, Cronenberg gives us young Chris Stuart, whose megalomaniac father insists on a hockey practice on an only partially frozen pond even after John Smith has warned him not to. Two boys Chris's age drown as a result. Although it is possible to view the shift from roadhouse to hockey as simply an acknowledgment of Cronenberg's Canadian roots, when viewed through the lens of racism, it is so much more. Cronenberg claims he "hate[d] the boy in the [novel]; he's eighteen, and has a Corvette and a swimming pool and he's blond. I hate him" (Rodley 114). Yet, I argue the shift away from the slightly homoerotic tutor/student relationship between Johnny and Chuck is necessary because, as a child, Chris Stuart does not "see" Smith's blackness and thus is more capable of accepting him. He (Chris) can touch Smith, can be friends with Smith, can see him without a sense of revulsion, in a way that the older Chuck, in Cronenberg's version of this story, would not be able to do. He (Chris) can read sections of Poe's "The Raven" to Smith and not recognize the parallels between his tutor and the text—Cronenberg needed the innocence of the child to allow Smith some human contact that is not mediated by visions or voyeurism. This is clearly demonstrated in the scene where Chris asks, "why are you crying, Johnny?" following Smith's encounter with Sarah and her husband as they campaign for Stillson. Chris has not yet learned the racism and revulsion that dictates the reaction of the adults to Smith, but the filmic text suggests, once back under the officious eyes of his conservative father, Chris soon will.

As the antecedent to other Cronenberg films that depict their heroes as monsters, Jeff Goldbloom in *The Fly* and Jeremy Irons in *Dead Ringers*, Christopher Walken's Smith both fascinates and repulses—viewers are drawn to these characters and yet absolve themselves with the realization that they are not like those men. There is a striking similarity between John Smith and sexual psychopath Frank Dodd. They come from similar homes and have mothers with overlapping characteristics. Beard argues that in a sense the two figures are parallel and linked, and makes much of the scene in the film where Dodd looks out his prepubescent bedroom window, sees Smith in the street below, and nods (*Artist as Monster*, 182). Although Bannerman has ordered Smith to stay outside, after this cryptic exchange, Smith enters the house. What is fascinating about Dodd is his choice of apparel: the slick *black* raincoat he wears to shield his body from the frantic and desperate attempts by his victims to stop the inevitable. Smith also wears a *black* coat, collar up to shield his face when he is in public. Shots of him in the film use the coat as a central focus, not his face, so viewers are left with an impression of blackness rather than Smith himself. Are we to read these two men as *doppelgängers*? Beard would like to see these two in this way, a connection back to the Dr Jekyll and Mr Hyde mask that Johnny is wearing in the opening pages of the novel (186–187). I, too, see a connection between these two characters, but, if so, they are much more yin and yang. White Dodd, in his black coat, is the sadistic rapist and murderer, whereas Smith, as personification of blackness, is the hero who stops the serial killer and who, it can be argued, pushes the policeman to his grotesque and horrific suicide in the bathroom. In this case, black in the monstrous body and person of Smith triumphs over evil personified in the normative naked white body of Dodd, suggestive once again of Smith's construction as the antecedent to John Coffey's black Christ.

If we are to read John Smith, no middle initial, as a redemptive Christ figure as his final pose in the *mis-en-scene* of his death would suggest, he must be read as a sacrificial Christ figure ostracized and marginalized by his difference and the inability of the society around him to go beyond recognizing and actually embrace that difference. As a cultural commentary, then, this is a reactionary film that condemns an America that is "off kilter" with regard to racial relations; moreover, it is a challenge to change the vision of racial Armageddon that Smith "sees" when he shakes hands with Stillson and that perhaps Cronenberg, from the relative security of Canada, "sees" when he considers Reagan's America.

Notes

1. In the novel, the cocaine references serve to contextualize the text in the Reagan years; in the movie, instead we are given photos and veiled echoes of Reagan's policies.
2. Interestingly, King claims *The Dead Zone* is "the least offensive film I have made" (Rodley 114) and yet Rodley tells us that since *The Dead Zone* "also touched on politics, a subject Cronenberg hadn't dealt with before in the strict sense of the word[,] [s]ome critics . . . were uneasy with *The Dead Zone*'s (subordinate) political implications" (118).
3. In 1983, King was in rehab for his cocaine habits; it is fascinating to consider the ubiquitous snow through the lens of his drug addiction given that "snow" is one of the many slang terms for cocaine.

4. Much has been made of the use of Poe's "The Raven" in this text, but the text also calls to mind another Poe text: *The Narrative of A. Gordon Pym*, whose fear of the unknown whiteness can be clearly linked to the predominance of white images in Cronenberg's text.

5. While it must be noted that there aren't any clearly defined black or minority characters in the book, it does seem problematic that in the various crowd scenes in this movie, there is an almost complete absence of color.

6. With the exception of the already noted Asian American in the band who appears only briefly in a shot that pans the members of the bands; in a latter and more prolonged shot of the band, his head is obscured by the raised arm of the white man standing next to him, in a sense erasing his difference, as, from the neck down, he looks like all the other white members of the band.

7. Cronenberg claims that "Stephen King's own script was terrible . . . It was basically a really ugly, unpleasant slasher script" (Rodley 113).

Chapter 12

The Feminist King

Dolores Claiborne

Colleen Dolan

In the world we live in, feminism is a commitment and entertainment can be a luxury. My writing is entertainment.

Stephen King (Owen 47)

Dolores Claiborne has aged well. Now in my mid-fifties, I see this character as something of a role model. In some ways, I am Dolores. Mind you, I did not murder my ex-husband, but I have to admit the thought did cross my mind. I admire the way Stephen King fashioned a female character unfettered by others' opinion of her. He crafted a woman with a brusque surface, but a deep underlying sense of love and purpose. She is a character who acted with intensity and evolved over time. Her story pivots around the year 1963. Stephen King chose the year well. That was the year a full solar eclipse crossed Alaska, central and eastern Canada, and Maine. The event drew a great deal of media attention and a beautiful article about the eclipse appeared months later in the pages of the November 1963 issue of *National Geographic* (Espanek). One can imagine a young Stephen King perusing the article. Coincidently, that was also the year feminism reemerged from its years of remission after women's suffrage in 1920. It was the year feisty young women who grew up in "a man's world" would be presented with the option to "become the men we wanted to marry" (Steinem 263). Betty Friedan's *The Feminine Mystique* was released in 1963. It was also the year of the Equal Pay Act and the publishing of the *Report on the President's Commission on the Status of Women*, chaired by Eleanor Roosevelt until her death in 1962. Women had the vote, but it still seemed the status of women was second class and falling fast.

Set in the 1960s and 1980s, *Dolores Claiborne* is the story of a woman who reclaimed her selfhood through a violent act and rescued her daughter from a tidal wave of resultant neuroses. In setting the story tone, Dolores's employer, Vera Donovan, artfully played by Judy Parfitt in the movie *Dolores Claiborne*, said, "It's a painfully masculine world we live in, Dolores." Stephen King, our prolific chronicler of nightmares, observed the injustices directed toward women and captured the essence of it in Dolores's story.

Of course, no trend or movement is birthed with perfect shape or design intact. Stephen King wrote Dolores's story with the clarity of 22 years hindsight. I doubt, as a writer of popular fiction, he crafted female characters with the single intent of supporting a cause. Rather, he is a novelist who reflected upon what jarred our sensibilities and shriveled our guts. Many women failed to thrive under the oppressive conditions of the 1950s and 1960s. Still others suffered physical and emotional pain. The rights withheld from women at the time now seem so basic that young women may assume they have always been in place. As Ariel Levy notes,

> The women's movement introduced revolutionary ideas that caught on so thoroughly they now seem self-evident. That women don't automatically have to be mothers or (even) wives. That women are entitled to their constitutional guarantee of equal protection under the law. That women ought to be eligible to attend top schools (Princeton and Yale did not begin admitting female students until 1969; Harvard shared some classes with the women of Radcliffe as early as 1943 but did not fully integrate until 1972; Columbia was all male for undergraduates until 1983). That women should not be discriminated against in the workplace. That there is such a thing as a clitoris. (85)

King's writing reflected on the absurd attitude at the time that women could not handle even family finances. The bank scene in *Dolores Claiborne* attests to the institutional discrimination inherent in a male-centric society. The film version of *Dolores Claiborne* brought King's views on women to a wider audience. King may have used his storytelling skills to entertain us, but this story of Dolores's dilemma highlighted the inequalities that inspired second-wave feminism.

Dolores Claiborne, played perfectly by Kathy Bates in the film, was the wife of an abusive husband and father. King has pointed out to us on several occasions the tension inherent in sexual relationships. The sexual relationship of marriage equals male power (as is evident in the more realistic fiction King has published: *Gerald's Game*, *Dolores Claiborne*, *Rose Madder* and, more recently, *Lisey's Story*). Marriage can be a very dangerous institution. Dolores fought back. She told her husband that if he ever hit her again one of them would end up in "the bone yard." That act of courage and her statement foretell the action to follow. King placed the story of domestic violence within his own particular genre. As a gothic writer, King discerns our darkest, most evil intent, and digs in with his pen. An abused woman may imagine the death of her abuser, but would never commit the act. King allowed Dolores to take that imaginary death a step further and plan her husband's true demise.

Dolores is not an endearing character. In fact, King describes all the women of *Dolores Claiborne* with their foibles and faults intact. But he also shows us their innate strengths. King honors women by portraying us honestly. A misogynist would only respect a "perfect" woman . . . and that woman does not exist. For women to be accepted as we are in our most natural, awful, complex states, is to acknowledge our humanity and thus our equality with men. Had Dolores been an attractive, charming woman, would this book have held the same core of truth? Would Dolores, in the words of Carol A. Senf, have had an "authentic" voice? Senf writes in her essay "*Gerald's Game* and *Dolores Claiborne*: Stephen King and the Evolution of an Authentic Female Narrative Voice": "King creates plausible women characters who relate their own stories. It is as though King wants the reader to believe that he as novelist has turned the stories over to his women characters" (96). I agree. Stephen King obviously listened to several strong-willed women in his day and has a fine-tuned ear for the truth as filtered through a gothic story line. We read King's work to experience terror and exact revenge. In this case, we want Dolores to survive.

Although Dolores's point of view is central to the film and King's novel, this is a story of relationships: mother/daughter, employer/employee, pursuer/pursued, and that special form of love: friendship. The fluidly intertwined life cycle of women—daughter, mother, and crone—are represented in the three main characters: Selena St. George (Jennifer Jason Leigh), Dolores Claiborne (Kathy Bates), and Vera Donovan (Judy Parfitt). The format of the movie exposes us to Dolores's relationship with the other two women more so than does King's original story structure. In the novel, Dolores narrates a deposition, readily insulting and belittling the men in the room. With the exception of one quote from her dead husband, Joe, and a blurb in the local paper at the end, the novel is written entirely in Dolores's words. Unlike King's more convoluted narratives, such as *The Stand* or *Lisey's Story*, Dolores Claiborne's story is a straightforward accounting of events. She tells the truth: she killed her husband more than 30 years ago. She did not kill her employer, Vera Donovan, yesterday. Tony Gilroy's screenplay took this woman's words and adapted them into a visually satisfying series of flashbacks.

The film adaptation goes a step further, by placing Dolores's dilapidated house outside the village on Little Tall Island. The structure of Dolores's rough colloquial language and her working-class background in both the novel and the film demonstrates her differences from the literate reader and filmgoer. She alienates the people, especially the men, of Little Tall Island with her snappish tongue and sarcastic wit. Stephen King crafted Dolores as one of those steely-headed, truth-telling old women who make the rest of us cringe. Her tact filter is missing. She says whatever comes to mind and it is usually the ugly, critical truth. It is uncomfortable to watch onscreen and even sorrier to deal with in person. Women like Dolores repel us, perhaps because she is what Kathleen Margaret Lant and Theresa Thompson refer to as "the alien who lives with and within us—who frequently is 'us'—yet remains always Other to a male-centered culture: This creature is, of course, woman" (6). Dolores is the worst offender: an older, unattractive woman. Our present cultural morass notwithstanding, women, and especially older women, long held an archetypal presence as bearers of wisdom and truth. Since the medieval transformation of wise elder woman into witch, women who lived on the edges of civilization were deemed evil. "By persecuting them as witches, men sought to deprive them even of the last right of self-expression that powerless men claim for themselves: bitching" (Walker 138). That concept lingers on the edge of this film. The concept of a crone, an old woman living alone, easing pain and ushering in birth and death, carries the weight of centuries of negative advertising: "The real threat posed by older women in a patriarchal society may be the 'evil eye' of sharp judgment honed by disillusioning experience, which pierces male myths and scrutinizes male motives in the hard, unflattering light of critical appraisal" (Walker 122). Dolores is a modern witch, the independent, opinionated bitch. Vera, Dolores, and Selena share the quote, "Sometimes being a bitch is all a woman has to hold onto." Most of us have known women forged by life's abuses, and we tend to admire them . . . from a distance.

It is the simpler task to assign Dolores the role of witch than accept her in sisterhood. Yet, who among us has not suffered at the abusive hands of a bully and grown a bit tougher as a consequence? Or worse yet, who of us has not been a bully at one time or another and grown colder as a result? Are we really so very different from Dolores? Or

Joe? Edward F. Edinger writes in *Ego and Archetype*, "[A]t the root of violence of any form lies the experience of alienation—a rejection too severe to be endured" (44). Neither Joe nor Dolores is all that likable, nor has either of them had an easy time of it. Both commit violence. We are not privy to the details of Joe's fall from grace, but we do learn he came from wealth and now lives from hand-to-mouth, comforted by his vices. It seems possible that each of us, male and female, has the potential for becoming a Stephen King character.

So how does one live an *authentic* life without losing one's place in society? None of the three women in *Dolores Claiborne* is willing to choose "normal" polite behavior over self-preservation. Yet, they persevere and grow in strength in spite of and perhaps because of their ornery ways. What they lose is acceptance. Although the nature of normal behavior may be fluid and Dolores's standing in the Little Tall Island community is strained, the nature of abnormality is not. Quirky or abrasive as she may be, we can sympathize with Dolores because we have a common cultural understanding of certain behaviors as falling outside our boundaries. We can agree that emotional, physical, and sexual abuse is unnatural and unacceptable. We also agree that a mother may behave heroically to save her children. And so Dolores, while living outside our explicitly shared, mostly polite experience, picks up a structured sympathy because of her circumstances—she and her daughter have been abused by Joe St. George. Our second common agreement, that motherhood may take on a heroic role, opens the door for our acceptance of Joe's murder. Dolores had to save both herself and, more acceptably, her daughter, Selena. This dynamic was seen in real life at the time of the release of the movie (1995) adding to its popularity and relevance. Newspapers in 1987 carried daily columns devoted to a domestic abuse drama. Hedda Nussbaum, a New York woman, was vilified for *not* saving the life of her daughter, Lisa Steinberg. The victim of years of abuse at the hand of her husband, Joel Steinberg, numbed Hedda to the needs of her children. We were repulsed by her weakness and inability to remove herself and her children from the domestic terror perpetrated by Joel. We were sickened by her lack of response when little Lisa was lying unconscious on the bathroom floor. Later, Lisa died of her injuries (Shoos 157). We would never tolerate repetitive, horrific abuse. Dolores was also separate from the wholesome middle-class reader, but in this case we could rally to her side more readily than we could claim sisterhood with the punch-drunk, cocaine-numbed, weak-willed Hedda Nussbaum. Gloria Steinem remarked about the Nussbaum case, "Either you allow yourself to realize that it could have happened to you or you're so invested in making sure it couldn't happen to you that you reject the victim" (Shoos 57). Television and newspapers were inundated during the 1980s with stories of "battered wife syndrome." Dramatized accounts of their tragedies would inspire limp, made-for-TV movies. The media of the day could not come up with a satisfactory heroine in the face of domestic abuse, but the release of the film *Dolores Claiborne* did a short time later. King put homefront terror smack in the middle of Dolores's story and this time the heroine did rescue her daughter and we all sighed with collective relief. The mother/murderer had saved her child. Interestingly, the film version eliminated Dolores's two sons from the novel and presented her as the mother of an only daughter. As Sally Owen said in *The Progressive Women's Quarterly*, "[T]he bottom line in a King novel is good triumphs, peace reigns, the tyrant must be vanquished. Stephen King may not call himself a feminist but he surely has raised consciousness about the lives of women and children. And he'd like to see us fight back. While King's children characters often fight in groups, his women are isolated and nearly always fight alone" (47). Most often. Dolores needed an outsider to push her beyond her weepy, "Oh, I couldn't do that . . ." limits. Vera is the crone who prodded her into action by relaying her own experience with spousal disposal. "Sometimes, Dolores, an accident can be an unhappy woman's best friend." This sobering moment of intimacy signals the start of a very long friendship.

In defense of Dolores's actions, archetypal imagery is used to solidify our reaction to her plight; first by King and then taken up beautifully by director Taylor Hackford throughout this film, giving it a vertical, precultural form of visual/visceral identification. Symbols are "the system of living, subjective meaning . . . the releaser and transformer of psychic energy" (Edinger 109). The solar eclipse, the abandoned well, and the expressive use of character's hands are all symbolic references to innocence vs experience and give the film more depth than the plot would allow on its own. Even the familiar gothic twist—the haunted house—draws our attention away from the cold plot of a murder investigation and into the deeper, more human dichotomy that exists between the present, chilled by lies, and an emotionally wrenching past, remembered.

The solar eclipse is central to both the plot and the meaning of the story. While the event moves the action forward, the symbology gives it depth. When faced with a total eclipse of the Sun, all bets are off. Darkness descends and light retreats. An eclipse defines the lapse of natural law. It is the perfect moment for a woman to murder her husband. If natural law can be overlooked for six and a half minutes, can't human law look away, too? Eclipses have been known throughout the ages to inspire wars, peace, panic, and abnormal human behavior. An eclipse is seen "[a]lmost universally, as an ill omen." It is the "dominance of the feminine Yin principle over the masculine Yang principle"; it is the feminine lunar blocking the masculine solar power (Tressider 163). Dolores is mesmerized by the beauty of it, even in the midst of murdering her husband. Her attention to the eclipse draws in our attention to its significance. We even get a glimpse of eclipse as seen from the bottom of the well . . . Joe's grave. It is a second eclipse, for the round light as seen from the bottom of this womb-like hole is blotted out in death. Joe's evil life ends as the Sun is extinguished. Then Dolores's face reflects the return of the light and her life. It is the moment of her resurrection. After that brilliant moment, her life continues in domestic drudgery, but she does have her moment in the sun.

In killing her husband, Dolores, who has also died an emotional, spiritual, and intellectual death from abuse, then rises from this death to become strong and whole again. History is replete with examples of women who manage to pull themselves out of abusive marriages, save their children's futures, and go on to create clean, decent lives for themselves. Our neighborhoods are full of these women. This hero/mother is what I like to call an archetypal phoenix woman. One life has been burned beyond salvation, but she begins anew with clarity, strength, and dignity. Dolores Claiborne commits murder and saves the life of her child. The cost is dear, both to Joe, whose life ends, and to Dolores, who becomes a brittle, life-calloused outsider. She did what she had to do, then continued on with her life, minus the abuse and worry, unaware of Selena's buried memories and pain. Should she have left Little Tall Island and moved to Bangor after murdering Joe? Should she have found a job as a waitress or housekeeper in some New England Holiday Inn? Hardly. King's decision to keep her in place is what gives Dolores's story that touch of reality. Living with Vera Donovan was not all that bad. Sure, it was the life of a domestic, but it was what she knew and Dolores truly cared for Vera. She had a routine. Living with an abusive partner makes one wary of surprises. Her renewed life brought Dolores stability until Vera Donovan decided she wanted to die. In Dolores and Vera, we see the camaraderie of crones. The crone figure in mythology is the wise woman who eases the pain of sickness, childbirth, and death. As Dolores confesses to wanting to help Vera die, we understand her compassion. Through their mock-bickering companionship, it is

obvious that Vera and Dolores have traded in cruel relationships with
men for nonsexual love between female friends. As Dolores says in the
novel (but not the movie), "Love is about the only thing I do believe
in." In King's stories, sexual relationships are fraught with danger and
male domination. Dolores's and Vera's nonsexual friendship was safe.
Dolores continued to thrive, in spite of Vera's complaints. Dolores
kept Vera in line if she got too bossy: "Don't go too far, Vera." They
buried any guilt they may have had within the cloistered walls of
Vera's elegant home. Selena, on the other hand, moved out into the
larger world arena, bringing crippling guilt and sorrow with her. For
15 years, Dolores was blind to her daughter's pain. Once aware,
Dolores found a way to mother Selena back to health by exorcising
Joe's ghost. In the end, Dolores had a motherly/crone role. She was
a phoenix woman whose new life had once been reflected in the wings
of light at the moment of eclipse.

The abandoned well is another plot device that touches our collective nerves. Joe is a man of vices: alcohol, rage, thievery, and incest.
Dolores kills him by feeding him his vices. She brings him a bottle of
Black and White (good vs evil?) Scotch in a brown paper bag and
seductively pulls the paper bag down like a strip-tease, knowing he will
consume it all. When he is drunk, she pokes at him verbally about his
sexual inadequacies, tells him (falsely) she has recovered the money he
stole, and taunts him about his abuse of his own 13-year-old-daughter.
She knows this will provoke his explosive rage, just as she knows he
will kill her unless she can kill him first, reminding us of her earlier
line, "You hit me again, one of us is going to the bone yard." He does
hit her again. She is committed to the act of murder with her use of
taunting words. Words are her weapon. Dolores kills Joe indirectly by
allowing him to succumb to his own vices; he falls into his own dark,
evil hole and dies. Is this murder? She leads him knowingly to the
place he would go anyway. She murders Joe with knowledge (shades
of Eve?). She jumps over the black hole of his rage and vices and
allows him to fall into his own pit. Dolores has been codependent
her entire marriage. In Al-Anon and Co-Dependents Anonymous
literature, one must "neither help nor hinder the addict's progress."
Dolores got it wrong on both ends. She interfered. She was Joe's
enabler and his executioner. She overlooked his shortcomings and
failures up until the point of physical and sexual abuse. Dolores stops
him there. She attempted to leave, but the male-dominated bank
sided with Joe in his theft of Dolores's and Selena's back account.
Dolores was faced with more abuse and no escape. Vera provided the
answer: "Sometimes, Dolores, an accident is an unhappy woman's

best friend." In the end, Dolores definitely shows Joe the path to his own destruction and he goes for it. Still, because he participates so predictably in the vile behavior that leads to his death, it seems a lesser form of murder. The archetypal image of a well is one of knowledge (Tressider 515). Dolores knows all. She knows what Joe has done. She knows about the dark abyss, and she knows that it will be Joe's deathbed. An abandoned well is the image of abandoned knowledge. Joe abandoned the knowledge of his role as loving father and husband and fell in. As Dolores says, "The minute I knew what he'd done, he was already dead." The terrifying monster of King's story is the arche-typal father: shown as solar power and civil law (Tressider 179). King does not portray Dolores as a murderer, but rather an avenging angel. She never looks more breathtakingly beautiful than when the eclipsed sun emerges behind her, illuminating what she has done, mocking marriage with its Diamond Ring imagery. Dolores turns her face to the sun and is awash in brilliant light and color. The music softens and she breathes in a slight whimper. Her tearful eyes close in calm relief. This image of the avenging Dolores is the most striking of the movie. She fought back and won. The memory of this moment is relived with Selena's return.

Even in his most realistic fiction, King does not stray far from his gothic roots; he provided Dolores with a haunted house. After Vera's death, a surly Selena and Dolores must return to their decrepit, aban-doned, family home. Unbidden, the ghosts of the past return to haunt Dolores. As the women first enter the threshold, Dolores sees a vision of the men searching for her dead husband's body. The men, washed in warm colors, form a semicircle closing in on her and the young Selena. It's a man's world. When they find the body, little Selena turns to Dolores and cries, "Mommy! What did you do to him?" Dolores lies, "Nothing, baby. I promise you." That lie keeps the two women apart for 22 years. Selena always knew her mother killed her father. She could not trust her. Shortly thereafter, we see a Magritte-like image of Dolores's reflection shattering along with shards of broken window glass. The image she has created for herself is broken by the memory of what really took place. Placed by circumstance back in the location of her true history, Dolores must give up the ruse. Her carefully crafted persona is shattering. She must right the wrongs done to Selena by her lies. The house is haunted by ghosts of Joe, a softer, gentler version of herself, and a sweet, young, fun-loving Selena. The memories are so vibrant with rich colors that they are more alive and real than the emotionally drained, blue-filtered present. While Dolores remembers with emotional intensity, Selena has forgotten everything. "Frequently, such memories [of incest] are so painful that they don't surface until years after the events occurred" (Steinem 163). Like the chafing Maine weather in which she finds herself, Selena's life is cold. Dolores finally sees in the haunted house that her daughter is not the bright, successful, healthy Vassar alumna she thought she was. Dolores had hoped that in sending Selena to Vassar she would have a future. There was a promise in those years of women's liberation. In 1963, women noted their unequal status, as Dolores and Vera did. Twenty years later, Selena lives the life our second-wave feminists demanded; she has a thriving, creative career in journalism, transposable relationships, and a driving will to succeed. She also has pills, alcohol, and "a lot of nobodies" in her life. She is following her father, Joe, into the same pit of self-destruction. Like a second eclipse, Dolores must once again intervene. She must come between Joe's male behavioral traits picked up by Selena and bring her safely into the light. It is time to guide Selena out of the dark confusion caused by the death of her father and heal the pain and anger she feels toward her mother and herself. During their entire stay, Dolores is inundated with visions of what was both good and bad. She shares these visions with Selena, hoping to explain to her why her father was not just an innocent drunk whom Selena believes cannot defend himself. She wants Selena to see the truth. Only when Selena has her own haunting on the ferry, does she remember the sexual abuse. Only then, does she understand her mother's actions. They both needed to revisit the past and face their own truths. The haunted house forces them to do that.

An endearing symbolic touch, used by King and Hackford, is the play of hands throughout the work (Magistrale, *Hollywood's Stephen King*, 75–76). We see a close-up of Dolores's hands as she is hanging up the sheets ("six pins, not five, Dolores"). At first we see a young Dolores and her young hands applying the clothespins. Then, as she smooths out the sheets we see her hands are gnarled and cracked and the camera returns to a gray-haired Dolores 22 winters older. When Dolores touches Selena's face with her rough hands and says, "You're still my good girl," Selena pulls away. This reaction makes sense later in the film. "I guess if you want to know somebody's life, you look at their hands," she says, and we believe her. Selena, who is still relatively young, foretells later scenes by paying inordinate attention to rubbing and softening her hands. When Selena remembers the molestation scene on the ferry, we only see Joe's hands at first purchasing coffee for himself and hot chocolate for young Selena. Then we find out young Selena's hands are cold. Joe rubs them and pulls on them as she struggles to get free. He prevails and insists she satisfy him sexually using her hands, "You remember how I showed ya? Selena, please, come on . . . you're my good girl." Then, in his death scene, Joe's hand thrusts out and grabs at Dolores's ankle. Finally, at the end of the film, after Selena has successfully defended Dolores against Detective Mackey's charges, she offers her open hand to Dolores as a gesture of support and capitulation. She then leads her mother by the hand out of the judge's office toward freedom.

King is an insightful man. He speed-reads cultural fear and transcribes it back to us. He uses symbolic and structured language to show us our own truth. The women's movement will continue on its bumpy path with or without him. Once upon a time we, like Dolores and Vera, thought that by disassociating from men, getting tough, and joining with other women, we could change our view of ourselves. We could climb out from under the missionary position of wanting to please men for no other reason than to gain their approval. Vera and Dolores, in a strident mimicry of militant second-wave activists, killed off their husbands. Selena is the microcosm of second-wave feminism's successes and failures: she busied herself with independent pursuits while stifling her emotional needs. Her story may have been more relevant in 1987, though I believe Dolores's story makes more sense today. We have backpedaled some and need a crone's wisdom to set us straight. The stale trend of some third-wave feminists claiming male pornographic fantasies as our own is as ineffectual a way to gain power as were the mannish navy blue suits with shoulder pads back in the 1980s. Adopting male affect is not equality. Of course, any progressive movement will have its moments of backsliding, but a mother wants her daughters to move beyond our realizations, not rejoin the old struggle. We, of the second and third wave of feminists, have built up a wall of conflicting language that slogs down our children's progress toward gender equality. Stephen King cannot tear down this wall. That is not his job. He is a prolific chronicler of our fears, but not the solution to them. His stories cannot abscond with the momentum of the women's movement, nor does his rendering of female characters represent a hatred or misunderstanding of us. King simply does what he always does best: he crafts a female character tortured by fearful circumstances, a brave woman who comes to her own rescue and that of her children. What we could use now is another brave woman who speaks the truth: Send in the crones.

Chapter 13

Only Theoretical

Postmodern Ambiguity in *Needful Things* and *Storm of the Century*

Mary Pharr

Stephen King is a paradox: a pop cultural icon as well as a significant literary artist. For over thirty years, he has been a celebrity, instantly recognizable from commercials and movie spots. King has long acknowledged his own identity as a brand name; more truthfully, he has encouraged it. Within a different context, however, King's delight in his celebrity has always been a detriment to his literary stature: he is so openly American middle class (often generous, sometimes vulgar, always opinionated) and he has been so consistently successful that critics have sometimes found his public persona a large and tempting target. But it's the art that really matters, and time has confirmed King's artistry. Like the author, the art of Stephen King personifies contemporary America, its postmodern mixture of fear and hope, greed and decency. Over the years, manifesting these qualities primarily through the horror genre has allowed King to reach the very audience his characters represent—a techno-oriented, mass-market audience that might otherwise never have considered the themes King presents. Today, those themes are more complex than ever.

If postmodernism is the *mentalité*, the *zeitgeist* of the contemporary era, King really is emblematic of postmodern attributes: its blending of author and audience, its focus on the ordinary made extraordinary, its celebration of disorder and polysemy, its obsessions with technology and celebrity, and its recognition of the violent instability that has broken whatever moral certainties once underpinned our culture. Many of the figures in his fiction reflect the lack of self-awareness that permeates this world. As Carroll F. Terrell says, King writes about "typical people in our own culture going about their daily lives, most of them trying to get ahead and keep out of trouble" (11). Accurate depictions of the human comedy, these "regular" folks are largely concerned with their own well-being while yet convinced of their fundamental goodness. With only minimal philosophical or theological curiosity, they tend to believe what the authority of the moment tells them. As Americans, they like stuff; getting it is another matter. Although they want the good life, King's masses of supporting characters tend to react to events rather than initiate them. When their fuzzy notions of self-actualization come in conflict with ethical crises, their responses define postmodern ambiguity—the absence of absolute codes in a democratic universe. The results, highlighted by the gothic paraphernalia littering King's horrorscape, exemplify pathos, chaos, and death. Like many within King's print and film audience, I find myself both disturbed by and sympathetic to these benighted supporting characters even as I wonder if I am really empathizing with them.

In line with his paradoxical genius, however, King is also heir to the older tradition of American Romanticism. His main characters have more awareness and, ultimately, more ethical angst than their philosophically limited and materialistic neighbors. With valor and insight during horrific times, these main characters must make choices that isolate them from their peers. They stand upright but alone. As Tony Magistrale notes in *Landscape of Fear*, King's protagonists are linked to those of Hawthorne and Melville both by a central theme of the "discovery of evil" (21) and by the "knowledge that moral maturity is a possible consequence from contact with sin" (22). Although they come from the disordered universe, King's heroes move beyond it. Thus, King's work—literary and cinematic—seems to agree with Vaclav Havel's assertion that the "only real hope of people today" is "self-transcendence" ("Need for Transcendence"). A lingering question remains: if self-transcendence is not experienced by ordinary people but only by the exceptional individual, will it ever translate to the wider community?

Film has always been a good medium for King, almost all of whose fiction has been adapted for the big screen or for television. Although these adaptations have been inconsistent, they have included notable films such as *Carrie, The Shining, Stand By Me, Misery, The Shawshank Redemption, Dolores Claiborne,* and *The Green Mile.* In style and fidelity to their print origin, these films vary; some, like *Carrie, The Shining,* and *Claiborne,* use postmodern structures and devices; others, like *Misery* and *Shawshank,* adhere more to the formulas of classical cinema. But one element these films have in common is a sense of the continual challenges to our communal humanity that resonates throughout their source material.

The ambiguity inherent in King's examination of communal humanity and in the way film has visualized that examination is not just found in his most popular movies. In particular, the film version of *Needful Things* (1993) and the telemovie *Storm of the Century* (1999) reflect this ambiguity, most especially the deconstruction of ethics in contemporary society. Granted, neither work attracted a blockbuster audience; together, however, these films demonstrate King's vision of the mass collapse of American moral codes and the imperfect solace of the few who defy the many. Directors Fraser Clarke Heston and Craig R. Baxley have distinctly different styles, but both use King's narrative insight to create emblems of something very unpleasant in our world. Their ultimate challenge is to show that unpleasantness to the very audience engaged in it, to make a movie with a hard message that informs rather than repels its audience. While *Needful Things* falters and *Storm of the Century* had trouble holding its viewers, both deserve attention.

Published in 1991, the novel *Needful Things* begins with the ominous (and reflexively postmodern) statement, "You've been here before" (1). "Here" is Castle Rock, Maine, the site of the separate—and mostly horrific—events detailed in *The Dead Zone, Cujo, The Body*, and *The Dark Half*. A site seeded with natural and unnatural corruption, the Rock is yet more than dark ground; "here" is also small-town America: "[C]all it Peyton Place or Grovers Corners or Castle Rock, it's just folks eatin pie and drinkin coffee and talkin about each other behind their hands" (6–7). Its denizens argue over religion, yearn for love, keep secrets, and hold grudges; but "Castle Rock is still a pretty nice place to live and grow, as the sign you see when you come into town says" (8). The sign suggests that the scattered dark seeds of the past do not foretell the future—but they do. A demon comes to town under the name of Leland Gaunt and seduces a number of the inhabitants by selling them "needful things" (from the name of his shop), worthless curios that stimulate their most secret fantasies. Whatever the objects, however, Gaunt knows the truth: he really always sells his customers weapons "and they always bought" (548). As for price, Gaunt has his customers pull "pranks" on their neighbors, leading to murder and mayhem as the center of the town literally blows apart, torn to shreds by the obsessions and fury of its inhabitants, who invariably blame the wrong parties for the humiliating tricks played on them. Sheriff Alan Pangborn is one of the very few to (barely) escape the devil's enticement, but he cannot reverse what has already happened. Near the novel's close, Alan rescues a bag full of lost souls from the demon, but the Sheriff has not likely saved the obliterated soul of the Castle Rock community. Alan is last seen heading away from the Rock, thinking, *"It was my town. But not anymore. Not ever again"* (685; emphasis in the original).

According to Sharon Russell, "By taking apart Castle Rock [King] investigates what held it together. . . . In *Needful Things* he details the process of destruction" (122). Detailing the process is, by definition, intricate: the novel runs almost seven hundred pages. Translating it to the big screen, single-film format requires an encapsulation that threatens to trivialize the process, abandoning many of its particularities for an overview of its spectacularly theatrical results. As adapted by veteran screenwriter W. D. Richter, Heston's film succumbs to the threat. At 2 hours in the theatrical release cut, its portrait of the town is more an adroit sketch than a broad canvas, lighter and softer than King's design. King himself was disappointed in the movie as released, preferring a longer alternate version (actually the unexcised first studio cut) that was shown on cable television in 1996. Of the theatrical release, he has said, "When edited down to 'movie length,' it's almost indecipherable because it doesn't have time to tell all the stories and do all the setups" (quoted in Magistrale, *Hollywood's Stephen King*, 8). To be fair, none of the cinematic adaptations of King's novels—not even the miniseries—can do justice to the intimate texture of his characterizations. In truth, despite King's concerns, Heston's movie is not incoherent; rather, its design self-consciously refuses reflection as it rushes the audience through a frenzied excursion into consumer greed gone mad. With a harder edge, a sense of *gravitas*, the movie might have worked as satire or as the tragedy of King's novel, but it settles for parody.

Repeatedly, the film exemplifies its cleverness and lack of subtlety. Virtually every indoor location in the movie is filmed with the sets (windows, blinds, doors, picture frames, wall edges, building arches, etc.) serving as interframes within the larger frame of the shot, rectangles inside rectangles that create a formal proscenium effect. Technically sharp and quite pleasing to the eye, this theatrical focusing effect was used by Vincent Minnelli to great acclaim in *Meet Me in St. Louis*, but in a nonmusical film that derives from horror fiction, the precision of this repositioning of reality by the *mise-en-scène* is curiously relaxing. We are distanced rather than involved in the action. The framing does, however, work efficiently to indicate the breakdown of the community. At one point, for example, the camera uses the blinds of a diner's window to frame Brian Rusk, a 11-year-old boy who has bought into Gaunt's evil, standing outside in the night like a solitary ghost, repositioned from community youth into archetypal lost child.

In both novel and film, Gaunt uses two flawed women as test cases for his demonic plans. Both victims of vicious pranks they mistakenly blame on each other, these women, Nettie Cobb and Wilma Jerzyck, square off at Wilma's home in a duel predicated on a dead dog and a vandalized house—but really on the seething resentments of unstable personalities. Fighting with knife and cleaver, the women madly hew each other, ending impaled together after falling out an attic window. Composer Patrick Doyle sets the violence of this fight-to-the-death (framed by curtains and lit by lightning) against the counterpoint of Schubert's "Ave Maria," creating a scene that is vivid but less meaningful than in King's book. In print, the women duel and die on the corner of two neighborhood streets, "like gunslingers in a spaghetti Western" (274). Their mutual murder is more public in every sense, symbolic of the nastiness lurking below the communal surface of Castle Rock, where everyone—even Alan Pangborn—has an ugly secret festering inside. Everyone is guilty of something that could be damnable and only the town's hypocritical social structure holds its surface together. When people go to the shop Needful Things, they are trying to buy distraction from their guilt. In effect, they seek momentary salvation from the devil, but as the sheriff's girlfriend warns Alan when he almost buys Gaunt's wares, "*He makes you buy back your own sickness, and he makes you pay double!*" (668; emphasis in the original). *Needful Things* the novel is an indictment of the moral sickness within contemporary humanity, a sickness that breaks through to the surface and overwhelms Castle Rock. Leland Gaunt is the catalyst, but the novel suggests that he only speeds up the town's destruction, that like Nettie and Wilma, Castle Rock self-destructs. Only a few escape. The novel's ambiguity lies within the tragedy of communal greed and hypocrisy.

Besides distancing the viewer stylistically, the movie drastically softens the theme, allowing at least the possibility of broader moral survival. At the film's climax, Gaunt has lured Castle Rock's Catholics and Baptists into fighting one another, ostensibly over pranks but actually over their mutual religious bigotry. Simultaneously, Dan Keeton, a mentally ill politician turned embezzler and murderer, blows up the center of town. As Gaunt watches, road rage erupts and people riot in the streets, while a storm rages around them and buildings explode. The mayhem effects are good, with a church steeple shearing off in a shower of sparks and its cross plunging precipitously into the ground. But then, as the priest and the minister face off, as the town hovers on the brink of final ruin, Sheriff Pangborn steps in. Rather than shooting the clerics to restore order (as Gaunt audibly suggests), the lawman fires into the air and cries, "No!" Most improbably, things quiet down as Alan proclaims, "No more killing! Not in Castle Rock!" The Big Speech has begun.

In the novel, Alan is grieving for a dead wife and son, but he also has physical magic at his command, magic he uses at the conclusion against Gaunt. It's typical of King's print fiction (*The Stand* being the most notable example) that the supernatural exists, but the demonic is opposed by the magical rather than the theological. The end of the movie *Needful Things*, however, eschews both magic and theology. The cinematic Alan (who seems unscarred by the past) is a naturalistic hero whose probity is clear. Rapidly convincing the townspeople that Gaunt has used hate to "turn us all against each other," Alan watches as the priest helps the minister to his feet, while people publicly admit the pranks they pulled for Gaunt. "You're finished in this town," Alan tells Gaunt, who responds with an act of stupidity: he taunts the despairing and dynamite-laden Dan Keeton, who turns in fury on the demon, blowing them both up in an impressive explosion that somehow does not pulverize anyone else in its slow-motion glory. Unsurprisingly, this last explosion embarrasses Gaunt, who steps out of the bomb site to announce wryly, "Not my best work." The demon then predicts a happy marriage for Alan and his girlfriend, but adds before leaving that he will deal with their grandson in 2053! Off goes Gaunt, the camera backtracking up and away from the town over the lighthouse and across the ocean—the reverse of the way it rolled into town at the opening—and the largest frame in a frame-filled film.

Every omission from the novel lessens the film's thematic weight: for example, Gaunt has no valise of trapped souls, and the body count is much lower. But the sins of the movie's Castle Rock fester just beyond its stylish frames. Gaunt's evil prophecy hinges on Alan's mortality: he will not always be around to resurface the community. The Rock's folks are not wholly evil, according to their sheriff, but theirs is the tragic ambiguity of a postmodern community full of thoroughly respectable Americans who secretly value comfort more than ethics, who cannot communicate with their neighbors, and who descend into violence as the most obvious solution to any conflict. In both King's book and the movie, there is little hope for any permanent recovery of communal cohesion. *Needful Things*, is, after all, subtitled "The Last Castle Rock Novel."

In 1996 King conceived the idea of *Storm of the Century*, an original novel for television that would avoid the discomfort he has felt about the adaptation process altogether. In the Introduction to the filming draft of the screenplay, King argues that *Storm* is not a "TV drama" or a "miniseries"; it is "a genuine novel, one that exists in a different medium" (xi). The argument is valid: *Storm of the Century* is certainly a much stronger work than the movie *Needful Things*, mostly because as a primary novel, *Storm* is King's narrative vision, unaltered (hence its full title—*Stephen King's Storm of the Century*). This vision, moreover, sees beyond *Needful Things'* indictment of communal hypocrisy to gaze full into the tragedy of communal doubt. Both works deal with the collapse of moral codes and the rise of chaos within postmodern America, but the TV novel looks far more deeply into the agony inherent in that collapse when those involved really are fundamentally decent but so devoid of moral certainty that they do not know how to follow what they say they believe rather than what they see. The ambiguity in *Storm* is more profound than that of *Needful Things*, for it uncovers the skull beneath the skin of contemporary American ethics. Filmed under the auspices of journeyman director Craig R. Baxley and shown in February 1999 on ABC, this large-budget ($35 million), tripartite novel for television is, perhaps, not only King's bleakest work, but it is also among his most challenging and most moving commentaries on our world.

Set in another familiar part of King's fictional universe, Little Tall Island, Maine, *Storm of the Century* occasionally references Islander Dolores Claiborne, who made and paid for the moral compromise of justified murder, an open secret among older Islanders. But the pit Dolores dug for herself when she tried to protect her children by killing their abusive father is but a sandbox compared to the hell waiting for the residents of the island during the Blizzard of 1989. Narrated by Mike Anderson from the perspective of 1998, most of the film is a flashback to 1989, when Mike is Little Tall's general storekeeper and part-time constable (a combination of jobs that says volumes about islanders' sense of homeland security). Geographically separated from the mainland by a reach, Little Tall is psychologically separated from it by overwhelming public unity. Weathered Yankees, islanders feel prepared for the coming storm. True, most of the village's kids are stranded (though safe) at school on the mainland when the storm strikes, but eight preschoolers are left snug with their parents on the island. Little Tall is not prepared, however, for the storm-timed arrival of a demon who calls himself Andre Linoge. First brutally killing a harmless old woman so that he can be arrested, then driving other villagers to suicide and murder, Linoge effortlessly spreads fear and the repeated message that he first tells Mike as the nervous constable waits to lock up him up in the island's hand-welded jail: "Give me what I want, and I'll go away" (75). No one understands.

But they do understand that their situation is worsening. Cutting off communication with the outside world, the storm isolates Little Tall from all orthodox authority, leaving the island literally a land unto itself, a community no longer under the auspices of federal or state control—a body of men and women who must not only fend for themselves physically but also morally. In emergency quarters at the town hall while the storm wreaks havoc on their streets and busi-nesses, the 200 stranded villagers find that Linoge is using both their isolation and their cohesiveness for his own purpose. After slipping away from jail, the demon snatches more islanders as they watch their lighthouse topple during a whiteout. If that lighthouse were the friendly sentry whose previously reliable beacon symbolized Little Tall's connection to mainland values, its loss suggests that islanders are now morally as well as literally in the dark. A single, terrified survivor returns to warn the rest that Linoge will make his demand clear in a town meeting that night. By then, he has thrown the preschoolers into a controlled coma, reducing the adults to hopeless panic. All the while, Mike has tried to maintain order, but the most important thing he has deduced about Linoge is the least comforting: his name is an anagram for the Biblical devils *Legion*.

At the meeting, Linoge quietly demands the unthinkable: a single child from among the eight. Although ancient, he is not immortal, and he wants to pass on his heritage. If the islanders agree, he will take the child and leave; if they refuse, he will obliterate every one of them—children and all. The outside world will find a deserted island—like Roanoke in 1587. In the 30 minutes that Linoge gives the town to decide, Mike argues strenuously, urgently against the proposal; but everyone else—even the local minister and even Mike's wife—finds reasons to accept it. Little Tall legally votes to give a child to a demon. Ralphie, Mike's son, is selected by lottery and taken by Linoge. As the flashback ends, Mike notes how he left wife and town and started a new life in San Francisco. Some islanders had regrets and some died badly, but most just hid the truth. In 1998 California, however, Mike inadvertently glimpses Ralphie with Linoge. Mike cannot catch them, cannot do anything really, but he sees enough to know that Ralphie has grown to look like his foster father.

Thanks to Baxley's production team, *Storm* is as visually compelling as it is thematically challenging. Unlike the conventionally rich Hollywood tones of *Needful Things*, much of the telefilm's color is blue-white, the color of winter snow, frozen death, and chilled consciences; its inside scenes are hued in the realistic tones of small-town, middle-class habitats, cozy enough to belie the decisions made within them. Rather than use precise framing within his scenes, Baxley has his cinematographer shoot some scenes from a slightly canted angle, not slanted enough to be immediately noticeable but just barely askew—the way real life is. The cinematography and the mechanical effects also present an unusual depth of field, allowing viewers to see more background details than the characters may notice—just as we may see more implications of their situation than they do. Baxley takes particular care with the visual effects within the storm that enshrouds the chaos Linoge introduces into the community. Although much of the movie was filmed in Canada and Maine during warmer months, the winter storm scenes are intense, the snow realistic and the destruction profound, matching the moral misery of the island's communal body. Matching King's vision of Linoge is more problematic. Actor Colm Feore plays Linoge as a figure of quiet menace, and in his DVD commentary, director Baxley praises Feore's performance as an example of "What restraint can do. Less is more." A quiet demon is certainly an alternative to the cosmopolitan Gaunt. However, according to Heidi Strengell, in dress, name, and power, Linoge must be equated with Randall Flagg, the Dark Man of *The Stand* and *The Gunslinger* (145). Under Baxley's direction, only in the town meeting scene does Feore's performance achieve the intensity needed for the Dark Man's grip to be felt by the audience as surely as the islanders—but that scene is riveting.

Caveat aside, *Storm of the Century* pulls few punches during its 4-hour presentation of the inadequacy of postmodern social structures to handle crises. Rather than merely repeating the pattern of desire mistaken for need that dominates *Needful Things*, King's telemovie presents the contemporary belief in everyone's right to nitpick over ethical questions—even the loss of a child's soul. When different voices do finally pull together under pressure to find a way out of an ethical impasse, "the idea of 'community' seems on this occasion not to warm the heart but to 'chill the blood'" (King, Introduction to *Storm of the Century* ix). Watching *Storm*, I find that part of what chills and enthralls me about it is the haunting ambiguity that lies within the conflict between individual righteousness and communal compromise. There is something archetypally American within this conflict: democracy is based on the collective will of the majority, but America, especially postmodern America, is also predicated on the right of the individual to assert his own will, even when it goes against the collective judgment. Reinvigorating the philosophical opposition of Thoreau vs Hawthorne, King presents the most extreme situation he can possibly conceive of to delineate the agony of the ambiguity within contemporary moral choice. Ultimately, no one is satisfied with the results. The American determination to allow everyone's opinion to matter equally is tested in excess in this novel for television not as a *reductio ad absurdum* but as a tragedy of the postmodern condition.

Linoge's power is immense and it is not just physical; he knows everyone's private sins—an especially powerful weapon in a community so sure of itself that before Linoge arrives, Mike annoyed by the lack of discretion on Little Tall declares to Ursula Godsoe, the town's bedrock administrative assistant who stands for all the townspeople's strength, "No secrets on the island" (41). Ursula represents all the positives of island life, but she knows there are secrets here, secrets that Linoge will tear out just as he tears out insecurities and uses them to make islanders kill. "I cannot take," Linoge says, "although I can punish" (328). Early on, the demon punishes Ursula's own husband for augmenting the income from his failing fish business by selling marijuana on the sly: he forces the hapless Peter Godsoe to hang himself. Inevitably, the dreadful imbalance of Lingoge's power (imagine if no Mother Abigail existed as a counterpart to Flagg in *The Stand*) is unnerving. When the meeting comes to decide what to do about Linoge's ultimate threat, it is attended by 200 believably terrified people. We have seen enough of them to know they are ordinarily tough and—unlike many of the denizens of Castle Rock— fundamentally stable. Yet, they begin the debate by wasting time on a discussion and preliminary vote about whether or not they believe Linoge. As they haggle, Mike warns them to eschew even this preliminary vote, since "once we start down this road, every step gets easier" (332). Yet they go on, knowing that as a tight-knit group they *can* together affirm Linoge's reality. Appallingly, they have nothing else to fall back on, no philosophical or theological code with which to defend themselves against the hideous reality they have affirmed.

As the debate moves closer to the question, Mike tries to bring the faith they supposedly all share into the issue. He suggests that they refuse Linoge as a community: "Stand against him, side by side and shoulder to shoulder. Tell him *no* in one voice. Do what it says on the door we use to get in here—trust in God and each other. And then . . . maybe . . . he goes away. The way storms always do, when they've blown themselves out" (333; emphasis in the original). Everyone demurs as if Mike is talking nonsense. All Rev. Bob Riggins can say is "Render therefore unto Caesar the things which are Caesar's" (333)—the Bible become a hymn to raw power. Mike tries to counter with another biblical reference to shunning Satan, but the islanders already know about the devil, about his superiority. Trying to maintain some sense of their own autonomy, they revert to arguing about the lesser of evils: better one die than all, better the chosen one live as a demon than die a child, better they give in than risk living without their children. "God help us, but let's give him what he wants" (337), says Ursula, who has already lost her husband to Linoge and does not want to lose everything. As Ursula, transformed by Linoge's actions from moral pillar to forlorn widow and frantic mother, capitulates, the town's fate seems to me to be sealed. Her reference to God helping them all even as she gives in to the devil is both expedient and despair filled; it is the call of someone who believes in momentary rather than eternal survival. Desperate, Mike tells his neighbors, "This is damnation" (338), but they are already feeling damned. They vote yes to evil, the "lesser" evil.

In his DVD commentary, King says that the ending to his telemovie evokes the moral bankruptcy of millennial America—a "go along to get along" perspective. He worries that the islanders' terrible fate may be waiting for all of us, that while the cost of doing the right thing is "very, very high," the cost of doing the wrong thing is "ruin." But *Storm* itself evokes more sympathy than its author may have intended. In the meeting, the townspeople truly want to do what is best for everybody. "What's a community for," cries one woman at the climax of the debate, "if it isn't to help people when something terrible happens? When none of the choices look good?" (338). Tragically, however, for these postmodern Americans with no overriding codes, the ambiguity of any decision is excruciating. As I watched *Storm of the Century*, I realized that I do not know if I would have had the wisdom or the foresight or the fortitude to side with its hero rather than with the collective perspective of the community. Under pressure, they choose expediency rather than morality, and everyone, Mike included, suffers. I also find myself almost as worried about his splendid, desolate isolation from the town's damnation. Life without community is not much life.

Tony Magistrale has suggested several reasons that the ratings for *Storm of the Century* were not as high as initially anticipated: its demographically awkward winter broadcast dates, its "bloated midsection" in which Linoge exerts his power from jail, its structural requirement that the audience wait 3 days to learn Linoge's demand, and its stiff competition (acknowledged by King) from the likes of *E.R.* (*Hollywood's Stephen King,* 211). *Storm's* message may also have been more severe than many in its intended audience wanted to confront directly. The absence of the numinous within the narrative film reality of *Storm of the Century* suggests that, for many Americans, any human code of ethics is only theoretical within the awe-filled and awful vastness of the postmodern universe. Yet, those who stayed with the telemovie may have experienced a Sophoclean catharsis that moved them—us—past horror into understanding. The storm that blows Little Tall asunder is a far cry from the one in which the dead of another Maine Island, Goat Island, join hands with Stella Flanders to pull her into the comforting community of Infinity. But that was "The Reach" in 1981. King's millennial storm blows us into a dark no-man's-land—a harsher place than usual for his most constant audience to visit. But better visit this Hades than be trapped there.

Chapter 14

Rose Red and Stephen King's Hybrid House of Horrors

Dennis R. Perry and
Carl H. Sederholm

Commentary on the work of Stephen King usually provides a litany of his shortcomings as a writer. Harold Bloom, for example, insists that he "cannot locate any aesthetic dignity in King's writing" ("Introduction" 3). Moreover, S. T. Joshi dismisses King as an unoriginal hack, "a panderer to the cheapest of middle-class tastes" (63). King certainly has his shortcomings as a writer, but such claims confine King's work within strict definitions of authorship. They ignore King's experiments not only with genre and authorship but also with his broad use of different media. By focusing on King's weaknesses in writing, King's critics overlook an even deeper problem—how do King's own notions of authorship help us understand his larger project? As Linda Badley argues in *Writing Horror and The Body*, King deliberately distances himself from traditional conceptions of authorship. In fact, King writes for so many different kinds of venues and media that broad terms like "novelist"—or even "writer"—may not apply to him very well at all. Badley goes so far as to suggest that King's work ought to be defined in terms of performance. In Badley's view, "King sometimes seems to prefer performing his fictions . . . more than writing them" (40). The result is that King "might be better defined as a figure or phenomenon whose impact goes far beyond any genre or medium" (xi).

Badley's claims are useful, particularly given that King sometimes makes claims that seem to agree with her directly. In fact, he sometimes promotes himself as a kind of master of ceremonies rather than as a traditional writer. In his preface to the screenplay of *Storm of the Century* King hints at his own playful sense of authorship. He admits that "I assumed that if I wrote *Storm of the Century*, it would be a novel. Yet as I prepared to sit down to it, the idea kept insisting that it was a movie. Every image of the story seemed to be a movie image rather than a book image" (x). According to King, authorship serves as a means of discovering how stories want to be told, no matter how he would prefer to write them. *Storm of the Century* insisted on a visual medium. King, obedient to the logic of his dreams, followed along. As he suggests in *On Writing*, King often conceives of his plots visually:

> My books tend to be based on situation rather than story. Some of the ideas which have produced those books are more complex than others, but the majority start out with the stark simplicity of a department store window display or a waxwork tableau. I want to put a group of characters . . . in some sort of predicament and then watch them try to work themselves free, or manipulate them to safety—those are jobs which require the noisy jackhammer of plot—but to watch what happens and then write it down. (*On Writing*, 164)

For King, authorship begins with learning how to "watch what happens" and only then attempting to record the events as they unfold (164). The result is a conception of writing that readily combines verbal and visual techniques in unique and playful ways.

In her recent study, Heidi Strengell contributes to this discussion by noting that King's fiction is both an "arena of spectacle" and a series of "generic hybrids" that deliberately challenge conventional boundaries of genre (22). Strengell states, "In combining elements of the gothic tale with other genres—such as realism, literary naturalism, myths, fairy tales, romanticism, and other elements of the fantastic— King enriches his fiction at the same time as he challenges the traditional limits associated with these genres" (Strengell 22). Although Strengell correctly emphasizes King's genre-crossing style, she largely overlooks not only King's visual sense of authorship, but also his tendency toward a kind of humorous playfulness. Such playfulness serves as an essential dimension not only of King's hybrid writing style, but also in helping us further understand how King ought to be understood as a writer. The result, we suggest, will be something far greater than further claims regarding King's lack of "aesthetic dignity."

Having argued for a wider view of King's authorship, we now examine the ways his 2002 ABC miniseries *Rose Red* demonstrates the complex interactions of authorship, genre, and hybridity. We argue that *Rose Red* is a particularly playful and subversive hybrid, one that freely mixes themes and allusions from many sources, including some from King's prior work. In fact, *Rose Red* may be read as a series of conversations concerning the nature of haunted houses, the conflicts between scientific investigation and belief in the paranormal, and the problem of human survival.

We begin by discussing the way *Rose Red* transforms traditional haunted house stories. From the beginning, *Rose Red* does not seem to fit within the standard conceptions of what a haunted house story ought to be. After all, King locates Rose Red squarely within a busy section of Seattle. King further complicates his sense of place by modifying his own conception of the haunted house as a Bad Place. King's use of this archetype stems back to his descriptions of both the Marsten House (*Salem's Lot*) and the Overlook Hotel (*The Shining*). As he writes in *Danse Macabre*, Bad Places are supposed to challenge readers to look beyond the simple "haunted house" iconography of "the fallen-down house at the end of Maple Street with the weedy lawn, the broken windows, and the moldering FOR SALE sign" (252). Bad Places exist in spite of their surface appearances. They represent the reality of evil and tend to feed off of the troubled and complex collection of wicked memories, corrupt voices, and relentless evils of generations past. Though human behavior does not create a Bad Place, it contributes to what King calls the "psychic residue" that lurks within the house.

King's states Rose Red's identity as a Bad Place quite clearly when Annie Wheaton (Kimberly J. Brown) refers to it directly as both a "bad house" and a "Bad Place." Moreover, Joyce Reardon (Nancy Travis) suggests that Rose Red, like Shirley Jackson's Hill House, was "born bad." But, unlike Jackson's house (and also unlike King's own Marsten House and the Overlook Hotel), Rose Red's sinister history emphasizes the female rage that underscores the largely male-centered acts of murder, betrayal, lust, and revenge that usually characterize King's Bad Places. Indeed, Rose Red's "psychic residue" is deeply embedded within Ellen Rimbauer's dark resentment toward John Rimbauer's sexual dalliances; in particular, she hates John for infecting her with syphilis, the disease that likely caused April Rimbauer to be born with a withered arm. Ellen's rage lies at the heart of Rose Red. In fact, her anger toward John's libidinous desires for Sukeena causes her to throw him through a beautiful stained glass window. So pointed is this female rage that Rose Red noticeably divides its victims by gender. Joyce explains that "there has always been a difference between the ways Rose Red treats the ladies and the gentlemen."

Indeed, male victims tend to die violently while females tend to disappear. As Joyce concludes, "Rose Red has always been particularly fond of the ladies." Unfortunately, King does not develop nor sustain this female-centered theme very carefully.

King moves even further away from the connection between Ellen Rimbauer's anger and Rose Red at the beginning of parts II and III. In both cases, he introduces a broad exposition on bad houses spoken by Joyce Reardon (Nancy Travis). Here we learn that "Houses are alive. This is something we know—news from our nerve endings. If we're quiet, if we listen, we can hear houses breathe. Sometimes in the depth of the night we hear them groan. It's as if they're having bad dreams." Joyce goes on to suggest that "a good house cradles and comforts; a bad one fills us with instinctive unease. Bad Houses hate our warmth and our humanness. That blind hate of our humanity is what we mean when we use the word 'haunted.'" Later, Joyce qualifies the term "haunted" further by explaining that it really refers to the unthinkable mental state of the house itself—that the house itself "has gone insane." Joyce states further,

> A house is a place of shelter. It's the body we put on over our bodies. As our bodies grow old, so do our houses. As our bodies may sicken, so do our houses sicken. And what of madness? If mad people live within, doesn't this madness creep into the rooms and walls and corridors, the very boards? Don't we sometimes sense that madness reaching out to us?

King's notion that haunting and insanity are synonymous alludes to ideas originally developed by Edgar Allan Poe and later extended by Shirley Jackson. Both writers explored in their most celebrated works—"The Fall of the House of Usher," and *The Haunting of Hill House*, respectively—the idea that houses may be rendered as complex symbols of the self. Moreover, both writers sought to develop an analogy between houses and the human mind. In *Rose Red*, King likewise expands on this now-familiar theme that houses share a physical connection to our own bodies.

The problem with King's development of Rose Red as a variant of the Bad Place is that it never really adds up to anything comprehensive. Not only does King confuse the theme by casting the house's anger in terms of feminine fury, he likewise asks viewers to think of the house as both something capable of insanity and as a kind of architectural vampire. At the end of the film, King further complicates matters by showing the zombie-like Ellen Rimbauer holding a hammer inviting

Steve Rimbauer to help her "build." The result is to distance viewers further from their preconceptions about haunted house stories generally. At this point in the film, King seems more interested in the visual effects of the film rather than exploring the deeper meanings behind Ellen's relentless building.

One of the most telling ways King renders *Rose Red* completely unstable is through his recurrent allusions to works such as William Shakespeare's *A Midsummer Night's Dream*, Herman Melville's *Moby-Dick*, and Bram Stoker's *Dracula*. As with those works, *Rose Red* may be broadly characterized as a plot that features a cast of characters who willingly leave their ordinary lives to enter an enchanted space in which identity is always suspect and where invisible powers manipulate events in ways beyond the comprehension of the guests.

Throughout *Rose Red*, King regularly juxtaposes natural and supernatural events in ways largely reminiscent of Shakespeare's *A Midsummer Night's Dream*. In that play, as in *Rose Red*, the audience first meets the characters in the ordinary world, only to be quickly introduced to the enchanted forest world, and, finally, to a kind of hybrid space in which the two worlds come together. In *Rose Red* King suggests a similar kind of hybridization by showing the house's uncanny relationship to the surrounding traffic and commerce of nearby Seattle. As Tony Magistrale writes in *Hollywood's Stephen King*, this juxtaposition demonstrates that "the two worlds . . . do not interface very well" (214). Moreover, much of *Rose Red* features external shots of the house that highlight the supernatural space that Rose Red occupies. Unfortunately, such visual tours are frightening only to the extent that audiences are able to recoil at things like empty rooms and lifelike statues of Ellen Rimbauer. Unlike Robert Wise's skillful use of red filters and distorting lenses to create a sense of strangeness and dread in *The Haunting*, the shots of *Rose Red* create only a sense of hope that the interior of the home will be more frightening than the exterior. Once inside the house, however, Joyce takes her team on a tour that turns out to be about as scary as a tour of Disneyland's Haunted Mansion, complete with a strange hall with hidden doors, a library with a mirrored floor, the apparition of April Rimbauer's (Julia Campbell) ghost, the guide rope inexplicably going through a wall, and an upside down room—all of which evokes more awe and wonder than terror. The house is presented as a historical anomaly, not a haunted house. Even the guests seem to enjoy Joyce's ride; during the tour, they actually beg her to tell them more about the house's fascinating history.

The haunted fun-house quality increases after the tour during the pizza party sequence. As if hinting at us how far his tongue is in his cheek with this story, King himself appears in a cameo as an over-the-hill pizza delivery boy bringing treats to enhance the party. Again, at the party, the supernatural is taken as a matter of course, more in a fantasy vein than something horrific. Annie causes the defunct record player to work, playing Glen Miller music as some of the team dance while floating on air. The party's atmosphere perfectly captures the juxtaposition of the light and the dark that characterizes *Rose Red*. But this is not just any party—during the festivities, Joyce's high-tech, spirit counter registers the attendance of unseen party crashers who soon wreak havoc by popping lights, blowing violent wind, and causing the fire to rage.

In *Rose Red*, King seems to be trying to frighten his audience through the regular juxtaposition of such light and dark moments. Nevertheless, King does not maintain a strong balance between the two sides. At times, the film seems almost overwhelmed with comic verbal play, even in some of the tensest sequences. For example, Nick Hardaway (Julian Sands) baits Emery's selfishness by asking him "What do you want big boy? Nymphs to kneel at your feet and offer you delicacies from silver platters?" Other examples of the film's verbal comedy include Emery's insistence that the ghosts cannot frighten him as long as he has bills to pay ("try warning someone who doesn't need the money"), and the way Mrs Kay Waterman (Laura Kenny) abuses Professor Carl Miller (David Dukes) as they try to get onto the property ("Get the gate would you? Come on; put your back into it"). In addition Steve Rimbauer (Matt Keeslar) repeatedly makes wise-cracks (particularly the phone message he leaves Professor Miller), and Professor Miller himself serves as an example of ridiculous pomposity (his answering machine message states: "Remember your Shakespeare: Brevity is the soul of wit").

King's use of black humor throughout *Rose Red* serves as an overt nod to the fun that lays beneath all the pretend bloodbaths, monsters, violence, and supernatural pyrotechnics that fill the average horror tale. In *Rose Red* King foregrounds this comic dimension regularly, even though the film is not an all-out comedy. The point of such a gesture, we suggest, has to do with playing with the well-known intimate tie between humor and horror. After all, both horror and play are characterized around destabilizing fixed categories of meaning. As Noël Carroll writes, humor, like play, "is bound up with transgressive play with our categories, concepts, norms, and common place expectations" (249). Likewise, Dani Cavallaro notes that "there is something simultaneously tantalizing and disturbing about play's propensity to subvert existing structures of meaning through its imaginative manipulation of symbolic signs since it intimates that no system is unproblematically stable." Even play things share in this ambivalence. As Cavallaro writes, toys, "especially dolls . . . combine the attributes of innocent and timeless beauty with darker qualities related to their artificiality, their utilization by black magic and their representation of humanity as a gallery of more or less grotesque dummies" (137).

In *Danse Macabre*, Stephen King argues for the connection between humor and horror by writing that the former is "implicit" in the latter (124). Throughout his career, King has drawn on images of play and toys to emphasize the uncanny horrors of everyday life. Pennywise, the clown from *It*, serves as a classic illustration of this point, as does the central image in the short story, "The Monkey," in which a cymbal-clashing toy monkey induces fear and panic in its owners. Both images, of course, function in a playfully uncanny way— both clowns and monkeys entertain us in part because they are anthropomorphic figures that cross the boundaries of discreet human behavior. King has also played with the connection between humor and horror in much of his original work for film. Two of King's anthology films, *Creepshow* (1982) and *Cat's Eye* (1985) are filled with playful dark humor. In the *Creepshow* segment entitled "The Lonesome Death of Jordy Verrill," King himself stars as a hilariously hick farmer who touches a substance from outer space he finds in his yard, soon covering him and his world in green grass (shades of Lovecraft's "The Colour Out of Space"). "The Crate," also from *Creepshow*, presents a deliciously dark revenge by a henpecked husband on his shrewish nagging wife, introducing her to a man-eating monster locked up in the science building. *Cat's Eye* offers similar fare. "Quitter's Inc.," for example, is a humorous story starring comedian Alan King, about how the threat and fulfillment of torture and mutilation can curb the tobacco habit in a hurry.

More recently, King's television series *Kingdom Hospital* seems more radically interested in combining serious suspense and horror with a cast of strange characters and scenes of utterly absurd humor. Here the contrast between humor and horror seems to be the point— and seems the next logical step after something like *Rose Red*. As Alfred Hitchcock himself noted, "Fear, you see, is a feeling that people like to feel when they are certain of being in safety" (quoted in Gottlieb 143). In other words, feelings of fear can be entertaining so long as viewers are not asked to identify too much with the actual threat. Hitchcock further stated that "any carnival man will tell you the rides that attract the greatest clientele are those that inspire the greatest fear" (quoted in Gottlieb 117). Surely this blend of horror with entertainment is part of the reason that most horror movies, no matter how poorly acted, directed, or produced, usually turn into box office gold.

In keeping with Hitchcock's likening of terror to a roller coaster ride, *Rose Red* seems to be taking that concept to its logical limits. As important as anything else the film does to generate its peculiarly playful tone (for a haunted house story) is its horrendous pace. Generally, the more chilling moments are paced too quickly to build up the necessary atmosphere of dread that would truly horrify viewers. Since King is a master of the rules for scaring viewers, we can only imagine that *Rose Red* is a deliberately transgressive gesture toward the standard rules. For example, at one and the same time, King juggles several sets of somewhat confusing scenes: Vic being led away by Pam Asbury's (Emily Deschanel) ghost, Kay Waterman's wandering wildly through the woods, and a lost and frantic Professor Miller coming upon the (probably) dead Kevin Bollinger (Jimmi Simpson). Such cross cutting between various people in frenzied predicaments is reminiscent again of comic spectacles like *A Midsummer Night's Dream*, or, more to the point, children's shows like *Scooby Doo*.

King's juxtapositions between horror and humor suggest that Rose Red is dominated by two distinct presences, one embodying the dark side, the other, the light. While Ellen Rimbauer represents the more sinister elements of the house, the Puck-like imp with the small horns and the wry smile whose statue overlooks the house and all that happens in and around it represents the lighter side. This figure, invoking the playful use of supernatural spells and confusions that harass the unwitting forest visitors in *A Midsummer Night's Dream*, suggests the black humor of both the house and the narrative itself. To some extent, we can argue that *Rose Red* is largely a variation on Shakespeare's story of Lysander's and Demetrius's running blindly after each other as King creates his own aimless, yet somewhat comic, ramblings of multiple characters within and without Rose Red. King's uses of visual sequences in a Shakespearean mode are foreshadowed by his own use of Shakespeare as a model for his own performance-based writing. As he writes in his introduction to *Storm of the Century*: "And I would remind you that the man most students of literature believe to be the greatest of English writers worked in an oral and visual medium, and not (at least primarily) in the medium of print" (xviii). King's hint of his Shakespearean intentions appears in *Rose Red* directly through Professor Miller's admonition to "Remember your Shakespeare." Indeed, we can easily imagine the imp-like figure who sits atop Rose

Red directing the house's ghosts with the words: "Up and down, up and down, / I will lead them up and down; / I am fear'd in field and town. / Goblin, lead them up and down" (3.2.396–398). Indeed, much of *Rose Red* stresses a kind of endless chasing about. Just as Professor Miller and Emery's mother chase around the grounds, Emery, Cathy Kramer (Judith Ivey), and Nick find themselves running aimlessly throughout the house. If horror provides a kind of rehearsal for death, such fruitless rambling demonstrates the vain human desire to escape not only death but also its rehearsal. The limits of mortality, in other words, cause many of us to behave strangely—as Shakespeare has it, "Lord, what fools these mortals be" (3.2.115).

Another important narrative link between *Rose Red* and *A Midsummer Night's Dream* is the way they shift point of view between the mortals and the spirits. Shakespeare's play regularly invites the audience to see the action from the perspective of the fairies who are manipulating it. Similarly, *Rose Red* shows some of its story through the eyes of the ghosts, thereby inverting the usual haunted house device of having the audience experience the horrors alongside the protagonists. This goes beyond merely identifying the camera automatically with the house. An example of this point-of-view shift occurs when the young college reporter, Bollinger, disappears inside the house. As Bollinger approaches and enters the yard, he is filmed in a way that we see and feel right along with him. He opens the iron gate and we see him from behind, looking small against the large house. We then see a low-angle close-up as he nervously views the house. This is when the perspective begins to change. From his glance up to the house, the film cuts to the horned imp on the roof looking and smiling down on Bollinger. We now see him from the extreme high angle of the house—as if from the imp's standpoint. Bollinger then goes to the door and is welcomed by Sukeena (Tsidii Leluka), the ghost of a character the audience first saw in flashback. As Bollinger is ushered inside, Sukeena disappears, even though her disembodied voice continues bidding him to come "this way." As he enters the great hall, we again see Bollinger from an extreme height— now understood as one of the house' points of view. He is then led into the solarium—a stand-in for Shakespeare's own enchanted forest. He then begins calling out for Sukeena only to find himself completely alone. Importantly, because he has proven unlikable, working for an even more unlikable and obsessive Professor Miller who is out to ruin Joyce, we are encouraged to see Bollinger from the point of view of the house. We are not that fearful for him. Rather we are, with the house, amused over the developing justice unfolding. We enjoy his growing unease upon seeing the bugs on the floor. Then, like a character from Shakespeare's comedy, he begins to cry out: "Very funny, but I want to leave"; "Hey . . . I could use a little help!" Even he seems to acknowledge the house's presence—and prescience. Upon feeling a drip on his shoulder he looks up, at which point the camera zooms down at him from the house' high-angle point of view and the scene ends as we see Bollinger's legs shoot up suddenly in a disappearing act straight out of a Bob Hope or an Abbott and Costello comic "horror" movie. Importantly, the comic aspect of this equally horrific sequence comes from seeing it through the eyes of the house. This hybrid scene pulls us both ways simultaneously, balancing our sympathies for an essentially innocent young man and our dark glee at seeing how the little smart-mouth punk gets his comeuppance.

King's other major hybrid allusions and borrowings share equally in his project to both scare and amuse. In an interview featured on the *Rose Red* DVD, he suggested that he wants *Rose Red* "to be a sort of *Moby Dick* haunted house story, if you will. Something that's big and scary—that sticks in people's minds as '*the* haunted house movie'" (emphasis mine). In other words, the shadow of *Moby-Dick* serves as a sly and effective means of hybridizing some of *Rose Red's* narrative and characters. Most obviously Melvillean is King's development of Joyce Reardon as an Ahab-like figure with her crew of psychics standing in for Ahab's own "knights and squires." In this case, Joyce's elusive quest is to capture the "white whale of haunted houses" by recording the hard scientific evidence she needs to prove the existence of ghosts to her skeptical colleagues—and she does not care who dies in the process. *Moby-Dick* is particularly appropriate since it, too, mingles gothic tropes with playful and comic passages. Another hint at a borrowing comes late in the film when Steve declares that the house itself is a vampire, and considering the range of vampire imagery in *Rose Red*, King might have claimed *Dracula* as well as *Moby-Dick* for a narrative model. Indeed, Rose Red claims the lives of others so it can regularly renew itself. Moreover, like Dracula, Rose Red also has its active and dormant periods and is able to entrance the living into obeying its will. Ellen Rimbauer, the chief "vampire," even shows her fangs in the portrait Kathy sees. The film's structure also mirrors important elements from *Dracula*, including the castle haunted by seductive "brides" and the way it is shut up in such a way as to prevent the team from leaving.

Probably the most recognizable source for *Rose Red* is Shirley Jackson's *The Haunting of Hill House*. Indeed, King's story clearly draws on Jackson's story of a scientific investigation of a haunted house. Joyce, for example, oddly serves as a combination of both Dr Montague and Eleanor Vance. Other connections to Jackson's novel include Cathy's automatic writing (resembling Mrs Montague's Ouija board) and the multiple sequences in which people get easily lost and disoriented. Also important, however, is the constant return to the theme of "Summer Place," a clear reflection of Eleanor Vance's own romantic and hopeful thought that "Journeys end in lovers meeting." Another obvious borrowing from Jackson comes in the shower of stones sequence at the beginning of the film. In these scenes King presents a rather long sequence of events that tie the falling stones to Annie's emotional and perhaps physical states, and like Bollinger's abduction, invokes the dark glee of vengeance realized in a particularly spectacular way.

In *Rose Red*, humor, horror, and play are blended seamlessly, at-once incipient and fulfilled. The audience, along with King, is invited to play with the haunted house genre, to see how many ways it can be tweaked through conversations with other texts. King's is a language that multiplies sources by drawing on living narrative forms—just like Rose Red, it exists mainly by drawing out the blood of the living in order to remain alive.

Chapter 15

Gardening for a New Generation of Horror in *Secret Window*

Benjamin Szumskyj

Background—the Novella

When first released, Stephen King's collection of four novellas entitled *Four Past Midnight* (1990) received mixed reviews. The works ranged from the strong to the mediocre and continued well-known themes from King's oeuvre. However, one work stood out amongst the rest: *Secret Window, Secret Garden*. Though not a masterpiece, King returned to a favorite theme, that of the author haunted by fame or personal demons. *The Shining, Misery, Bag of Bones, Lisey's Story, The Dark Half, Tommyknockers*, and *'Salem's Lot* are all notorious for having characters that are authors, most of whom are seldom depicted in a favorable light. *Secret Window, Secret Garden*, would join that list. The genesis of the story is worth quoting. King found a window in one of his homes and

> looked out. That window looks down on a little brick-paved alcove between the house and the attached sun porch. It's an area I see just about every day . . . but the angle was new. My wife had set half a dozen pots out there, so the plants could take a little of the early November sun, I suppose, and the result was a charming little garden which only I could see. The phrase which occurred to me was, of course, the title of this story. It seemed to me as good a metaphor as any for what writers—especially writers of fantasy—do with their days and nights. Sitting down at the typewriter or picking up a pencil is a physical act; the spiritual analogue is looking out of an almost forgotten window, a window which offers a common view from an entirely different angle . . . an angle which renders the common extraordinary. The writer's job is to gaze through that window and report on what he sees. (*Four Past Midnight*, 306–307)

The above comment is interesting, in that King was clearly having a writer's block the late fall of 1987 and, through an accident, he uncovered something new, something that had eluded him for over a decade. Minor as it may appear to a person who is not a writer, King stresses that "the angle was new." These four words alone could easily promote much of the author's oeuvre, as much of his work taps into well-known themes and creations that are delivered in a new fashion. King's metaphor manifests itself quite clearly in the novella as well as the film.

Secret Window, Secret Garden is easily summarized. It is the story of Mort Rainey, a hermitic author who lives in a cabin after finding out his wife has been having an affair. One day, Rainey is confronted by an individual named John Shooter who claims the author has stolen his story. Throughout the novella, Rainey is haunted by Shooter and believes he is dealing with a madman, at the same time, reflecting on the claim of plagiarism. By the end of the story, it is revealed that John Shooter is, in fact, an imaginary figure created by Rainey as a psychological reaction to his guilt of an early unrelated act of plagiarism. Rainey himself has been the one committing recent murders, vandalism, and acts of self-persecution. In the final scenes of the novella, Rainey psychologically *becomes* Shooter and tries to kill his wife Amy, but is killed by an insurance agent who suspected Rainey was mentally unstable.

From Paper to Reel—Cinematic Adaptation

Secret Window, Secret Garden was not considered a bankable King adaptation until director David Koepp was given a copy of *Four Past Midnight*: "I'd been working with Columbia on a couple of movies and the executive there had bought the novella and said, 'You should direct this.' And I said, 'Yes, you're right. I should.' I guess I just really am drawn to guy-in-a-house-going-crazy movies. *The Tenant* is obviously a great inspiration for this movie and *Rosemary's Baby*. . . . I like somebody spending a lot of time in their home and then finding their home turning on them in a way. I like that kind of confinement. I like bad things happening in your living space" (Koepp, "*Secret Window*: From Book to Film"). This remark is worthy of consideration for it appears that from the very moment Koepp decided to adapt this film, he was not only aware of Mort Rainey's descent into madness, but this aspect of the novella was also his *main* interest, as opposed to any other aspect (e.g., the role of the writer, the breakup of his marriage, the issue of recurring plagiarism). Koepp freely admitted this later, stating that the "writer aspect of it was actually one of the least appealing elements to me. Because I think that writers are just very boring people" (Koepp, "*Secret Window*: From Book to Film"). Whether Koepp's portrayal of Rainey's descent into madness was a success or not is an issue I address later.

At the time, David Koepp was a relatively new director who had been applauded for his directorial and script work on movies such as *Death Becomes Her* (1992), *Carlito's Way* (1993), *The Paper* (1994), *Mission: Impossible* (1996), *Jurassic Park: The Lost World* (1997), *Stir of Echoes* (1999), and *Panic Room* (2002). It is perhaps the last two movies listed here that helped Koepp secure direction of the King adaptation, for despite their flaws, both were well received. The former is loosely based of a Richard Matheson novel; Koepp wrote the screenplay for the latter.

Secret Window's cast of actors was perfectly chosen. Johnny Depp, one of the modern generation's finest living actors, has proven to audiences over and over again that he is more than capable of immersing himself in the foreboding characters he plays. The dark overtones of *Secret Window* were a fine fit, in light of his performances in *Sleepy Hollow*, the underrated *Ninth Gate*, and even the eccentric nature of the Jack Sparrow character in the *Pirates of the Caribbean* trilogy. Depp's ability to portray authors is impressive, as displayed in the several movies in which he plays a writer: *Fear and Loathing in Las Vegas* (as Raoul Duke, Hunter S. Thompson's alter ego), *Finding Neverland* (as Sir James Matthew Barrie), and *The Libertine* (as John Wilmot, second Earl of Rochester). John Turturro's decision to play John Shooter was likewise a good fit, for both his physical and verbal presence matches the character perfectly. Timothy Hutton's portrayal of Ted Milner is superb, while Maria Bello played Amy Rainey surprisingly rather well, as *Secret Window* served as her introduction to the horror genre. In an interview for the film, she states that she is "a huge fan of Stephen King and a huge fan of thrillers" (Bello, "*Secret Window*: From Book to Film").

Direction—Understanding the Heart
of the Story

Koepp is clearly a fan of Stephen King's work, something that is important as too often modern directors lack enough appreciation for the literary texts they adapt for screen. In *Secret Window, Secret Garden*, Koepp "felt like the characters were really vivid. What you think you're gonna get from Stephen King material is not what you actually do. What you get [from King] is extremely well-developed characters and really well-thought-out psychology" (Koepp, "*Secret Window*: From Book to Film"). King's characters often share something from the writer's life; in this case, an accusation of plagiarism raised over King's publication of the novel *Misery*, a falsehood that was dismissed accordingly (Beahm 160). Soon after, a schizophrenic man broke into King's house, confronting King's wife Tabitha with a fake bomb. Although early reports painted him as another person claiming plagiarism, it was later clarified that he only wanted to write a book with the author (Beahm 162).

Koepp acknowledges that "Shooter is the alter ego, the pure artist, the uncompromising artist. Mort is the commercial artist, the one who wants to please an audience. Shooter couldn't give a shit if he pleases an audience or not. He wants to write the right story" (Koepp, "*Secret Window*: From Book to Film"). As a commercial writer who is also capable of producing first-rate art, this discussion is immediately relevant to King's work, as many of his author-heroes engage a meta-textual struggle with the dichotomy between real art and commercial success. Several of King's critics find that he writes *just* for the reader, as opposed to writing for the reader *and* himself, and as a result, as one critic puts it, "has more in common with [Judith] Krantz, Danielle Steel, Sidney Sheldon and other purveyors of popular sentiment than he does with Poe, Lovecraft, and Blackwood, let alone Hawthorne and Faulkner" (Joshi 94).

Koepp admitted in a press release that he paid homage to director Stanley Kubrick in the making of *Secret Window*, an ironic acknowledgment in light of King's well-known public disparagement of Kubrick's adaptation of *The Shining* ("A Nod to Kubrick"). The Kubrick influence is most apparent near the end of the movie, when the name Shooter and words "Shoot Her" appear reminiscent of Redrum and "Murder" in *The Shining* (Koepp, "*Secret Window*: Secrets Revealed"). Interestingly, one reviewer hinted that *Secret Window* is slightly Hitchcockean in its direction: "Rainey appears to be the classic Hitchcock hero, an Innocent Man Wrongly Accused" (Ebert 2004).

Novella and Film—Comparing and Contrasting

Secret Window (its title was shortened so not to conflict with Frances Hodgson Burnett's *Secret Garden*) begins slightly different than the novella. While the novella begins with the line: "You stole my story" (308), Koepp felt the audience needed to understand the main character of Mort Rainey first, by referring to a past event that made us sympathize with him; in this case, as the victim of an adulterous partner. This event that opens the movie is only mentioned much later on in the novella (451). Koepp chose this course of plot evolution because he "wanted the movie to snap onto the screen" (Koepp, "*Secret Window*: A Look Through It").

Aside from its ending, Koepp's cinematic adaptation of King's novella is relatively fair. Throughout the movie, several scenes are identical to those in the novella. In the novella, Rainey's former wife Amy unconsciously comes across as his literary muse; since the divorce, he "hadn't written anything worth a damn" (314). In Koepp's adaptation, however, she is in many ways the reason for his writer's block, as he only begins to write again after she is killed at the end of the movie. John Shooter is slightly more fleshed out in the novella, something Koepp may have avoided in order to create more of melding between the two characters. Koepp changed Amy's pet cat Bump to a dog in the movie, a somewhat perplexing move when we learn that Koepp did so because he feared that a cat might raise questions about Rainey's masculinity. In the novella, Rainey refuses to inform the local police of Bump's murder (363), while in the movie, Koepp has him doing so, portraying the cop in the stereotypically autocratic mold that is often found in modern horror movies. In order to minimize the number of characters from the novella, Koepp replaces Rainey's security officer Greg Castairs (365) and literary agent Herb Creekmore (370) with the character of Ken Karsch, a private investigator. In the novella, King has Shooter wanting Rainey to write an entirely new story for publication (398), as opposed to the film's demand that he rewrite the ending of "his" plagiarized work.

The ending of *Secret Window*, however, differs greatly from the novella. In an interview, Koepp states that "What was challenging is trying to make this ending work because [it] is different than it was in the novella" (Koepp, "*Secret Window*: From Book to Film"). After the success of *The Sixth Sense*, many scriptwriters and directors felt that the audience of horror movies expected twists. In some cases, the villain or forces of evil often triumph (such as in the film *Identity*). It appears Koepp aligns himself with this school of thought, as Rainey is not shot and killed as he is in the novella (466), but retains his John Shooter persona and kills both Amy and Ted in a gruesome fashion by "implied violence but not a lot of actual violence just because I don't think there's that much artistry in it" (Koepp, "*Secret Window*: Secrets Revealed"). This alternative ending is, by no means, in poor taste or badly acted. The problem is that by ignoring King's ending, Koepp undermines the whole moral behind the story of Rainey's descent into madness as a consequence of his guilt concerning plagiarism. This is most frustrating as interviews with the director indicate that he understands the issue of Rainey's alleged plagiarism as paramount to the story, saying, "I think for a writer to be accused of plagiarism is to be accused of being nothing" (Koepp, "*Secret Window*: Look Through It").

Secret Window—A Bakhtinian Dream

Mikhail Bakhtin (1895–1975), author of books such as *Discourse in the Novel, From the Prehistory of Novelistic Discourse,* and *Forms of Time and of the Chronotope in the Novel,* might have appreciated both King's narrative and Koepp's film. King's novella is told in third-person narration, allowing us to hear the words and thoughts of Mort Rainey; he is the only character whose thoughts we read in the novella and hear throughout the movie. As such, the reader/viewer is limited to one point of view, voice, and form of language, precluding a second (and outside) opinion from which we might form a more balanced reality (rather than a singularly enforced one). Koepp's *Secret Window* dramatizes this by entering—and later retreating from—a mirror in Rainey's house at the beginning and end of the film. However, one must see Rainey's thoughts as being neither a singular motivation nor specifically targeted. The narrative is a psychological commentary that delivers a moral and seeks to define a deeper understanding of why the story began (and ultimately ends). In a Bakhtinian manner, Rainey has made clear his identity, his subject position. In many ways he is both purging his sin and justifying his actions, going so far as to clarify the psyche of what is really a madman who honestly believes that he did no wrong to a cinema audience who could never conceive of committing such a crime (e.g., John Shooter is seen and heard as being psychotic as opposed to Mort who, for most of the film, is normal). This killer is housing more than one voice.

The formation of the subject, in accordance with Bakhtin's writings, occurs by way of forces outside human control. To make this clearer, his belief is that in order to define ourselves as a subject, one must adopt the view of another person so that we can make clear of what our *being* is and what our *self* is. In finding the *self*, the individual must work together with more than one other person (to gain a broader understanding of who he is and perceived to be). If you desire to create a sense of *being* you cannot do so alone, as we understand our place through the eyes of others. It is by this notion that we are made aware of external factors unseen that can only be interpreted by someone other than the self.

Taking King's *Secret Window, Secret Garden* and Koepp's adaptation of the novella into consideration, the dialogical formation of the subject is created from several different elements. There is King's interaction with Mort Rainey, the reader's interaction with Mort Rainey, Mort Rainey's interaction with the other characters (Amy, Ted, John, Tom, etc.), and last, but certainly not the least important, Mort Rainey's own life portrayal. The narrator in both film and novella is unpredictable in that he does not tell the reader what they should know or understand and the main voice is subjected to change. Amusingly, the title is also double voiced. *Secret Window* is the name of the story that is at the center of plagiarism in the novella and is also the name of a window and garden loved by Amy.

In King's book we have an author writing about a fictional narrator, which then becomes a meeting between the fictional narrator and the reader, which is, after all, a shadowed meeting between author and reader. This illustrates Bakhtin's notion of polyphonism (in which there are many different voices, i.e., personas). Double voicing (what the subject thinks and what it says are two very different matters) and polyphonism can coexist, as there will always be a difference between thought and speech in which a single person gives life to many different types of voices. Even though it is written in first person, there are two distinct voices to be read: that of the narrator *describing* (impersonal in the sense that they are merely describing what is experienced by them) and that of the narrator's *consciousness* (personal in the sense that they are voicing their thoughts and it is something that we cannot see or understand unless otherwise told). This is clearly seen in *Secret Window* through Mort Rainey leading to conflicting bodies of interest: *Insane* vs *Sane*, *Good* vs *Evil*, *Law Abiding* vs *Crime Committing*, *Innocence* vs *Guilt*, and *Intelligence* vs *Stupidity*. One may feel free to consider these conflicting bodies as a part of Bakhtin's belief in hetroglossia, in which several different languages and/or discourses can be heard as oppositional voices. This seems to abide by Bakhtin's statement that there is always a struggle within language and the acting out of different but equal subject positions. *Secret Window* would be most favorable to him, as it presents a character that cannot easily be read through a single defining voice.

The closing scenes of Koepp's cinematic adaptation of *Secret Window* are predictably Bakhtinian, as the narrator sets himself toward an inevitable ending. Although we begin with a man who appears to be free of guilt and is a victim of a confused psychopath, we witness his own undoing as a result of his conflicting personae. Self-conflicting dialogue eventually undermines his personal vision and attempts to justify what he has done. It is through dialogue that we come to interpret and understand the narrator's sense of place in the world and his role in it, allowing a personal experience to enlarge into social commentary. We finally come to realize that a dialogical relationship is established between narrator and the character that is internalized in both book and film (leading to no synthesis of conflict).

Conclusion—Closing the Window

In adapting *Secret Window, Secret Garden*, Koepp is gardening for a new generation of horror fan. Current audiences are flocking to see horror movies in which either evil conquers, or one in which a hero survives but at a great cost. While there is an abundance of theories for this change, from those advanced by popular culture commentators to sociologists, let us simply acknowledge that this is a phase in cinematic horror and is a reflection of social uncertainty and convergence (or even reinterpretation) of "good" and "evil." In reflecting on the current state of the horror market and his own place in it, King shares his interpretation on the issue:

> Horror is something that appeals to young people. I've said this before. Because young people feel healthy, they view it the way they view amusement park rides: it's a thrill, it's a kick, it's a gas, but you don't really think it's going to happen to you.
>
> But now my generation is reaching an age where we don't really need the hidden cancer metaphors of a movie like *Alien*. When we have friends who are coming down with the disease or we are worried about the disease ourselves. A lot of the fears, a lot of the terrors and a lot of interest that drive a movie like *Scream* or *Scream 2* or *I Know What You Did Last Summer* is closer to the sensibility of such juvenile novels as the Goosebumps books, the R.L. Stine phenomena. In fact, I think that, in America, the *Scream* movies are driven by people who cut their teeth on R.L. Stine rather than Stephen King and are now old enough to get into "R" rated films. ("The Man Who Would Be King," 185)

This is a difficult statement to assess, as King seems to imply that the allegorical nature of past horror movies (such as *Alien*, which has been interpreted as being everything from a metaphor for cancer to asexual rape) is lost on modern audiences simply because they are healthy, fearless, and possibly desensitized. It would be safe to say that *Hostel* or the *Saw* trilogy would not be possible decades ago without an

X rating (yet interestingly, the sequel to *Basic Instinct* had to be less sexually explicit than its predecessor). More so, very few modern horror films showcase allegory or social commentary, and even when they attempt to do so, they often fail miserably. It is refreshing that Koepp endeavored "to show implied violence but not a lot of actual violence just because I don't think there's that much artistry in it" (Koepp, "*Secret Window*: Secrets Revealed"), as this seems to be a trait many other directors fail to appreciate sufficiently (such as the *Texas Chainsaw Massacre* remakes).

Is *Secret Window* a failure? By no means. Is it, then, a faithful adaptation of King's *Secret Window, Secret Garden*? No, but in saying that, Koepp's adaptation is far better than many in the last decade and does not detract too much from the original source. Although it is virtually impossible to adapt a text, word for word, onto the big screen, it remains important that both the director and scriptwriter (in this case, Koepp was both) appreciate its original source. In this instance, Koepp created a new interpretation, but did so without ruining a great story by Stephen King.

Chapter 16

Plucking Stems, Pulling Strings, and Pushing Agendas

The Consistency of Personal Failure and Mental Frailty in *The Mist*

Patrick McAleer

As a species, we're fundamentally insane. Put more than two of us in a room, we pick sides and start dreaming up ways to kill one another. Why do you think we invented politics and religion?

Ollie Weeks, from *The Mist*

Stephen King's fiction and films have consistently brought his readers into a variety of realms, from nightmarish dreamscapes of alternative worlds to everyday American towns overrun with supernatural monsters or monstrously deplorable humans. As King shows quite the range of plots, locations, characters, and themes, a majority of his writing can be seen as centered on real concerns of great social magnitude. And while the Stephen King canon is one that may have shadowed areas that few wish to approach (*Dreamcatcher* being one of the most common targets for criticism and ridicule, both as a text and as a film), his body of work is quite powerful as it not only brings readers into intimate contact with tales of horrific and perhaps even questionable content, but also provides numerous spotlights that illuminate dark recesses of humanity that need attention and action. Indeed, King often places his audience into the role of a student, suggesting an instructive or harshly didactic element to his craft. For example, in an English writing course I recently taught, with *Different Seasons* (1982) as the primary fiction selection, many of my students became rather numbed and stupefied regarding the novella *Apt Pupil* as they read of Todd Bowden's continual degeneration into a monster, and ultimately they had to consider Stephen King's lesson that we all possess the potential to transform into a monster like Todd. This shocking lesson that Todd is simply "one of us"—just another all-American brute that has succumbed to the lures of evil that represent the human legacy in Stephen King's America—found quite a bit of resistance from my students. Many balked at the idea that America, whether in the 1980s or even in the new millennium, contained and even bred *real* people that purportedly served as source material for or reflections of Todd Bowden, a boy whose fascination with the Holocaust illustrated a disturbing detachment from his society and from any semblance of normalcy, or sense of ethics. However, several other students were less reluctant to face the reality of this horror and were bold enough to confront the uncomfortable and disturbing reality that Todd Bowden is not entirely a character of pure imagination, and that his personal failings mimic and mirror our own potential for discord and misanthropy, which is the primary theme running through Stephen King's 1980 novella and Frank Darabont's 2007 film, *The Mist*.

From *The Shining* (1977) and Jack Torrance's losing battle with alcohol and the Overlook Hotel to *The Dark Tower* series (1982–2004) and the gunslinger Roland Deschain's failure to breach the door at the top of the Dark Tower itself, the chaos King creates and asks his characters and readers to navigate suggests a constant and almost unwinnable battle against failure. And in *The Mist*, failure takes on numerous faces and forms, ultimately providing a sobering look into the very core of the American Everyman and Everywoman and their perpetual struggles against myriad obstacles. Regardless of how one wants to view America and its populace, King and director Frank Darabont remind us of a human being's constant propensity for folly all throughout *The Mist* and challenge their audience to hold up and look into a mirror of judgment and truth, complete with a dreary reflection that offers little hope. Although all remnants of hope are not necessarily removed from *The Mist*, especially as the original text ends with a suggestion of survival, the film does tend to walk within the boundaries of destitution rather than optimism.

When one thinks of failure within the Stephen King canon, there are, again, numerous examples to pull from. *The Stand* (1978) sees an entire nation become fractured and fragmented, while *Storm of the Century* (1999) explores the inner workings and failures of a small town, where, as Tony Magistrale claims, "The supernatural and horrific presence of [Andre] Linoge is merely an extension of the town's general propensity for malevolence" (Magistrale, *Hollywood*, 208). *The Mist* takes up this microcosm of the small town (one that King revisits over and over again, especially within *The Tommyknockers* [1987] and *Under the Dome* [2009]) and condenses this even further, trapping desperate and confused Mainers within a grocery market after a strange and terrible mist descends upon the community. In terms of the location where much of the film takes place, perhaps there are criticisms of consumerism lurking in the aisles of the Food House, but the main draw and purpose of this location is that it is one in which people tend to gather for items of actual *need*. And as such, the supermarket would seem to be a place that fosters humanity through common ground, whereas locating this tale within an electronics store or a tavern might not have the same effect. The name of the grocery store itself (which is altered from the original text— Federal Foods Supermarket—suggesting an eerie governmental influence among the marketplace) reminds us of the necessities of life: food (Food) and shelter (House). And with clothing cast aside as a third necessity, there is a fourth necessity to survival that emanates from the film: decency.

Decency, and its closely related practices of courtesy and compassion, is one of the key tools at the disposal of the "supermarket survivors" to be used in the battle stemming from the film's tagline that appears on the original movie poster: "FEAR CHANGES EVERYTHING." In the face of fear, and the unknown, *The Mist* asks its characters to embrace their humanity and their ability to care for one another as this humane bonding and banding together is likely a more effective tool than isolation or uncouthness. However, etiquette and sympathy are not always instruments that humans wield well. For example, in the text version of *The Mist*, fear pushes the main character, David Drayton (played by Thomas Jane in the film), into the sexual embrace of Amanda Dumfries (played by Laurie Holden in the film), indicating that fear certainly changes everything, so much so that wedding vows are compromised but are done so as to find solace in the face of despair. To be sure, the abrupt and somewhat unsurprising sex between David and Amanda displays a human connection that is desired when one is in the throes of despair, and such is an understandable attempt at creating harmony out of discord. On one level, this is an act of compassion that provides a semblance of hope, or decency, in a story that is rather pessimistic: it is "a spontaneous act that underscores the need for human interdependency" (Magistrale, *Second Decade*, 91). But this interdependency smacks of pessimism, a failure to believe that they will truly escape the nightmare of the mist alive and that their shared sexual embrace is their last tether to the lives that they once knew. And, as such, the foundations for the film version are laid, despite King and Darabont's decision to cut the sex scene between David and Amanda from the film, in that the people of the Food House in *The Mist* tend to look for any excuse to avoid personal responsibility or embrace the possibilities of the irrational world that has clearly surrounded them and necessitates intelligent, ethical, and hopeful action. In short, *The Mist* is hardly an uplifting film, suggesting that while the monsters from the mist have limited time on the screen, the film's horror stems from the follies and dubious actions of the film's citizenry, and that their unscrupulous deeds are more than just troubling—they are based in reality.

Setting the Stage

Amanda Dumfries: "Don't you have any faith in humanity?"
Dan Miller: "None whatsoever."

The Mist, as a film, has certainly received its share of attention among King critics and scholars, and one such scholar is Mark Browning, whose work is obsessed with chiding other scholars for their apparent lack of familiarity with, and understanding of, the nuances of film studies. Browning, author of *Stephen King on the Big Screen and Stephen King on the Small Screen*, seems to take issue with literary critics offering ideas and insights into the films of Stephen King—"Tony Magistrale shows little sign that he is aware of the academic disciplines of Film Study and more particularly Television Studies" (*Small Screen*, 7–8). Browning claims that analyses and criticisms of film must be contained or circulated only from within film studies circles. In an attempt at providing a complete examination of all of King's fictions that have been adapted for the screen, Browning looks at *The Mist* in his 2011 text *Stephen King on the Small Screen*. Although his unscholarly and haphazard inclusion of a film in a text that examines King's television ventures is forgivable (while his failure to examine *The Dead Zone* television series is not), Browning aims to provide an analysis of *The Mist* that he feels is superior to those untrained in film studies, but, ironically, he fails to do so.

Indeed, Browning has taken his shots at King scholars, like the editor of this volume, and has boldly if not arrogantly claimed a corner on the market of studying King's cinematic and television adaptations. Browning's own offerings, however, are certainly limited and uninspiring, as he claims his first book, "takes an original look at King adaptations through the prism of intertextuality and a closely-related concept—genre" (*Big Screen*, 11). Such approaches are not reserved for the film critic, nor are they the sole property of literary critics. Assuredly, Browning's only real cinematic discussion regarding *The Mist*, beyond linking the film to numerous other movies (many notably of the "B" variety) in an attempt at providing an intertextual analysis that is mainly limited to brief musings and plot summaries, is this almost random note about the picture window of the Drayton house: "Looking through the window constitutes a screen-within-a-screen, creating a depth field and suggesting that the cinema screen might also be penetrated" (96). This note is akin to merely commenting upon the nearly constant gray hue that encapsulates the film, providing an almost ubiquitous presence of the physical mist that hides the monsters of the Arrowhead Project. Such an observation may be interesting, but given Browning's failure to develop it into something more substantial, it becomes a dead end.

Further, and perhaps most importantly, among the debatable comments that Browning provides concerning *The Mist*, he makes the claim, "Explanations about the source of the threat are less important than how the characters react to it" (*Small Screen*, 92). Despite the ranking of importance concerning characters versus information, one cannot dismiss the reported or factual information regarding the mist itself, and the monsters it shrouds. When Browning claims, "Knowledge here [in *The Mist*] provides no help in trying to survive," I would have to wholeheartedly disagree (*Small Screen*, 95). From a broad generic standpoint, science fiction (which is just one of the potential labels that can be attributed to *The Mist*) concerns itself not just with other worlds and technological innovations, but also with *learning*. The knowledge one acquires when a science fiction character is, say, on a scouting mission to Mars, or engaging in laboratory experimentation, propels such characters and their colleagues/companions toward a better, but not always full or entirely clear, understanding of the problems and obstacles that they face. Even when some knowledge seems unlikely, unhelpful, or even unbearable, *some* semblance of knowledge is certainly important for one's survival in an unfamiliar or strange situation.

For example, although David Drayton and his companions learn little about the nature of the mist and the Arrowhead Project from Private Wayne Jessup before he is murdered by Mrs. Carmody and her gaggle of scared, mindless followers, they receive a sense of confirmation that the world outside is no longer completely under their control or umbrella of understanding. The knowledge that the world has been reshaped and has shifted under the great weight of the monsters that now roam the streets, and because of the gravity of the government's callous indifference to the catastrophic outcomes of their misguided experimentations, does help David and his group of survivors in knowing that their survival depends upon innovation and quick thinking because they have truly experienced nothing like the mist before. Also, knowledge of the government's attempt to clean up their mess, so to speak, would have undoubtedly aided David in his precarious position of being the Angel of Death in the film's final moments; knowing that efforts were being made to rectify the problems of the Arrowhead Project just may have saved the lives of Billy Drayton (David's son), Amanda Dumfries, Irene Reppler, and Dan Miller. But, as Tony Magistrale argues (and which will be discussed in detail later in this chapter), mistrust of the American government runs rampant through this film, ultimately clouding David's judgment and his perceived knowledge or belief that the government and the military might actually try to rectify the problem of the mist, providing the film with its provocative conclusion and a foregrounding of the importance of knowledge that Browning apparently misses, or, even worse, chooses to dismiss.

Knowledge is certainly a fickle thing, yet it is often more of a boon rather than a burden to the characters in *The Mist* as well as to the audiences watching this film. As for the audience, knowledge of King's other works helps one navigate the film. Case in point, the first scene of the film shows David Drayton hard at work in his painting studio, and the audience sees a painting, or a movie poster, that depicts Roland Deschain of *The Dark Tower*. Knowledgeable viewers know that this is not just a nod toward King's other works, or a tongue-in-cheek moment of subtle import; this is a reminder to the audience that one had better be informed before watching this film as King takes great care in his *Dark Tower* series to posit the notion that there are multiple worlds surrounding our world, and that a simple doorway can lead into dark and dangerous unknown worlds, or allow beings to walk into our own world, just like in *The Mist*. With these alternative realities in play, Mark Browning once again provides a questionable understanding of King when he states, "King ducks the potential difficulty of creating alternative worlds and universes by locating most of his fiction firmly in the world he knows well" (*Small Screen*, 104). The point of *The Mist*, however, is not to create an alternative reality or even explore it, as one experiences in Mid-World of *The Dark Tower* series. Although dependent upon the notion of alternative realities while its own multiple realities are informed by one's knowledge of King's other works, *The Mist* is purposefully and primarily concerned with the real world, the world in which the Arrowhead

Project exists, and not the world into which the faceless scientists cast their gaze. Further, *The Mist* is focused on the real people that populate the real world, the world we all know, along with their common and frightening responses to not just fear, but to one another as well, and what happens when reality is invaded by an unknown or overwhelming force (which certainly parallels the anxiety concerning terrorism in twenty-first century America). And many of the unpleasant interactions that King's characters experience occur not necessarily because of the threat of monsters or an inability to look into and thoroughly explore an alternative dimension, but rather through the inability to look into and understand one another. Without doubt, the failure to be knowledgeable, or to direct one's queries toward information that will actually be of use, and a failure to be understanding and decent to one another is costly in *The Mist*, as it is nearly everywhere else in King's canon.

Plucking Stems: Ignorance Is Bliss, or, Evidence, Schmevidence

Ollie Weeks: "Denial is a powerful thing"

The function of the mind, or the gathering of information and either creating or ignoring knowledge, whether by design or accident, serves as the critical axis on which *The Mist* turns. As a member of the audience, for instance, much of our interaction with the film comes from a lack of knowledge and not just about the plot (i.e., if we have not read the original text version). But beyond the basic and common absence of knowledge regarding the potentially unfamiliar story of a film for a viewer, the unknown becomes the primary backdrop for *The Mist*. From monsters that are unfamiliar as a result of their inexplicable physical existence to the hidden thoughts and machinations of those contained within the Food House, King's brand of horror reigns supreme in that the monstrous horror of *The Mist* is not the only horror in the story. As Douglas Winter says, "We are disturbed by 'The Mist' because, like its narrator, we do not know exactly what to do when confronted by its horrors" (91). However, and this resembles many of King's characters, when most of us are confronted with the unknown, rarely do we shrink and curl up into a fetal position to await passively for some sort of cruel end to sweep us away. For instance, the character Jim, one of the locals who chooses to decry otherness and education, is still an active participant in the game of survival that all must play. He is, of course, a malleable character whose weakness is exploited by the religious fervor and persuasion of Mrs. Carmody. But Jim's desire for some sort of order, which is a function of knowledge, is satiated not by information, or the information that the mist poses a real and terrible threat; he, instead, finds solace in a lack of information, or the empty yet alluring promises and rhetoric of Mrs. Carmody. Jim is a scared individual, but one who does not buckle under the social trauma attendant to the mist and its monsters as he strives for a promise of relief, which he finds in his misguided but comforting faith that expiation will eliminate the threats that reside outside of the Food House. And although Jim is not the poster boy of intelligence, as evidenced by the words of his former teacher Irene Reppler, who calls him an "underachiever," and through his verbal sparring with David Drayton regarding David's college education and the presumed sense of superiority that accompanies an education, he nonetheless serves as a clear reflection of the constant struggles for and with information and knowledge in *The Mist*, and how education provides a rational avenue for applying knowledge and information to good use.

According to Bernadette Lynn Bosky, "The personalities seen in King's fiction walk a dangerous tightrope between dismissal of and obsession with the irrational" (260). This "tightrope" wraps itself into a scale of sorts that tips back and forth between Mrs. Carmody's congregation of sheep and Brent Norton's "Flat Earth Society," placing David Drayton and his companions, or survivalists, in a position as a fulcrum swinging between these two opposing forces. While both of these camps possess a clear trust and assurance in their beliefs, perceptions, and truths, each is blinded by their respective degrees of arrogance. Norton is a child of the Enlightenment, a rational skeptic whose own supreme confidence in what is real and his courtroom training (or at least his training to always be right and never be taken for a fool) leads to a denial of the absurd, the possible yet improbable, and this results in his demise. Moreover, the willingness on behalf of Carmody's followers to believe in anything besides the creatures in the mist, or believing in a force that will protect them from the creatures that they see yet still somehow deny, leaves David Drayton, Billy Drayton, Ollie Weeks, Irene Reppler, Dan Miller, and Amanda Dumfries (and, eventually, the store manager, Bud Brown, as well as one other character simply named Cornell) in a group of their own and on their own with lines of careful communication and genuinely critical discourse between other groups severed by ideology and hubris. While Drayton's group retains the rational skills that we associate with Norton, they are also capable of grasping imaginatively the vision that informs Carmody's understanding of the monsters in the mist.

Drayton's group is one that has a foot on either side of the line, the line of logic and disbelief that separates itself from faith and (misguided) hope, and this middle ground that neither accepts nor denies anything with absolute certainty; such a perspective serves as a model of survival that seems to be proportionally representative of Stephen King's America in which small numbers of people still manage to function in apocalyptic times without resorting to zealotry and extremism. Being without a definitive camp or ideology, be it religious or political, is so discomforting to many that they often adhere to radical thinking simply to feel as if they have control over something, like a belief that is perceived as truth simply because the majority is promoting it. Ignoring the middle ground, or the proposition that alternatives exist beyond "black" and "white," is a major concern for King and Darabont, who provide us with an ample number of characters that err on the side of being, in David Drayton's words, "willfully dense." In the numerous surface-level attempts at navigating the threat of the mist and the creatures hidden therein, the people of this film often appear as poor chess players who are only able to think one move ahead.

This failure in intellect and imagination leads to the first ostensible and visceral threat of the mist—the death of Norm, the bag boy. The lack of foresight or forethought involved is just one cause for Norm's death (along with his false sense of teenage bravado that prompts him to leave the apparently protective walls of the Food House). As David, Ollie Weeks, Norm, and other patrons of the Food House, Jim and Myron, move to the back of the supermarket to investigate a backed-up generator and "noises" that David claims to have heard, we witness a scene that is troubling for more reasons than Norm's failure to imagine the unimaginable and falling into the trappings of masculinity rather than survival. Indeed, the horror of the first visible death in *The Mist* is not entirely troubling for its blood, its gore, and the frightening alien tentacle that has much more than suckers attached to the limb; rather, the real horror lies within the inability of the human group, from which the victim emerges, to communicate with and comprehend one another.

After Norm is dragged out into the mist by several alien tentacles attached to an unseen body, leaving a bloody streak to function as real, tangible evidence of something challenging our capacity to understand, the audience is left with David, Ollie, Jim, and Myron, all dumbstruck and dumbfounded about what has just taken place. Jim's reaction, beyond shock, is to blame David for not being clear in what he heard outside the loading dock—"You shoulda said what you meant better"—essentially blaming David for Norm's death. David's response, besides giving in to his base instincts and punching Jim, is to chastise Jim and Myron for being irresponsible adults—"Are you guys being willfully dense?" We sympathize most with David here because we recognize, or at least should recognize, that Norm's ploy for bravery and glory found support from Jim. Almost amusingly, David's chastisements, including the observation that Norm's childish pride is understandable because of his age, whereas Jim and Myron (two adults) should know better, are on par with Andy Dufresne in *The Shawshank Redemption* asking Warden Norton, "How can you be so obtuse?" As we see in *The Mist*, many of the characters consciously choose to be dense, or obtuse, allowing and perpetuating division among themselves based on several factors, like the class distinctions that separate not only David from Jim, but also David from Brent Norton, whose skin color ultimately becomes less important than his profession as an affluent urban lawyer.

Brent Norton, as a lawyer, is depicted as a rational, skeptical man of not necessarily law, but of logic. And while logic is a crucial tool to utilize in situations of uncertainty, logic undoubtedly has its limits. To wit, Norton's response to the mist is that it is "obviously a natural disaster," to which one of the survivors replies, "There ain't nothin' obvious about this sumbitch." As David, Ollie, Jim, and Myron attempt to show Norton the evidence he requires so that he might arrive at a workable conclusion to the conundrum of the mist—a severed tentacle from a creature in the mist—his pride suggests to him that these men are merely playing a joke on him, like they are trying to convince him that the tooth fairy is real, and that they have its wings on display in the back room of the store. Norton, just like many of us, is, in his own words, "just not that stupid." Norton's approach to the mist is not unheard of; in fact, his approach—unless the evidence *directly* and *convincingly* suggests otherwise—is the foundation for action that most rational people would (and often should) adhere to. Just as we would criticize an adult who is convinced that Santa Claus or the Easter Bunny is real, Norton is critical of David and those who are proposing that mythical or imaginary creatures, those that have not yet been seen or known to exist, are actually real and pose a real threat. Of course, King and Darabont are hardly suggesting that the key to survival in a world gone mad is to attach oneself to the first abnormal notion that is presented; to do so would be utter lunacy. But to dismiss completely the *possibility* of a faceless voice speaking to a street preacher, or the *possibility* that there are creatures in the mist waiting to eat and devour anything that dares to become a lower link on their food chain, is a mirror to the madness of Mrs. Carmody and her cult, who ultimately form their perceptions on what they *want* to believe, or what someone else instructs them to believe. This belief is ultimately a matter of *disbelief*—they are unable to confront the possibility that there is no God at hand to battle the creatures in the mist, or that their God is unwilling to interject on their behalf. But even more than serving as a fail-safe of mental comfort, religion, especially for Mrs. Carmody, becomes an instrument, or a tool, with which she enables failure: a failure to think or conceive of the reality of horror that is natural to deny. She takes the strings that have been placed into her hands and controls those who are primed for manipulation not solely because of reliance upon faith, but because of the tendency to deny horror at any cost and through any means, *especially* through faith.

Pulling Strings, or "For the Bible Tells Me So": Carmody's Cult

Dan Miller: "You scare people badly enough, you can get 'em to do anything."

Although Stephen King has gone on record noting that he is a believer in a higher power, he has also indicated that he nonetheless has his concerns about organized religion. And while *The Mist* certainly carries a critical gaze toward religion, this film, however, is not a veiled, or overt, attempt to discredit those of religious belief or to deny the existence of God. Of course, it would be appropriate to remove a benign deity from the universe in which *The Mist* takes place, and the universe from which the creatures in the mist call home, suggesting that a universe without a benevolent overseer is an acceptable explanation as to why the creatures in the mist exist, and why they are now on Earth. Then, again, according to Ross Douthat, "King's God isn't a well-meaning weakling, holding our hands and hoping things turn out OK; rather, he is so far *above* the various adversaries, from Tak to Randall Flagg, that the possibility of their winning passing victories concerns him not at all. The demons are a means to chastise and test a struggling humanity, not a threat to God himself" (19). This distance, rather than nonexistence, that God (and, for that matter, the US government) has in relation to the people who populate the world, and who end up trapped in the Food House, certainly poses problems for the religious elements of the film, perhaps pushing some to conclude that *The Mist* is a film aimed at engaging the audience to a point where a dislike, or even hatred, of religious fervor (and government disinterest and incompetence) is promoted. Undeniably, this is just one of the strings pulled when watching *The Mist*.

More to the point, and briefly returning to Brent Norton, the role of logic is often rendered moot unless emotion is placed into the mix, usually acting as a counterweight to logic (and also as a target for ridicule). Yet, emotion is not absent in people of almost complete logical thinking and dependence, and emotion has its negative aspects, even when blanketed by logic. Norton may be a man of great intellect, but he is an outsider, and, moreover, he is black, a noteworthy casting decision that is of *some* importance and carries certain implications in the bickering and confrontation between him and David from the onset of the film to Norton's death. To clarify, with Norton as an outsider on three distinct levels—he is an out-of-towner, he is a man of logic as displayed through his dialogue and profession as a lawyer, and he is black—he is established as a man prone to anger and backlash. And perhaps it is his predilection toward emotive outbursts coupled with a desire to be *right*, a desire fueled through his ostracized position (and his ongoing legal and personal feuds with David), that ultimately leads to his death. This final emotional straw, so to speak, stems from the last verbal exchange between Norton and David, as the latter, sounding almost like an accusatory preacher, asks Norton about his assured belief about the mist posing no harm and questions, "What if you're wrong?"

From one angle, David's question for Norton is simply a matter of concern; and while Norton's response hardly seems to carry any observable tone of anger—"Then, I guess, the joke would be on me after all"—Norton is nonetheless falling prey to the blinding mist of emotion. One could easily envision Norton retorting to David "What if *you* are wrong?" indicating a defensive and emotionally charged response to a question that is perceived to be one of challenge rather than compassion. But Norton's response and perception of a prank playing out, especially as Norton believed that David had tried to trick him earlier in the film by asking him to look at the severed tentacle in the back of the supermarket, reveals just one example of the emotion that is played out in this film. Norton believes that David is questioning his logic, his common sense, and even his manhood, and, almost like Norm the bag boy, Norton feels the need to prove his mettle and his intellect by stepping into the fog. He is, in essence, answering a challenge that has actually not been laid out, and he is foregoing any consideration of doubt or alternatives to his predicament. Norton, like those who fall under the nearly literal spell of Carmody, is allowing his emotional (and logical) strings to be pulled and played. He is unwilling to enter into further dialogue, whereas David is, of course, more than willing to admit that he does not necessarily have any concrete evidence himself as to the nature and origin of the mist, yet is willing to engage in discussion and dialogue, to find a solution rather than have one miraculously fall into his lap or present itself through undependable tools like logic and faith.

Despite some of the implications put forth in *The Mist*, a lack of knowledge or faith does not equal a lack of power or volition. But when tried and tired means of understanding the world are proven unreliable, a third alternative is hard to find, or even imagine. However, David and his group do dare to *imagine*. Indeed, imagination is not just the muse that King listens to when crafting his works; it is an indispensible tool throughout his canon, from *'Salem's Lot* (1975) for those who concede the possibility of vampires to *IT* (1986) where the child's mind attuned to the powers of imagination serves as the metaphorical sword that helps to slay the beast after which the book is titled. This is not to say that imagination is the only weapon at one's disposal in the battle against the unknown. But, for example, when King looks at his own world through the eyes of Roland Deschain, the gunslinger of *The Dark Tower* series, King utilizes a character who comes from the alternative reality of Mid-World to the real world (New York City) only to find, "Wonder had run out: here, in a place of miracles, he saw only dull faces and plodding bodies" (King, *The Drawing of the Three*, 366). Whereas Brent Norton and the "Flat Earth Society" are examples of those whose imaginations and sense of wonderment blind them to the possibility of monsters, Mrs. Carmody is one whose sense of wonder—or faith—foregoes the rational thought process that seeks some sort of concrete, rational answers for the impossibilities occurring outside of the supermarket. Again, while this does not necessarily lead to a critique of religion as a whole, this is still a matter of an individual seeking a crutch on which to rest his or her mind, and once that support has been provided—no matter how plausible or implausible it may be—a marriage of convenience, and power (especially for Mrs. Carmody), is established.

Both subtly and directly, *The Mist* provides a critical examination of the rhetoric that dominates American thinking, namely, the tired and empty phrasings like "You are either with us or against us." This is the same type of thinking, and appeal to the emotional desire to belong to a group, that suggests that automatic acceptance of what the American government asks its citizens to believe is patriotism, while dissent flirts with terrorism. Such binary, black-and-white thinking that is complicated further with emotional manipulation, while troubling and despicable when used as a tool of control and indoctrination, is the startling reality of *The Mist*. Even when faced with critical reason and counterarguments that, regardless of their accusatory tone, warrant consideration, Carmody and her cult fall into the failures of literal ignorance: by ignoring alternative points of view. For example, during one of Carmody's early sermons, or tirades, Irene Reppler throws a can of peas at Carmody, hitting her in the head and stating, "Stoning people who piss you off is perfectly okay. They do it in the Bible, don't they?" While this approach is not a peaceful one, it challenges Carmody and her followers to consider the potential foibles and flaws of their perceptions and accepted truths. But neither Carmody nor her cult is receptive to this challenge; they are also unwilling to consider that Carmody's God is neither the answer to their plight nor the actual entity about which Carmody preaches. As a biker who braves the mist to retrieve a physical, tangible tool to use against the creatures—a shotgun—says to a hysterical Carmody, "I believe in God, too ... I just don't think he's the blood thirsty asshole you make him out to be." Between challenges to suspect use of scripture and an insistence upon a God who is vengeful and in need of blood in order to free the people in the Food House, Carmody actually faces little intellectual challenge to her growing popularity, and the growing belief in her word and her visions ultimately provides a repetitive reminder as to the constant failures in thinking that are more common than balanced, reasonable acts of cognition.

The only challenge to Carmody's ranting and raving, ironically, is a bullet to her stomach and head, suggesting that in the worst of times, peace will not prevail among humankind (especially as audiences actually applauded Carmody's death when *The Mist* was in theaters, indicating that they, too, would not have fought for a peaceful resolution). This failure to think, to talk, and to carefully and genuinely consider the numerous options and explanations available is, of course, not surprising. The discord that forms the core of the human experience in *The Mist* is a very real failing that finds more and more traction the more frightened and uncritical the masses become. And it is with this nod toward the general disposition of the American population that Carmody finds herself in league with the very monsters behind the mist: the American government. As Tony Magistrale argues: "Her [Carmody's] insistence on a collective level of compliance parallels the action of the military that originally unleashed the monsters. As such, Carmody and the American military represent dangerous versions of institutionalization—both establish power from fear and the use it as a means for intimidating and controlling those who are unable to cope with the situation" (*America's Storyteller* 55). This submissiveness, alongside a detachment from any semblance of responsibility or courage, while deplorable and a key ingredient of horror that seeps into *The Mist*, is really just a matter of course, but nonetheless it haunts the audience, and perhaps more than whatever lurks inside the mist itself.

Pushing Agendas: The (Faceless) Overlords of the Mist

Private Wayne Jessup: "It wasn't me. I'm not responsible. Hell, I'm a local."

Despite the final scene of *The Mist* showing the military at work removing the threats within the mist (as well as the mist itself), the film is still very critical of the armed forces and the government to whom they answer. While the text version of *The Mist* only speaks of the military and the government through whispers and speculation, the film highlights and foregrounds the presence of the military, from the military policeman cocooned in King's pharmacy blurting, "It's our fault. It's all our fault," to the mob murder of Private Wayne Jessup for his perceived role in the mysterious Arrowhead Project. The increased attention to the military in the film is noted and is examined as a critical alteration: "The mist itself becomes a metaphor for the U.S. government's effort to obfuscate and hide the truths of Iraq and the scientific machinations of the Arrowhead Project from its people, as well as the country's willingness to invest the military establishment with an undeserved blind trust" (Magistrale, *America's Storyteller*, 57). And when *The Mist* wraps contemporary concerns with government betrayals alongside religious undercurrents and technological collapses, the somewhat didactic message of failure becomes hard to ignore. Whether or not one views *The Mist* as a horror film or a venture into science fiction, complete with the meshing and melding of strange and possibly supernatural creatures alongside attempts to explain the science behind their entry to Earth, approaching *The Mist* as a generic hybrid, much like the *Dark Tower* series, helps one peel back the layers of the film.

To return to the concerns of agendas and those behind the military uniforms and indifferent god-like governmental positions, we are drawn to the science and technology behind the Arrowhead Project. This scientific misadventure is only described in the film through a scared Private Jessup's fragmented speculations: "They thought that there were other dimensions [...] other worlds around us, and then the wanted to try and make a window, you know, so they could look through and see what's on the other side [...] [the scientists] must have ripped a hole open by accident. This other world came spilling through to ours." Such a doorway between worlds is not entirely unfounded, especially for those familiar with King's *Dark Tower* series, but the actual science of the Arrowhead Project is, in essence, unimportant information. It serves as more of a symbol, a distanced component of the film that is meant to function as a conduit. Or, in the words of Douglas Winter, *The Mist* aligns itself with "the contemporary horror story [that] often utilizes an exaggeration or extrapolation of modern technology as its surrogate for the unknown, operating as a cautionary tale that simultaneously rejects technology while reassuring the reader that things could nevertheless be worse" (87). Just as the mystery of King's *The Colorado Kid* purposefully remains a mystery when the murder of the title character is never solved, so too does the mystery of the mist remain as an intentionally vague inclusion, standing in as an axle, or a nexus, about which other key concerns turn. To reiterate, the science in and of itself is unimportant as, "Conspicuous by its absence from 'The Mist' is a stock character of the 'technohorror' nightmare—the scientist. We are offered only straw men: two young soldiers trapped within the supermarket who commit gruesome suicide in confirmation of the feared source of the disaster [and one soldier who is murdered by the mob]. The culprits of the Arrowhead Project remain as faceless and opaque as the mist itself" (Winter, 89). What is important, then, in *The Mist* is connecting the people using the tools of science to forward their dangerous designs, and learning not of the numbers or calculations behind the Arrowhead Project, but learning of the intentions and learning ways to cope with the fallout. In other words, one of the key goals in this film for the survivors is a venture toward knowledge that can actually be useful rather than embracing an obsession with the absolute, or seeking knowledge that can be practical and helpful rather than just informative. Moreover, as King "considers civilization and its accomplishments precarious at best and dangerously delusive at worst," we must be careful in reducing the mist to just a critique of technology (Egan, 58). In short, "If we view *The Mist* primarily as a caution against technology and its dangers, we limit the story," but if we look at the failures that result of a misuse of technology, and look at the actions people take in the aftermath of progress run amok, we circle back to the mirror King and Darabont ask us to hold up when watching this film (Rickard, 179). In the foreground, we see ourselves, just as potentially monstrous as Carmody and her cult because of our own limits and patterns as humans seeking solace and comfort no matter the cost; and in the background, we see hazy images of the very same government at work in *The Mist*, a government that we allow to run rampant, creating quite the formidable pairing of monsters—those who take advantage of the masses (the government) and those who are complicit in that hostile and parasitic, but hardly symbiotic, relationship.

Just as Stephen King has become quite overt in the expression of his political leanings in recent years, *The Mist*, too, leans in a particular direction, seeking to unearth and highlight the numerous governmental failures of the new millennium. *The Mist* certainly parallels the economic downturn and recession as the people watching this film find themselves in familiar company as King's characters are responsible for the "public failure to monitor sufficiently a technocracy that has been given too many tax dollars and not enough accountability" (Magistrale, *The Second Decade*, 91). This sentiment most definitely illustrates governmental defense spending and its ventures into Iraq, the war that has received the most criticism and least support from the American population. From one angle, the role of the government is captured in the self-inflicted hanging of Privates Donaldson and Morales, along with the brutal murder of Private Jessup as "their [the soldiers] suicides and murder take on additional meaning in the context of how most Americans had developed severe misgivings about the course of the Iraq war at the time of Darabont's film production" (Magistrale, *America's Storyteller*, 56). Such dissent and distancing among the people and their government is captured quite well in *The Mist*, a film in which, "the American government and its military are portrayed as divorced from the American people" (Magistrale, *America's Storyteller*, 55). Moreover, when one compares the American government of King's actual world and the government in *The Mist*, one sees a connection between this group and Carmody's cult—a group limited by myopic visions and thinking, typically resulting from overly reactionary mental processes. Indeed, with the Iraq War, once messages concerning "weapons of mass destruction" were disseminated, enough decision makers supported the war based on convenient, appealing information and then decided to push forward. But what is important to note here is that this reflects, like Carmody's preaching, the *first* key piece of information to be presented, and like

Carmody's cult, the government is blind, or willfully ignorant, to other possibilities as they are enamored with the first option laid out, blinded by their hidden agendas. This failure in caution, discussion, and seeking alternative points of view not only visits tragedy and death on Brent Norton and his Flat Earth Society, but also leads to very similar ends for the American government at work in *The Mist*. To say the least, King and Darabont remind us that re-action is typically the mark of the mindless, leading to inexcusable actions.

Although *The Mist* eventually brings in a military force to disperse and destroy the monsters and the mist stemming from the Arrowhead Project, their absence throughout the first 95 minutes of the film is disturbing. The timeliness of their presence at the end of the film is heartbreaking considering what David Drayton had to endure not only moments before their arrival, but also in the previous two days. Without doubt, the eventual rescue efforts on behalf of the military are not to be seen as King or Darabont's softening stance toward the government and the military, in fact, it is quite the opposite. While the government and its military are seen attempting a cleanup of the horrific consequences of the Arrowhead Project, their separation from the people they are sworn and bound to protect is seen as two soldiers approach a devastated David Drayton, now a murderer (or, at best, a Kevorkian-esque character who is culpable in the assisted suicides of Amanda Dumfries, Irene Reppler, Dan Miller, and his son, Billy Draton). Seeing David's tears, the two soldiers do not attempt to help David to his feet, or even provide a feeble attempt at providing solace; instead, they simply look at one another, through gas masks that allow the faceless government and its underlings to maintain anonymity and a ruthless disconnect from the populace, and shrug, indicating both a lack of understanding for David's tears as well as a general disregard for his distress. The soldiers do not know what to do with the weeping man, show no signs of empathy or any other emotion, and the film ends almost exactly where it began—with the people of Maine outside the circles of the government and the military, and subjected to their whims, their weapons, and their (rescue) schedule(s) that were a mere 115 seconds too late to spare David Drayton from having blood on his hands.

In sum, the horrors of *The Mist*, or at least the horrors coming from the alternate worlds, should not have ever found a foothold on Earth. But, as we recall from the original text, we note, "In *The Mist* there are no bureaucratic or scientific representatives left to confront the consequences of their meddling and incompetence [...] [they are] faceless—and unresponsive to human suffering"

(Magistrale, *Landscape of Fear*, 33). One result of this purposefully hidden and emotionless identity involves passing blame onto the government's underlings, those who are only associated with the government: "In Darabont's version of *The Mist*, the soldiers in the supermarket are essentially held accountable for war crimes; they become scapegoats who accept blame for the misguided efforts of their political and bureaucratic superiors" (Magistrale, *America's Storyteller*, 56). Just as Carmody technically has no blood on her hands by the time David and his companions leave the Food House, the government positions itself to shoulder no blame for its role in unleashing the mist and its horrors, leaving the culpability to those who have been duped to do their bidding.

Conclusion: The Workings of Failure Realized and Human Frailty Exposed

Dan Miller: "We gave it a good shot. Nobody can say we didn't."

As *The Mist* comes to a close, with David Drayton, Billy Drayton, Amanda Dumfries, Irene Reppler, and Dan Miller sitting in David's jeep, out of gas and seemingly out of options, viewers are left with two distinct messages: that this group of pioneers *tried* to escape, and that they ultimately failed. The text version of *The Mist* certainly offers little in the way of a happy ending: "'The Mist' ends without much hope—so much so that King is forced to express that small sense of possibility explicitly in the final words, 'hope and Hartford'"— indicating that there just *might* be refuge several miles down the road in Connecticut (Collings, 17). The film, of course, is even more brutal in its conclusion. Perhaps even more troubling than the prospect of hearing the four gunshots that ring out, leaving David as the sole survivor of the suicide pact, is the final moment of life for Billy Drayton— the sudden opening of the child's eyes, wide and bewildered—that certainly haunts the audience as much as it haunts David, especially as he has to live much longer than the few minutes that he anticipated he would remain alive after killing his son. His level of pain is Shakespearean, and as the audience witnesses the army finally fortifying a presence in the town and destroying the creatures that have dominated the people and the land for only a few days, the father must live with more than the memory of nightmarish monstrosity; he must live with its reality for the rest of his life.

King's explorations throughout his canon and especially in *The Mist*, in his own words, remind us, "that I am not merely dealing with the surreal and the fantastic but, more importantly, using the surreal and the fantastic to examine the motivations of people and the society and institutions they create" (Magistrale, *The Second Decade*, 15). Further, King bluntly states, "We need to look around and recognize that we are really not solving any problems. We are simply turning lights on in more and more rooms and seeing more and more strange things" (Magistrale, *The Second Decade*, 15). King's commentary on the typical aimless wanderings of those who reside in the real world are captured quite well in the words of Amanda Dumfries who says, "I'd rather die out there trying than in here waiting." Either prospect poses little in the way of a solution to the dilemma at the core of the film, but this Scylla and Charybdis is an important plot device that asks people like Amanda and David, or even Mrs. Carmody and Brent Norton, to turn back from impossible or emotionally driven choices and make a rational decision to survive.

Bibliography

Abrams, M. H. *A Glossary of Literary Terms* (7th edn). Boston: Thomson Learning Academic Resource Centre, 1999.

Appiah, K. Anthony. "No Bad Niggers: Blacks as the Ethical Principle in the Movies." *Media Spectacles.* Edited by Marjorie Garber. New York: Routledge, 1993. 77–90.

Apt Pupil. Dir. Bryan Singer. Screenplay by Brandon Boyce. Perf. Ian McKellen and Brad Renfro. Phoenix Pictures, Canal+DA, Bad Harry, TriStar, 1997.

Badley, Linda. "Love and Death in the American Car: Stephen King's Auto-Erotic Horror." *The Gothic World of Stephen King: Landscape of Nightmares.* Edited by Gary Hoppensand and Ray B. Browne. Bowling Green, OH: Bowling Green University Popular Press, 1987. 84–94.

———. *Writing Horror and the Body: The Fiction of Stephen King, Clive Barker, and Anne Rice.* Westport, CT: Greenwood Press, 1996.

Bakhtin, Mikhail. *The Dialogic Imagination: Four Essays.* Edited by Michael Holquist, trans. Caryl Emerson and Michael Holquist. Austin: University of Texas Press, 1981.

Beahm, George. *The Stephen King Story.* Kansas City: Andrews & McMeel, 1991.

Beard, William. "An Anatomy of Melancholy: Cronenberg's *The Dead Zone.*" *Journal of Canadian Studies* 27 (1992–93): 169–179.

———. *The Artist as Monster: The Cinema of David Cronenberg.* Toronto: University of Toronto Press, 2006.

Bergson, Henri. "Laughter." *Comedy.* Edited by Wylie Sypher. Baltimore: The Johns Hopkins University Press, 1956. 61–192.

Biddle, Arthur W. "The Mythic Journey in 'The Body.'" *The Dark Descent: Essays Defining Stephen King's Horrorscape.* Edited by Tony Magistrale. New York: Greenwood Press, 1992. 83–97.

Bliss, Michael. *Brian DePalma.* Metuchen, NJ: The Scarecrow Press, 1983.

Bloom, Harold. "Afterthought." *Stephen King: Modern Critical Views* (updated edn). Edited by Harold Bloom. New York: Chelsea House, 2007. 208–209.

———. "Introduction." *Stephen King: Modern Critical Views.* Edited by Harold Bloom. Philadelphia: Chelsea House, 1998. 1–3.

Bogle, Donald. *Toms, Coons, Mulattoes, Mammies, & Bucks: An Interpretive History of Blacks in American Films* (4th edn). New York: Continuum, 2001.

Bosky, Bernadette Lynn. "The Mind's a Monkey: Character and Psychology in Stephen King's Recent Fiction." *Kingdom of Fear: The World of Stephen King.* 1986. Ed. Tim Underwood and Chuck Miller. New York: Signet, 1987. 241–276.

Browning, Mark. *Stephen King on the Big Screen.* Chicago: Intellect (U of Chicago P), 2009.

———. *Stephen King on the Small Screen.* Chicago: Intellect (U of Chicago P), 2011.

Carrie. Dir. Brian De Palma. Screenplay by Lawrence D. Cohen. Perf. Sissy Spacek, Piper Laurie, and Amy Irving. United Artists Corporation, 1976.

Carroll, Nöel. *Beyond Aesthetics: Philosophical Essays.* Cambridge and New York: Cambridge University Press, 2001.

———. *The Philosophy of Horror or Paradoxes of the Heart.* New York: Routledge, 1990.

"Caste." Def. 2, 4. *Webster's New Universal Unabridged Dictionary* (2nd edn). 1983.

Cavallaro, Dani. *The Gothic Vision: Three Centuries of Horror, Terror and Fear.* London and New York: Continuum, 2002.

Children of the Corn. Dir. Fritz Kiersch. Screenplay by George Goldsmith. Perf. Peter Horton and Linda Hamilton. Angeles Cinema Group, Gatlin, Inverness, Roach, 1984.

Christine. Dir. John Carpenter. Screenplay by Bill Phillips. Perf. Keith Gordon, John Stockwell, and Alexandra Paul. Columbia Pictures, 1983.

Clemens, Valdine. *The Return of the Repressed.* New York: State University of New York Press, 1999.

Clover, Carol. *Men, Women, and Chainsaws: Gender in the Modern Horror Film.* Princeton, NJ: Princeton UP, 1992.

Clover, Carol. *Men, Women, and Chainsaws: Gender in the Modern Horror Film.* Princeton, NJ: Princeton UP, 1992.

Collings, Michael, R. *The Films of Stephen King.* Mercer Island, WA: Starmont House, 1986.

———. *The Stephen King Phenomenon.* Mercer Island, WA: Starmont, 1987.

Collins, Patricia Hill. *Black Feminist Thought: Knowledge, Consciousness, and Politics of Empowerment.* New York: Routledge, 1990.

Conner, Jeff. *Stephen King Goes to Hollywood.* New York: New American Library, 1987.

Crane, Jonathan. "A Body Apart: Cronenberg and Genre." *The Modern Fantastic: The Films of David Cronenberg.* Edited by Michael Grant. Westport, CT: Praeger. 2000. 50–68.

Crowdus, Gary and Dan Georgakas. "Thinking about the Power of Images: An Interview with Spike Lee." *Cineaste* 26 (January 2001): 4–9.

Cumbow, Robert C. *Order in the Universe: The Films of John Carpenter* (2nd edn). Filmmakers Series 70. Lanham, MD: The Scarecrow Press, 2000.

Davis, Jonathan P. *Stephen King's America*. Bowling Green, OH: Bowling Green State University Popular Press, 1994.

The Dead Zone. Dir. David Cronenberg. Screenplay by Jeffrey Boam. Perf. Christopher Walken, Brooke Adams, and Martin Sheen. Dino De Laurentiis Corporation, 1983.

Denby, David. "San Fernando Aria." *New Yorker* 75 (December 20, 1999): 102–103.

Dolores Claiborne. Dir. Taylor Hackford. Screenplay by Tony Gilroy. Perf. Kathy Bates, Jennifer Jason Leigh, and Christopher Plummer. Castle Rock Entertainment, Columbia Pictures, 1995.

Douthat, Russ. "Stephen King's American Apocalypse." *First Things* Feb. 2007: 14–19.

Dreamcatcher. Dir. Lawrence Kasden. Screenplay by William Goldman. Perf. Morgan Freeman and Jason Lee. Castle Rock Entertainment, Village Roadshow Productions, 2003.

Dr. Strangelove: Or How I Learned to Love the Bomb. Dir. Stanley Kubrick. Perf. Peter Sellers and George C. Scott. Hawks Films Ltd., 1964.

Dyer, Richard. "Resistance through Charisma: Rita Hayworth and *Gilda*." *Women in Film Noir*. Edited by E. Ann Kaplan. London: British Film Institute, 1978/2005. 115–122.

Ebert, Roger. *Secret Window*. Movie Reviews. <http://rogerebert.suntimes.com/apps/pbcs.dll/article?AID=/20040312/REVIEWS/403120306> March 12, 2004.

Edinger, Edward F. *Ego and Archetype: Individuation and the Religious Function of the Psyche*. Boston and London: Shambhala, 1992.

Egan, James. "Technohorror: The Dystopian Vision of Stephen King." *Extrapolation* 29 (Summer 1988): 140–152.

Eisanstat, Stephanie A. and Lundy Bancroft. "Domestic Violence." *The New England Journal of Medicine* 12 (341): 886–892.

Eisler, Riane. *The Chalice and the Blade: Our History, Our Future*. San Francisco: Harper & Row, 1988.

Engels, Frederick. *The Origin of the Family, Private Property and the State*. New York: International, 1972.

Eppert, Claudia. "Entertaining History: (Un)heroic Identifications, Apt Pupils, and an Ethical Imagination," *New German Critique* 86 (Spring-Summer 2002): 71–101.

Espanek, Fred. *Eclipse Home Page*. NASA Goddard Space Flight Center. Greenbelt, MD. http://sunearth.gsf.nasa.gov/eclipse. Revised April 16, 1997. Retrieved May 31, 2006.

Fallaci, Oriana. *Interview with History*. Trans. John Shepley. New York: Liveright, 1976.

Fiedler, Leslie. *Love and Death in the American Novel*. New York: Stein and Day, 1966.

Figliola, Samantha. "Reading King Darkly: Issues of Race in Stephen King's Novels." *Into Darkness Peering: Race and Color in the Fantastic.* Edited by Elisabeth Anne Leonard. Westport, CT: Greenwood Press, 1997. 143–157.

Findley, Mary. "Stephen King's Vintage Ghost-Cars: A Modern-Day Haunting." *Spectral America: Phantoms and the National Imagination.* Edited by Jeffrey Andrew Weinstock. Madison: University of Wisconsin Press, 2004. 207–220.

Fiske, John. *Media Matters: Everyday Culture and Political Change.* Minneapolis: Minnesota Press, 1994.

———. *Understanding Popular Culture.* New York: Routledge, 1989.

Foucault, Michel. "What Is an Author?" *Language, Counter-Memory, Practice: Selected Essays and Interviews.* Ithaca, NY: Cornell University Press, 1977. 124–127.

Freud, Sigmund. "The 'Uncanny.'" *Sigmund Freud: Collected Papers* (vol. 4). Trans. Joan Riviere. New York: Basic Books, 1959. 368–407.

Gabbard, Krin. *Black Magic: White Hollywood and African American Culture.* New Brunswick, NJ: Rutgers University Press, 2004.

George, Nelson. *hip hop america.* New York: Penguin Books, 1998.

Ghosts. Dir. Stan Winston. Adaptation by Stephen King, Stan Winston, Mick Garris, and Michael Jackson. Screenplay by Stan Winston and Mick Garris. Perf. Michael Jackson. MJJ Productions, Sony Music Entertainment, 1997.

Gilda. Dir. Charles Vidor. Adaptation by Jo Eisinger. Perf. Rita Hayworth and Glenn Ford. Columbia Pictures Corporation, 1946.

Gottlieb, Sidney, ed. *Hitchcock on Hitchcock: Selected Writings and Interviews.* Berkeley: University of California Press, 1995.

Grant, Michael, ed. *The Modern Fantastic: The Films of David Cronenberg.* Westport, CT: Praeger, 2000.

The Green Mile. Dir. Frank Darabont. Screenplay by Frank Darabont. Perf. Tom Hanks, Michael Clarke Duncan, and David Morse. CR Films, Castle Rock Entertainment, 1999.

Hala, James. "Kubrick's *The Shining:* The Specter and the Critics." *The Shining Reader.* Edited by Tony Magistrale. Mercer Island, WA: Starmont House, 1991. 203–216.

Halberstam, Judith. *Skin Shows: Gothic Horror and the Technology of Monsters.* Durham, NC: Duke University Press, 1995.

"Happy Toyz Co." web site. http://www.geocities.com/happytoyzco/index.htm. February 28, 2007.

Haraway, Donna. *Simians, Cyborgs and Women: The Reinvention of Nature.* New York: Routledge, 1991.

Hardenberg, Friedrich von. *Novalis Schriften* (vol. 3). Edited by Richard Samuel, Hans-Joachim Mähl, and Gerhard Schulz. Stuttgart: Kohlhammer, 1968.

Harris, Joel Chandler. *Uncle Remus: His Songs and Sayings.* New York: Penguin, 1986.

Havel, Vaclav. "The Need for Transcendence in the Postmodern World." Speech at Independence Hall. Philadelphia. July 4, 1994. <http://www.worldtrans.org/whole/havelspeech.html>

Heldreth, Leonard G. "Viewing 'The Body': King's Portrait of the Artist as Survivor." *The Gothic World of Stephen King: Landscape of Nightmares.* Edited by Gary Hoppenstand and Ray B. Browne. Bowling Green, OH: Bowling Green State University Popular Press, 1987. 64–74.

Hester-Williams, Kim D. "NeoSlaves: Slavery, Freedom, and African American Apotheosis in *Candyman, The Matrix,* and *The Green Mile.*" *Genders* 40 (2004). 3–43 <http://www.genders.org/g40/g40_williams.html>

Hicks, Heather J. "Hoodoo Economics: White Men's Work and Black Men's Magic in Contemporary American Film." *Camera Obscura* 18 (2003): 27–55.

Holland-Toll, Linda J. *As American as Mom, Baseball, and Apple Pie: Constructing Community in Contemporary American Horror Fiction.* Bowling Green, OH: Bowling Green State University Popular Press, 2001.

Hoppenstand, Gary and Ray Browne. "The Horror of It All: Stephen King and the Landscape of the American Nightmare." *The Gothic World of Stephen King.* Edited by Gary Hoppenstand and Ray Browne. Bowling Green, OH: The Popular Press, 1987. 1–19.

Horsting, Jessie. *Stephen King at the Movies.* New York: Starlog Press, 1986.

"Intermittent Explosive Disorder." *Internet Crime Archives* May 15, 2006 <http://www.mayhem.net/Crime/intermittent.html>

Jackson, Shirley. *The Haunting of Hill House.* New York: Penguin Books, 1959.

Jameson, Fredric. *Signatures of the Visible.* New York: Routledge, 1990.

Jermyn, Deborah. "The Rachel Papers: In Search of *Blade Runner's* Femme Fatale." *The Blade Runner Experience.* Edited by Will Brooker. London: Wallflower Press, 2005. 159–172.

Jewett, Robert and John Lawrence, "Norm Demolition Derbies: Rites of Reversal in Popular Culture." *The Popular Culture Reader.* (3rd edn). Edited by Christopher D. Geist and Jack Nachbar. Bowling Green, OH: Bowling Green University Popular Press, 1983. 290–297.

Johnson, Kirk. "Papers Reveal Ruminations of Teenage Columbine Killers," *New York Times,* July 7, 2006, A13.

Jones, Stephen. "The Man Who Would Be King: An Interview with Stephen King." *Creepshows: The Illustrated Stephen King Movie Guide.* London: Titan Books, 2001. 174–185.

Joshi, S. T. *The Modern Weird Tale.* Jefferson, NC: McFarland, 2001.

Kael, Pauline. *Taking It All In.* New York: Holt, Rinehart & Winston, 1984.

Kakmi, Dmetri. "Myth and Magic in DePalma's *Carrie.*" May 2, 2006 <http://www.sensesofcinema.com/contents/cteq/00/3/carrie.html>

Kelso, Sylvia. "Take Me for a Ride in Your Man-Eater: Gynophobia in Stephen King's *Christine.*" *Paradoxa* 2.2 (1996): 263–275.

Kermode, Mark. *The Shawshank Redemption.* London: British Film Institute, 2003.

King, Stephen. *Apt Pupil. Different Seasons.* Movie Tie-In Edition. Signet: New York, 1998.

———. *The Body. Different Seasons.* New York: Viking Penguin, 1982.

———. "The Bogeyboys," May 26, 1999. Keynote Address at the Annual Meeting of the Vermont Library Conference, in http://www.stephen-king.de/interviews/interview6.html.

———. *Carrie.* 1974. New York: Pocket Books, 1999.

———. "Children of the Corn." *Night Shift.* New York: Doubleday, 1978.

———. *Christine.* 1982. New York: Signet, 1983.

———. *Danse Macabre.* New York: Everest House, 1981.

———. *The Dead Zone.* New York: Viking, 1979.

———. *Dolores Claiborne.* New York: Viking, 1993.

———. *The Drawing of the Three.* 1987. New York: Plume, 2003.

———. "The Dreaded X." *Gauntlet* 2 (1991): 69–83.

———. *Four Past Midnight.* New York. Viking, 1990.

———. "The Mangler." *Night Shift.* New York: Doubleday, 1978.

———. *Needful Things.* New York: Viking, 1991.

———. *Night Journey: The Green Mile, Part 5.* New York: Penguin/Signet, 1996.

———. *On Writing: A Memoir of the Craft.* New York: Scribner, 2000.

King, Stephen. *Pet Sematary.* New York: Doubleday, 1983.

———. "A Postscript to *Overdrive.*" *Castle Rock: The Stephen King Newsletter* 3.2 (February 1987): 1, 5.

———. *Rita Hayworth and the Shawshank Redemption. Different Seasons.* New York: Viking, 1982.

———. *Secret Window, Secret Garden. Four Past Midnight.* London: Hodder & Stoughton, 1990.

———. *The Shining.* New York: Doubleday, 1977.

———. "Sometimes They Come Back." *Night Shift.* New York: Doubleday, 1976.

———. *The Stand.* New York: Doubleday, 1990.

———. *Storm of the Century.* New York: Book-of-the-Month Club, 1999.

———. "Trucks." *Night Shift.* New York: Doubleday, 1976.

———. "You Don't Know Jackson." *Entertainment Weekly* 751 (February 13, 2004): 80.

Klawans, Stuart. "Y2K: The Prequel." *Nation* (January 24, 2000): 35–36.

Koepp, David. "*Secret Window*: A Look Through It." *Secret Window* [DVD]. America: Columbia Pictures Industries, Inc., 2004.

———. "*Secret Window*: From Book to Film." *Secret Window* [DVD]. America: Columbia Pictures Industries, Inc., 2004.

———. "*Secret Window*: Secrets Revealed." *Secret Window* [DVD]. America: Columbia Pictures Industries, Inc., 2004.

Lant, Kathleen Margaret. "The Rape of Constant Reader: Stephen King's Construction of the Female Reader and Violation of the Female Body in *Misery.*" *Journal of Popular Culture* 30 (1997): 89–114.

Lant, Kathleen Margaret and Teresa Thompson, eds. *Imagining the Worst: Stephen King and the Representations of Women.* Westport, CT: Greenwood Press, 1998.

Lee, Yale Bulletin Calendar March 2, 2001, 29:#21 www.yale.edu/opa/v29.n21/story3.html

Levy, Ariel. *Female Chauvinist Pigs: Women and the Rise of Raunch Culture.* New York: Free Press, 2005.

Lott, Eric. *Love & Theft: Blackface Minstrelsy and the American Working Class.* New York and Oxford: Oxford University Press, 1993.

Lowenberg, Bill. "The History and Future of the Demolition Derby." Online. *POV Films.* 2004. http://www.pbs.org/pov/pov2004/speedo/special_history.html. February 28, 2007.

Madden, Edward. "Cars Are Girls: Sexual Power and Sexual Panic in Stephen King's *Christine.*" *Imagining the Worst: Stephen King and the Representation of Women.* Edited by Kathleen Margaret Lant and Theresa Thompson. Westport, CT: Greenwood Press, 1998. 143–158.

Magistrale, Tony. *Hollywood's Stephen King.* New York: Palgrave Macmillan, 2003.

———. *Landscape of Fear: Stephen King's American Gothic.* Bowling Green, OH: Bowling Green State University Press, 1988.

———. *Stephen King: America's Storyteller.* Santa Barbara, CA: Praeger, 2010.

———. *Stephen King: The Second Decade, "Danse Macabre" to "The Dark Half."* New York: Twayne, 1992.

Marx, Karl. *The Communist Manifesto.* Edited by Frederic Bender. New York: W.W. Norton, 1988.

Maximum Overdrive. Dir. Stephen King. Screenplay by Stephen King. Perf. Emilio Estevez. Dino De Laurentiis Productions, 1986.

Misery. Dir. Rob Reiner. Screenplay by William Goldman. Perf. Kathy Bates and James Caan. Castle Rock Entertainment, Columbia Pictures, 1990.

The Mist. Dir. Frank Darabont. Perf. Thomas Jane, Marcia Gay Harden, Laurie Holden and Andre Braugher. Dimension, 2008. DVD.

Modleski, Tania. "In Hollywood, Racist Stereotypes Can Still Earn Oscar Nominations." *Chronicle of Higher Education* 46 (March 17, 2000).

Morris, Peter. *David Cronenberg: A Delicate Balance.* Toronto: ECW Press, 1994.

Moss, Larry. *The Intent to Live: Achieving Your True Potential as an Actor.* New York: Bantam, 2005.

"Movie Review: *Maximum Overdrive.*" Online. *efilmcritic.com* (November 1, 1999) http://efilmcritic.com/review.php?movie=2337. February 29, 2007.

Muir, John Kenneth. *The Films of John Carpenter.* Jefferson, NC: McFarland, 2000.

Müller, Jürgen. *Movies of the 70's.* London: Taschen GMBH, 2003.

Mulvey-Roberts, Marie. " 'A Spook Ride on Film': Carpenter and the Gothic." *The Cinema of John Carpenter: The Technique of Terror.* Edited by Ian Conrich and David Woods. London: Wallflower Press, 2004. 78–90.

Mustazza, Leonard. "Fear and Pity: Tragic Horror in King's *Pet Sematary.*" *The Dark Descent: Essays Defining Stephen King's Horrorscape.* Edited by Tony Magistrale. New York: Greenwood Press, 1992. 73–82.

Neale, Steve. "Masculinity as Spectacle." *Screen* 24 (1983): 2–16.

Needful Things. Dir. Fraser C. Heston. Screenplay by W. D. Richter. Perf. Ed Harris, Max von Sydow, and Bonnie Bedelia. Castle Rock Entertainment, New Line Cinema, Columbia Pictures, 1993.

Newhouse, Tom. "A Blind Date with Disaster: Adolescent Revolt in the Fiction of Stephen King." *The Gothic World of Stephen King*. Edited by Gary Hoppenstand and Ray B. Browne. Bowling Green, OH: Bowling Green State University Press, 1987. 49–55.

Newman, Kim. Review of *Apt Pupil* by Bryan Singer, *Sight and Sound* 6(1999): 35.

One Million Years. B. C. Dir. Don Chaffey. Screenplay by George Baker and Joseph Frickert. Perf. Rachel Welch. Hammer Film Productions, Seven Arts Productions, 1966.

Owen, Sally. "Even Stephen Gets Even" *The Progressive Women's Quarterly* (October 31, 1995): 47.

Pareles, Jon. "Film: By Stephen King, 'Maximum Overdrive.'" *The New York Times* (July 25, 1986) Online. http://nytimes.com. February 28, 2007.

Paul, William. *Laughing Screaming: Modern Hollywood Horror and Comedy*. New York: Columbia University Press, 1994.

Pet Sematary. Dir. Mary Lambert. Screenplay by Stephen King. Perf. Dale Midkiff, Fred Gwynne, and Denise Crosby. Paramount Pictures, 1990.

Place, Janey. "Women in Film Noir." *Women in Film Noir*. Edited by E. Ann Kaplan. London: British Film Institute, 1978/2005. 47–68.

Poe, Edgar Allan. "Dreams." *The Complete Tales and Poems of Edgar Allan Poe*. New York: Barnes and Noble, 1992. 22.

Powell, Anna. " 'Something Came Leaking Out': Carpenter's Unholy Abominations." *The Cinema of John Carpenter: The Technique of Terror*. Edited by Ian Conrich and David Woods. London: Wallflower Press, 2004. 140–154.

Rickard, Dennis. "Horror without Limits: Looking into *The Mist*." *Reign of Fear: The Fiction and Films of Stephen King*. 1988. Ed. Don Herron. Lancaster, PA: Underwood-Miller, 1992. 177–192.

Rodley, Chris, ed. *Cronenberg on Cronenberg*. 1992. Boston: Faber & Faber, 1997.

Russell, Sharon A. *Stephen King: A Critical Companion*. Westport, CT: Greenwood Press, 1996.

Said, Edward. *Orientalism*. New York: Vintage, 1978.

Sarris, Andrew. "Notes on the Auteur Theory in 1962." *Film Theory and Criticism* (4th edn). Edited by Gerald Mast, Marshall Cohen, and Leo Braudy. New York: Oxford University Press, 1992. 585–588.

Sax, Leonard. *Why Gender Matters: What Parents and Teachers Need to Know about the Emerging Science of Sex Differences*. New York: Doubleday, 2005.

Scheib, Robert. "Trucks." *Moria: The Science Fiction, Horror and Fantasy Film Review*. Online. http://www.moria.co.nz/sf/trucks.htm. March 9, 2007.

Schroeder, Natalie. "Stephen King's *Misery*: Freudian Sexual Symbolism and the Battle of the Sexes." *Journal of Popular Culture* 30 (1990): 137–148.

———. " 'Oz the Gweat and Tewwible' and 'The Other Side': The Theme of Death in *Pet Sematary* and *Jitterbug Perfume*." *The Gothic World of Stephen King: Landscape of Nightmares*. Edited by Gary Hoppenstand and Ray B. Browne. Bowling Green, OH: Bowling Green State University Popular Press, 1987. 135–141.

Scrase, David and Wolfgang Mieder, eds. *The Holocaust: Introductory Essays*. Burlington, VT: The Center for Holocaust Studies at the University of Vermont, 1996.

Secret Window. Dir. David Koepp. Screenplay by David Koepp. Perf. Johnny Depp, John Turturro, and Maria Bello. Grand Slam Productions, Columbia Pictures, Pariah Entertainment Group, 2004.

Sedgwick, Eve Kosofsky. *Between Men: English Literature and Male Homosocial Desire*. New York: Columbia University Press, 1985.

———. *The Coherence of Gothic Conventions*. New York and London: Methuen, 1986.

Senf, Carol A. "*Gerald's Game* and *Dolores Claiborne*: Stephen King and the Evolution of an Authentic Female Narrative Voice." *Imagining the Worst: Stephen King and the Representation of Women*. Edited by Kathleen Margaret Lant and Theresa Thompson. Westport, CT: Greenwood Press, 1998. 91–110.

Shakespeare, William. *A Midsummer Night's Dream*. *The Riverside Shakespeare* (2nd edn). Edited by G. Blakemore Evans, Heather Dubrow, William T. Liston, Charles H. Shattuck, Joseph J. Tobin, Herschel Bakee, et al. Boston and New York: Houghton Mifflin, 1997.

The Shawshank Redemption. Dir. Frank Darabont. Screenplay by Frank Darabont. Perf. Tim Robbins, Morgan Freeman, and Bob Guton. Castle Rock Entertainment, 1994.

The Shining. Dir. Stanley Kubrick. Screenplay by Stanley Kubrick and Diane Johnson. Perf. Jack Nicholson, Shelley Duvall, and Danny Lloyd. Warner Brothers, 1980.

Shoos, Diane. "Representing Domestic Violence: Ambivalence and Difference in *What's Love Got to Do with It*." *NWSA Journal* 15.2 (2003): 57–77.

Simmons, Rachel. *Odd Girl Out: The Hidden Culture of Aggression in Girls*. New York: Harcourt Books, 2002.

Southey, Robert. "What All the World Is Made Of." *The Oxford Dictionary of Nursery Rhymes*. Edited by Iona and Peter Opie. London: Oxford University Press, 1951.

Stand By Me. Dir. Rob Reiner. Screenplay by Raynold Gideon and Bruce E. Evans. Perf. Wil Weaton, River Phoenix, Corey Feldman, and Kiefer Sutherland. Columbia Pictures, Act III Productions, 1986.

Steinem, Gloria. *Revolution from Within: A Book of Self-Esteem*. Boston: Little, Brown, 1992.

Stephen King's Rose Red. Dir. Craig R. Baxley. Teleplay by Stephen King. Perf. Nancy Travis and Robert Blanche. Greengrass Productions, Victor Television, Mark Carliner Productions, 2002.

Stephen King's The Shining. Dir. Mick Garris. Teleplay by Stephen King. Perf. Rebecca De Mornay, and Steven Weber. Lakeside Productions, Warner Brothers Television, ABC-TV, 1997.

Stephen King's Storm of the Century. Dir. Craig R. Baxley. Teleplay by Stephen King. Perf. Tim Daly and Colm Feore. Walt Disney Television, ABC-TV, 1999.

Stowe, Harriet Beecher. *Uncle Tom's Cabin, or, Life among the Lowly.* New York: Penguin/Signet, 1998.

Strengell, Heidi. *Dissecting Stephen King: From the Gothic to Literary Naturalism.* Madison, WI: University of Wisconsin Press, 2005.

Sundquist, Eric J. *To Wake the Nations: Race in the Making of American Literature.* Cambridge, MA: Belknap Press/Harvard University Press, 1993.

Terrell, Carroll F. *Stephen King: Man and Artist* (rev. edn). Orono, ME: Northern Lights, 1991.

Top Hat. Dir. Mark Sandrich. Screenplay by Alexander Farago, Alodar Laszlo, Karoly Noti, Alna Scott, and Dwight Taylor. Perf. Fred Astaire and Ginger Rogers RKO Radio Pictures, 1935.

Tresidder, Jack. *[The] Complete Dictionary of Symbols.* San Francisco: Chronicle Books, 2005.

Trucks. Dir. Chris Thomson. Teleplay by Brian Taggert. Perf. Timothy Busfield. Credo Entertainment, Lion's Gate, Trimark, 1997.

Twain, Mark. *Adventures of Huckleberry Finn.* New York: Penguin, 2003.

Underwood, Tim and Chuck Miller, eds. *Bare Bones: Conversations on Terror with Stephen King.* New York: McGraw Hill, 1988.

Walker, Barbara G. *The Crone: Woman of Age, Wisdom, and Power.* New York: Harper Collins, 1985.

Weller, Greg. "The Masks of the Goddess: The Unfolding of the Female Archetype in Stephen King's *Carrie.*" *The Dark Descent: Essays Defining Stephen King's Horrorscape.* Edited by Tony Magistrale. Westport, CT: Greenwood Press, 1992. 5–17.

Wiater, Stanley, Christopher Golden, and Hank Wagner. *The Stephen King Universe: A Guide to the Worlds of the King of Horror.* Los Angeles: Renaissance Books, 2001.

Wiegman, Robyn. "Feminism, 'the Boyz' and Other Matters Regarding the Male." *Screening the Male.* Edited by Steven Cohan and Ina Rae Hark. London: Routledge, 1993. 173–193.

———. "Fiedler and Sons." *Race and the Subject of Masculinities.* Edited by Harry Stecopoulos and Michael Uebel. Durham, NC: Duke University Press, 1997. 45–68.

Williams, Linda. "Melodrama in Black and White: Uncle Tom and 'The Green Mile.' " *Film Quarterly* 55 (2001): 14–21.

————. *Playing the Race Card: Melodramas of Black and White from Uncle Tom to O.J. Simpson*. Princeton, NJ: Princeton University Press, 2001.

————. "When a Woman Looks." *The Dread of Difference: Gender and the Horror Film*. Edited by Barry Keith Grant. Austin: The University of Texas Press, 1996. 15–34.

Winter, Douglas E. *Stephen King: The Art of Darkness*. New York: Signet/ NAL, 1984.

Wiseman, Rosalind. *Queen Bees & Wannabees*. New York: Three Rivers Press, Random House, 2002.

Wood, Gary. "Stephen King: To Direct, Or Not To Direct." *Cinefantastique* 21.4 (1991): 47.

Wood, Robin. "The American Nightmare: Horror in the 70s" *Horror: The Film Reader*. Ed. Mark Jancovich. London and New York: Routledge, 2002. 25–32.

Wood, Rocky, David Rawsthorne, and Norma Blackburn. *Stephen King: Uncollected, Unpublished* (rev. edn). Victoria, Australia: Kanrock, 2006.

Young, Suzie. "Restorative and Destructive: Carpenter and Maternal Authority." *The Cinema of John Carpenter: The Technique of Terror*. Edited by Ian Conrich and David Woods. London: Wallflower Press, 2004. 128–139.

Index

AC/DC, 69–70, 77
"Acting *Carrie*," 17
The Adventures of Huckleberry Finn,
      119, 122–3, 124, 129, 134
Alien, 198
Appiah, Anthony K., 142
Apt Pupil, 3–4, 7, 27–40, 201–2
   homosexuality in, 32–3, 38
   Icarus, 39
   Jewish issues in, 31, 36–7

Badley, Linda, 72, 179
Bakhtin, Mikhail, 10, 74, 196–8
Bamboozled, 132
Basic Instinct, 199
Bates, Kathy, 94
Beard, William, 143–4, 145, 150,
      151–2
Bello, Maria, 193
Bergson, Henri, 78–9
Biddle, Arthur, 43, 48
Bloom, Harold, 2, 179
Bogle, Donald, 117
Bosky, Bernadette Lynn, 208
Browne, Ray, 94
Browning, Mark, 4–5, 204–6

Cage, Nicholas, 118
Carpenter, John, 65
Carrie, 1, 2, 5, 7, 13–25
Carroll, Noel, 137
Castle Rock, 169–70
Cavallaro, Dani, 184–5
Charmichael, Stokely, 119

children, 42–51
   bogeyboys, 26–8
   Carrie, 13–25
   death of, 51
   King's fiction, 7
   see also Apt Pupil, Pet Sematary,
      Stand By Me
Christine, 9, 53–66, 80
   capitalism, 58–9
   comparison of novel and film, 54,
      57, 63–5
   feminized machine, 54–5, 61,
      63–4, 66
   psychoanalysis of, 62
   rock music in, 65
   vampire-like, 58
Clemens, Valdine, 83–4
Cohen, Lawrence D., 15, 18
Collings, Michael, 24–5, 219
Collins, Patricia Hill, 136
Columbine killings, 7, 27–8, 35,
      36–7, 39, 40
Crane, Jonathan, 148
Creed, Barbara, 66
Creepshow, 185
Cronenberg, David, 143–53
      see also The Dead Zone
Cumbow, Robert C., 65

Damon, Matt, 118, 119
Danse Macabre, 22, 185
Darabont, Frank, 112, 117, 119,
      120, 126, 128
The Dark Tower, 206, 213, 216

The Dead Zone, 143–53
    novel, 3, 144, 152, 153
    setting of, 148–9
    The Defiant Ones, 133
Denby, David, 126
Depp, Johnny, 193
Dolores Claiborne, 7, 8, 155–65, 173
    novel, 2, 157–8, 162
    solar eclipse in, 160–1
    see also feminism
Duncan, Michael Clark, 118, 125,
        126, 129
Dyer, Richard, 107

Edinger, Edward F., 159
Egan, James, 9, 72, 216
Engles, Friedrich, 89
Eppert, Claudia, 36, 37

Fantasia, 32
Faulkner, William, 150
Faust, 32
feminism
    in *Dolores Claiborne*, 155–65
    in *Gilda*, 105–7
    in *The Shawshank Redemption*,
        105–9, 112
    in *The Shining*, 135
    Stephen King's relation to, 4,
        156–7
Feore, Colm, 175
Fiedler, Leslie, 134, 140
Figliola, Samantha, 133–4
film noir, 107
Findley, Mary, 65
Fiske, John, 70, 75, 81, 132, 134
Flagg, Randall, 175
Four Past Midnight, 191, 192
Friedan, Betty, 155

Gabbard, Krin, 118, 124
George, Nelson 143, 148, 149
Ghosts, 9, 140–2
Gilda, 105–7, 114
The Godfather, 2–3
Gothic, 112, 145, 147

The Green Mile, 7–9, 93–4, 97,
        117–32, 135–8, 140, 141,
        146, 152
    Christ persona in, 126, 127, 131
    comparison with *Huck Finn*,
        122–3, 129
    comparison with *Misery*, 99–102
    magical Negro themes in,
        118–21, 127, 131–42
    novel, 122, 128
    see also racial themes

Hala, James, 90
Halberstam, Judith, 144
Hanks, Tom, 118, 119
Happy Days, 81
Harris, Joel Chandler, 119, 125, 129
Hayworth, Rita, 105–6, 110, 111,
        114
Heathers, 13
Heldreth, Leonard, 48
Hester-Williams, Kim D., 121–2
Hicks, Heather, 123, 125, 127,
        133, 135
Hitchcock, Alfred, 73, 81, 185, 194
Hitler, Adolf, 28, 37, 147
    See also Apt Pupil
Hollywood
    and best sellers, 2
    King as director in, 67–8
Holocaust, 36, 40
Hoppenstand, Gary, 94

IT, 185

Jackson, Michael, 9, 140–2
    See also Ghosts, magical Negro
Jackson, Shirley, 181, 182, 188–9
Jameson, Fredric, 10, 83, 84
Jermyn, Deborah, 107
Jewett, Robert, 74, 76
Joshi, S. T., 179

Kelso, Sylvia, 66
Kermode, Frank, 4, 105, 106,
        110–11

King, Stephen
  death themes in, 42–4
  friendships in, 7–8, 34, 48, 157,
    160
  novels of, 3, 6, 10, 144, 152,
    153, 156–7, 162, 170,
    179–80, 195–7
  postmodern elements in, 167, 176
  social issues in, 6, 10, 134–6,
    176–7
  Spike Lee, 120, 134
  Vermont Library Conference
    Address, 27–8, 38
  See also children, Ghosts, feminism,
    magical Negro
Kingdom Hospital, 185
Klawans, Stuart, 122
Koepp, David, 192–4, 195, 198
Kubrick, Stanley, 83–92, 194
  see also The Shining

Lant, Kathleen, 94, 97–8, 158
Lawrence, John, 74, 76
Lee, Spike, 119–20, 129, 132, 134
The Legend of Bagger Vance, 118–19
Lenin, Vladimir, 85, 91
Levy, Ariel, 156
Lovecraft, H. P., 43

Madden, Edward, 59
magical Negro, 118–21, 127, 131–42
  see also Ghosts, The Green Mile, The
    Shining, Uncle Tom's Cabin
Magistrale, Tony, 1, 19, 24, 28, 30,
    40, 42, 43, 45, 48, 50, 54, 66,
    71, 75–6, 83, 94, 101, 120,
    126, 127, 131, 136, 146, 149,
    164, 168, 177–8, 183, 202–3,
    206, 214–15, 217–20
Markovic, Mihalio, 91
The Marriage of Figaro, 104, 108–9,
    114
Marx, Karl, 84–5, 88, 91
Maximum Overdrive, 9, 67–81
  auteur theory, 68–9, 79, 80
  comic elements in, 70–9

demolition derbies, 73–8
  Uncanny aspects of, 77–8
  see also "Trucks"
Melville, Herman, 37, 183, 188
Mieder, Wolfgang, 40
Misery, 8, 93–102, 194
The Mist, 201–20
  government in, 206, 215, 217–18
  novella, 203–4, 215, 219
  See also The Dark Tower
Modleski, Tania, 119, 132
Monroe, Marilyn, 111
Morris, Peter, 148, 149
Moss, Larry, 125, 126
Muir, John Kenneth, 66
Muller, Jurgen, 25
Mustazza, Leonard, 50

Needful Things, 10, 169–73
Newman, Kim, 39
The Night Porter, 29
Nosferatu, 30

On Writing, 98, 180
Owen, Sally, 160

Paranoid, 1
Pareles, Jon, 73
Paul, William, 77, 81
Pet Sematary, 18, 41–51
  comparison with Stand By Me,
    50–1
  criticism of, 49–50
  death theme in, 48–50
  Greek tragedy parallels, 50
Poe, Edgar Allan, 37, 83, 84, 145,
    151, 153, 182
Powell, Anna, 54
Psycho, 59, 66, 68, 150

racial themes
  in The Dead Zone, 9, 144–7, 152–3
  in Ghosts, 9, 140–2
  in The Green Mile, 9, 117–32
  in The Shining, 9, 136, 138
Rage, 28

Reagan, Ronald, 29, 143, 152–3
Rodley, Chris, 146–7, 148, 151, 152
Romero, George, 76, 81
Rosemary's Baby, 192
Rose Red, 3, 10, 180–9
  and American literature, 10
  comic elements in, 184, 187–8
  gender constructions, 181–2
  haunted house tradition, 181–3
Russell, Sharon, 170

Said, Edward, 133
Sarris, Andrew, 80
Sax, Leonard, 21
Schatz, Thomas, 69
Schroeder, Natalie, 50–1, 94
science and technology, 9–10, 72, 79
  see also Christine, Maximum
    Overdrive, "Trucks"
Scrase, David, 40
Secret Window, 10, 192–9
  novella, 191–2, 195–7, 199
  see also Bahktin
Sedgwick, Eve, 112, 139
Senf, Carol A., 157
Shakespeare, William, 183, 186–8
The Shawshank Redemption, 2, 7–8,
  93–4, 103–15, 139
  comparison with *Gilda*, 105–7,
    114
  comparison with *Misery*, 97–102
  gothic elements in, 112
  novella, 2–4, 105
  see also The Marriage of Figaro
The Shining, 2–3, 5, 9–10, 68,
  83–92, 135–8, 140
  capitalism, 10, 83–92
  children in, 6–7
  communism, 84–92
  family in, 88–9
  scrapbook (novel), 29–30
  television, 90–1

Simmons, Rachel, 13, 19
The Simpsons, 90–1
Springsteen, Bruce, 29
Stand By Me, 2, 7, 41–51
  comparison with *Pet Sematary*,
    50–1
  death themes in, 43–4, 47–9
Steinem, Gloria, 155, 159–60, 164
The Storm of the Century, 10,
  173–8, 179–80, 186
Strengell, Heidi, 50, 175, 180
The Summer of '44, 88
Sundquist, Eric J., 125

The Tenant, 192
Terrell, Carol F., 167–8
Top Hat, 128, 131
Tristan und Isolde, 33
"Trucks," 9, 68, 71–2, 76, 77, 80,
  81

Uncle Remus, 125, 129
Uncle Tom's Cabin, 117, 118, 120

vampire
  as automobile, 53, 58
  as house, 182, 188
  as machine, 76
Van Peebles, Melvin, 138
Verniere, James, 149
"Visualizing *Carrie*," 15

Welch, Raquel, 110, 111
Williams, Linda, 117, 119, 128,
  129, 132, 138–9
Winter, Douglas E., 51, 68, 81,
  207, 216
Wise, Robert, 183
Wiseman, Rosalind, 14
Wolfe, Tom, 74

Young, Suzie, 62